PERSUASIONS OF GOD

THE RSA SERIES IN TRANSDISCIPLINARY RHETORIC

Edited by
Michael Bernard-Donals *(University of Wisconsin)* and
Leah Ceccarelli *(University of Washington)*

Editorial Board:
Diane Davis, The University of Texas at Austin
Cara Finnegan, University of Illinois at Urbana-Champaign
Debra Hawhee, The Pennsylvania State University
John Lynch, University of Cincinnati
Steven Mailloux, Loyola Marymount University
Kendall Phillips, Syracuse University
Thomas Rickert, Purdue University

The RSA Series in Transdisciplinary Rhetoric is a collaboration with the Rhetoric Society of America to publish innovative and rigorously argued scholarship on the tremendous disciplinary breadth of rhetoric. Books in the series take a variety of approaches, including theoretical, historical, interpretive, critical, or ethnographic, and examine rhetorical action in a way that appeals, first, to scholars in communication studies and English or writing, and, second, to at least one other discipline or subject area.

Other titles in this series:
Nathan Stormer, *Sign of Pathology: U.S. Medical Rhetoric on Abortion, 1800s–1960s*
Mark Longaker, *Rhetorical Style and Bourgeois Virtue: Capitalism and Civil Society in the British Enlightenment*
Robin E. Jensen, *Infertility: A Rhetorical History*
Steven Mailloux, *Rhetoric's Pragmatism: Essays in Rhetorical Hermeneutics*
M. Elizabeth Weiser, *Museum Rhetoric: Building Civic Identity in National Spaces*
Chris Mays, Nathaniel A. Rivers, and Kellie Sharp-Hoskins, eds., *Kenneth Burke + The Posthuman*
Amy Koerber, *From Hysteria to Hormones: A Rhetorical History*
Elizabeth C. Britt, *Reimagining Advocacy: Rhetorical Education in the Legal Clinic*
Ian E. J. Hill, *Advocating Weapons, War, and Terrorism: Technological and Rhetorical Paradox*
Kelly Pender, *Being at Genetic Risk: Toward a Rhetoric of Care*
James L. Cherney, *Ableist Rhetoric: How We Know, Value, and See Disability*
Susan Wells, *Robert Burton's Rhetoric: An Anatomy of Early Modern Knowledge*
Ralph Cintron, *Democracy as Fetish*
Maggie M. Werner, *Stripped: Reading the Erotic Body*
Timothy Johnson, *Rhetoric, Inc.: Ford's Filmmaking and the Rise of Corporatism*
James Wynn and G. Mitchell Reyes, eds., *Arguing with Numbers: The Intersections of Rhetoric and Mathematics*
Ashely Rose Mehlenbacher, *On Expertise: Cultivating Character, Goodwill, and Practical Wisdom*
Stuart J. Murray, *The Living from the Dead: Disaffirming Biopolitics*
G. Mitchell Reyes, *The Evolution of Mathematics: A Rhetorical Approach*
Jenell Johnson, *Every Living Thing: The Politics of Life in Common*
Kellie Sharp-Hoskins, *Rhetoric in Debt*
Jennifer Clary-Lemon, *Nestwork: New Material Rhetorics for Precarious Species*
Nicholas S. Paliewicz, *Extraction Politics: Rio Tinto and the Corporate Persona*

Paul Lynch

PERSUASIONS OF GOD

Inventing the Rhetoric of René Girard

THE PENNSYLVANIA STATE UNIVERSITY PRESS
UNIVERSITY PARK, PENNSYLVANIA

Library of Congress Cataloging-in-Publication Data

Names: Lynch, Paul, 1971– author.
Title: Persuasions of God : inventing the rhetoric of
René Girard / Paul Lynch.
Other titles: RSA series in transdisciplinary rhetoric.
Description: University Park, Pennsylvania : The Pennsylvania
State University Press, [2024] | Series: The RSA series in
transdisciplinary rhetoric | Includes bibliographical
references and index.
Summary: "Explores René Girard's mimetic theory and
repurposes it to invent a post-Christian "theorhetoric" a new
way of speaking to, for, and especially about God. Advocates
a rhetoric of meekness that conscientiously refuses rivalry,
actively exploits tradition through complicit invention, and
boldly seeks a holiness free of exclusionary violence"—
Provided by publisher.
Identifiers: LCCN 2023047062 | ISBN 9780271097091
(hardback)
Subjects: LCSH: Girard, René, 1923–2015—Criticism and
interpretation. | Rhetoric—Religious aspects—
Christianity.
Classification: LCC BR115.R55 L95 2024 | DDC 210.1/4—
dc23/eng/20231122
LC record available at https://lccn.loc.gov/2023047062

Copyright © 2024 Paul Lynch
All rights reserved
Printed in the United States of America
Published by The Pennsylvania State University Press,
University Park, PA 16802–1003

© The Rhetoric Society of America, 2024

The Pennsylvania State University Press is a member of the
Association of University Presses.

It is the policy of The Pennsylvania State University Press to
use acid-free paper. Publications on uncoated stock satisfy the
minimum requirements of American National Standard for
Information Sciences—Permanence of Paper for Printed
Library Material, ANSI z39.48–1992.

For my daughters

Contents

Acknowledgments | ix

Introduction: An Alienated Theorhetoric | 1

1   The Meek Defense | 24

2   Friendly Injustices | 55

3   Overcoming Christianity | 84

4   Uneasy Holiness | 115

Postscript: Holy Envy | 146

Notes | 159

Bibliography | 189

Index | 203

Acknowledgments

I want first to express my gratitude to my late colleague Dr. Georgia K. Johnston. Georgia was an unstinting supporter of her colleagues in the Department of English, so it was no surprise that she left the department a substantial bequest at her death. That bequest created the Johnston professorship, designed for associate professors working on a second major project. I held the professorship from 2021 to 2023, and without it, I would not have finished this book. I extend similar gratitude to the entire Department of English, which endorsed the creation of the professorship from Georgia's gift. My colleagues have also offered copious insight, challenges, and encouragement as I have presented my ideas at our research colloquium. I am lucky to count myself among such generous scholars.

Thanks as well to the Saint Louis University Research Office for a 2022 Beaumont Award, which afforded me crucial time and support for completing this project.

I am particularly grateful to Nathaniel Rivers for his friendship, comradeship, and careful response to my work. His passion for the study of rhetoric has been a model for me. Another model for me, both intellectually and personally, is my friend and colleague Grant Kaplan, who has been unfailingly generous in sharing his expertise on Girard and theology. I am also indebted to the Girardian scholars James Alison and Sandor Goodhart for sharing their expertise with me in memorable conversations in Madrid and West Lafayette.

Other friends and colleagues whose comments improved the manuscript are Jeremy Cushman, Jeffrey Ringer, and Michael-John DePalma. I also want to acknowledge Richard Johnson-Sheehan and the Purdue University Rhetoric Program's invitation to present some this material as part of the 2018 Hutton Lecture Series.

Many thanks also go to my student Andrew Sweeso, who provided extraordinary research and editing assistance. I was also fortunate enough to teach a class on the rhetorics of sacrifice in spring 2021. My thanks to those students, including Andrew, whose thinking made mine better.

x   ACKNOWLEDGMENTS

The book is also better because of the manuscript reviewers, Steven Mailloux and Kyle Jensen. I am especially thankful to Steve for the many conversations in which he has responded so attentively and productively as I have sounded out my ideas. I am grateful for his friendship. I am also grateful for Kyle's incisive response, which pushed me to clarify my thinking in generative ways. Very special thanks also go to David Frank, who was kind enough to share his expertise on Girard, Jewish rhetorics, and Girard's relation to Judaism. In keeping with his fruitful study of argumentation, David persuaded me to rethink my own arguments. Just as I am fortunate to be a member of the Saint Louis University faculty, I am also fortunate to number among the guild of rhetoricians. Any remaining errors are mine.

I want to thank Archna Patel, Josie DiNovo, and Ryan Peterson at Penn State University Press. I am grateful to Archna and Josie for seeing this project through and to Ryan for his early interest in the project. I also want to thank Andrew Katz, Alex Ramos, and Laura Reed-Morrisson for their careful editing of the manuscript.

Of course, the most immediate and intimate thanks go to Melody, Beatrice, and Josephine for their patience, support, and love. AMDG.

Portions of chapter 2 were previously published in my article "Recovering Rhetoric: René Girard as Theorhetor," which appeared in the journal *Contagion* 27 (2020): 101–22, copyright © 2020 by Michigan State University. Portions of chapter 3 were also published in *Contagion* in "Rescuing Rhetoric: Kenneth Burke, René Girard, and the Forms of Conversion," 24 (2017): 138–59, copyright © 2017 by Michigan State University, and in "A Friendly Injustice: Kenneth Burke, René Girard, and the Rhetoric of Religion," which appeared in *Reinventing Rhetoric Scholarship: Fifty Years of the Rhetoric Society of America*, edited by Roxanne Mountford, Dave Tell, and David Blakesley (Anderson, SC: Parlor Press, 2020), 88–97. My thanks to Michigan State Press and Parlor Press.

Introduction | An Alienated Theorhetoric

God, whatever His other failings, is a great rhetorician.
—Mark Forsyth, *The Elements of Eloquence*

In her poem "On the Parables of the Mustard Seed," Denise Levertov revisits Jesus of Nazareth's famous analogy between a mustard seed and the kingdom of God. In Luke's retelling, Jesus asks, "What is the kingdom of God like? To what can I compare it? It is like a mustard seed that a person took and planted in the garden. When it was fully grown, it became a large bush and 'the birds in the sky dwelt in its branches'" (Luke 13:18–19).[1] The quote is from a description of cypress trees from the book of Ezekiel: "I in turn will take and set [in the ground a slip] from the lofty top of the cedar; I will pluck a tender twig from the tip of its crown, and I will plant it on a tall, towering mountain. . . . It shall bring forth boughs and produce branches and grow into a noble cedar. Every bird of every feather shall take shelter under it, shelter in the shade of its boughs" (Ezek. 17:22–23).[2] Jesus's repurposed images are usually understood to mean that the kingdom of God will flourish despite its insignificant beginnings.

That is not wrong, Levertov reflects, but it is not right enough. The point is not simply that something small grows into something large; the point is that mustard plants do not usually grow large at all. Mustard plants are more bushes than trees. More than simply drawing an arresting analogy, Jesus is imagining a miracle. "Faith is rare, He must have been saying, / prodigious, unique— / one infinitesimal grain divided / like loaves and fishes." This deeper lesson is easy to miss. "Glib generations mistake / the metaphor, not looking at fields and trees, / not noticing paradox." It is "*as if* from a mustard-seed / a great shade-tree grew."[3] Faith depends on the ability to say "as if."

The miracle that I am after here is not as prodigious as the kingdom of God. But it begins from a seed equally small. In this project, I pursue *theorhetoric*, a term employed by Steven Mailloux to designate the rhetoric used when we are talking "to, for, and about God."[4] Mailloux offers this brief definition on his way to making a larger point about Jesuit rhetorical practice. But this brief definition promises a new project for rhetorical studies, a project dedicated to the invention of theological questions, including the ultimate question of God. Trained by Kenneth Burke, rhetoricians have perhaps become too used to speaking of the rhetoric *of* religion, as though the entirety of religious rhetoric could be represented in a single prepositional relation.[5] The prepositions of theorhetoric, however, suggest multiple species. Theorhetoric-*to* might include rhetorics of prayer and liturgy. Inherently and etymologically precarious (L. *precarius*, dependent on another's will, uncertain—related to *prex*, prayer, request, intercession), theorhetoric-*to* requires the discipline of the open hand. Under theorhetoric-*for*, we might arrange the familiar rhetorics of preaching, catechesis, and evangelization. The basic office of the theorhetoric-*for*, as Augustine imagined it, is to "communicate what is good and eradicate what is bad, and in this process of speaking . . . win over the antagonistic, rouse the apathetic, and make clear to those who are not conversant with the matter under discussion what they should expect."[6] Theorhetoric may invite even more prepositional relations. In contemplation, one might observe theorhetorics-*in* God; in mysticism, theorhetorics-*from* God; in meditation, theorhetorics-*through* God. Pilgrimage goes *toward* God; discipleship follows *after* God; postmodern theologians imagine possible theorhetorics-*beyond* God. "Therefore let us pray *to* God," says Meister Eckhart, "that we may be free *of* God."[7]

Theorhetoric-*about*, the third of Mailloux's species, takes up the fundamental challenge of reflecting on who God may be. What is God? Where is God? Who is God? What does God want? Theorhetoric-*about* treats these questions as matters of persuasion rather than formal rationality or philosophic conceptualization. Theorhetoric-*about* is the rhetoric that invents God's *persuasion*, a word that carries a few different meanings. Persuasion can refer to ordinary, intentional appeals to the other—including the Wholly Other—but it need not be limited in this conventional way. Persuasion can also imply a more archaic sense of "the fact, condition, or state of being persuaded" (*OED*) and a sense of religious belief or commitment, as in "Professor Lynch is of the Catholic persuasion." This notion of persuasion-as-characteristic has also been casuistically stretched—with both humorous and hostile undertones—to include personal features that are not quite matters of choice, as in, "Professor Lynch is of the Irish-Catholic persuasion" ("and," the enthymeme might run, "you know what that means"). This usage suggests that "persuasion" paradoxically designates both matters of assent and matters of assignation; it suggests something like what Diane Davis calls "prior rhetoricity," an ontological notion of rhetoric in which the human person (though not only the human person) is shaped by an "affect-ability or persuadability."[8] For there to be any sense of ordinary or traditional persuasion at all, there has to be this ontology of persuadability in the first place.

Extended to the divine, these various nuances indicate that persuasion is something that God makes happen, something that happens to God, and something that suggests who God may be. Observing some of the available means of these persuasions can produce a theorhetoric-*about*. In this particular project of theorhetoric, I observe the persuasions of God through four key terms: meekness, sacrifice, atonement, and holiness. The persuasions of God could never be reduced to these four or any single list of terms; one might add a host of others—mercy, wrath, idolatry, forgiveness, justice, love. But any such list would certainly include meekness, sacrifice, atonement, and holiness as key topoi through which powerful religious rhetorics continue to be invented. The critical aim of this project is to track how these topoi have sometimes been invented in the past, and the creative aim is to imagine how in the present and future they might invent differently.

As I begin to theorize these theorhetorical topoi, I am cognizant of a remark offered by Thomas Rickert in *Ambient Rhetoric*: "We do not need a new rhetoric . . . ; rather, we must work anew with what has already been brought forward in rhetorical theory and practice." Such is my intention here. Rather than hatching entirely new ideas about rhetoric, I hope to work anew with what has already been brought forward. Key to that work is recognizing how the field's understanding of rhetoric has changed and how that understanding has stayed the same. "Rhetoric," Rickert continues, "can no longer be understood solely as a subjective, verbal, visual, or even performative art. These permutations should not be jettisoned, certainly; instead, we need to expand and rework them."[9] The idea of "permutation" (*per*, thoroughly + *mutare*, change) becomes significant here. Permutation suggests a change that maintains some relation to what is being changed from. To suggest new permutations is to suggest variations rather than rejections.

The tensive relation inherent in permutation articulates this book's *kairos*, method, and ethos. The book's *kairos* is the postreligious, postsecular, and post-Christian moment—a time in which certain kinds of Christian religious language have become unsayable even to many Christians and even as the effects of that older language (i.e., the practices and beliefs it prescribed) continue to linger. As with the terms "postmodern" and "posthuman," "post-Christian" suggests both a decisive break and an enduring influence. The term also has both descriptive and prescriptive import. It describes a changed relation to a cultural inheritance, but it also may indicate a more ethical stance toward that inheritance.

The book's methodology is likewise hinted at in the idea of permutation, both in the available means of invention and in its transdisciplinary approach. Regarding the former, the book practices a *complicit invention*, working through tradition and convention rather than against them. Such an approach is necessary for a post-Christian theorhetoric that would reclaim and reimagine ideas like meekness, sacrifice, atonement, and holiness. In addition, an archaic meaning of permutation as "exchange" or "barter" (*OED*) indicates the book's transdisciplinary approach, which draws on philosophy, anthropology, literature, and of course theology. Scholars from all these fields offer resources for the invention of a God-haunted inquiry that is distinctly rhetorical. Regarding theological ideas in particular, this project assumes that the most powerful post-Christian critique should proceed *from within* Christian tradition rather than outside it. In other words, this book presupposes that, insofar as many of the rhetorical effects of these topoi proceed from disordered Christian thought, better Christian thought can and should make repair.

Finally, the idea of permutation also suggests something about the ethos I perform here, an ethos that is recognizably Christian but is also oriented toward a post-Christian context in which traditional religious language has become moribund. Michael Hyde has reminded rhetoricians of an older meaning of "ethos" as "dwelling place," with implications of "haunt" and all that word connotes—familiar grounds, the places (terrain, topoi) to which we repeatedly return, and ghostly presences that dog us.[10] This ethos, which I later describe as "alienated," dwells within Christian tradition, even as it feels haunted within that tradition. It cannot quit the old dwelling place, but it must invent new ways to inhabit it.

For the remainder of this introduction, I expand on the book's *kairos*, method, and ethos. Concerning the book's actual approach, these three rhetorical conditions cannot really be separated, except for purposes of explication. Each is implicated in the others. The book's alienated ethos, for example, is reflected in a methodological approach that would recover ideas from, with, and within Christian tradition. The methodology is appropriate for a moment in which many traditional Christian ideas, and the appeals that proceed from those ideas, no longer seem persuasive. But the only way out is through.

A Post-Christian *Kairos*

It is an old story that the death of God has been greatly exaggerated. On the surface, Nietzsche's famous prediction appears to have come true, as empty churches are turned into supermarkets, floral shops, bookstores, and gyms.[11] Yet these structural conversions still indicate the long shadow of the once-living God, who haunts these secularized spaces in which people still seek their daily bread, purchase bouquets for private altars, gather the texts of personal liturgies, and practice the most self-denying asceticisms. God has appeared to survive the twentieth century's multiple assassination attempts: global warfare, genocide, atomic weaponry. In the wake of so much suffering, it should not be surprising that it might become difficult to imagine a deity both sovereign and benign. Scholars would eventually pose the "secularization thesis," the claim that WEIRD societies (Western, educated, industrial, rich, and—at least for the moment—democratic) were on an irreversible trajectory away from religion.[12] Yet the proponents of the secularization thesis would eventually be forced to admit that they had spoken too soon.[13] Religion would "return," as a social and historical reality, a political force, and a public philosophical question. Now, rather than speaking of secularity, it has become common to speak of the "postsecular," a term that suggests that religion retains tremendous political and cultural power even if it no longer enjoys an unquestioned political or cultural status.

Yet even if the case has been overstated, the death of God seems to have occasioned a "post-Christian" moment, characterized by the lingering effects of a diminished faith. For some people, this diminution is a cause of distress. Gabriel Vahanian, whose 1957 *The Death of God* helped set the stage for what would come to be known as "death of God" theology, argues that a post-Christian culture is one shaped by a Christianity that it no longer takes seriously. In the post-Christian era, "Christianity suffers 'not a torture death but a quiet euthanasia.'"[14] If God is dead, it is because God has become "neither necessary nor unnecessary."[15] This Christian morbidity has been caused by Christians themselves, who have settled for spiritual mediocrity.[16] "Is not indeed the literature of 'peace of mind,' of 'mental health,' a poison which is now attacking the head of Christianity—the heart presumably having stopped long since?"[17] There can be little doubt that some of the literatures of the present day—certain versions of "self-care," for example—might prompt the same bitter questioning.

6   PERSUASIONS OF GOD

For others, the euthanasia of Christianity is a relief. The Belgian art critic Thierry de Duve imagines that the post-Christian era will see "humankind freed from its subordination to the power of the father because it refers its fraternity—and its sorority—to the empty place of the symbolic father rather than the filled place of the incarnated son."[18] Out from under the nobodaddy, a formerly Christian culture can reach its full spiritual and ethical maturity. Others offer a more descriptive account of the post-Christian moment, arguing that, like it or not, Christianity is poised to supersede itself through a religiously induced secularization. This is the argument made by Marcel Gauchet, who describes Christianity as the preeminent "religion for departing from religion."[19] By this, he means that Christianity completes a process under way even before the so-called archaic religions gave way to the axial age, with its "mature" or "historical" religions. The emergence of religion *qua* religion—that is, as a phenomenon that is thinkable in and of itself—allows human beings to distinguish a transcendent or sacred sphere from an immanent or profane sphere. Once this division exists, the demise of religion is inevitable. Christianity's attempt to overcome this separation by universalizing its values, and thereby collapsing the distinction between "religious" and "ordinary" life, paradoxically sets religion on a terminal decline, though a decline that may take centuries to complete. Finally, there are some who argue that this secularization is precisely what Christianity should want. Gianni Vattimo makes the counterintuitive argument that secularization is "the constitutive trait of an authentic religious experience."[20] Secularization allows Christianity to shed what Vattimo sees as the reactionary superstition that has too long ordered and distorted its institutional expression. Christianity can then find its true vocation to love, freed from disordered attachments to miracle, mystery, and authority.

This small sampling of arguments indicates the range of interpretations of the post-Christian turn, which may be bad news, good news, or simply the news. Alternatively, secularization may not be happening at all. Much has been made, at least in the United States, of the rise of the so-called nones, the increase in the number of people who choose "none" when asked about formal religious affiliation. The nones are not "religious" in the conventional sense of the term (they do not belong to religious communities, they do not attend weekly services, etc.), yet they do not necessarily reject the idea of God.[21] Their search for the divine continues, even if their conventional religious identities are hard to track. Some scholars speak of the religiously "remixed," which includes not just the familiar "spiritual but not religious" but also the "faithful nones" and the "religious hybrids."[22] Other lists include categorizations as diverse as atheists, weak agnostics, strong agnostics, secular humanists, humanists, the secular, the spiritual, the spiritual-but-not-religious, and neopagans—along with the nothing-in-particular, the all-of-the-above, and the none-of-the-above.[23]

Many of these developments have been described by Charles Taylor in his landmark *A Secular Age*, which rejects any "subtraction story" of secularization. Subtraction stories are those that characterize modernity as nothing more than the society that emerges once a culture is drained of the murky waters of religion (thus revealing a Scandinavian-style paradise of confessional-free liberal flourishing). By Taylor's estimation, a secular age is defined neither by the dominance of nonreligious institutions nor even the vestigial religiosity of which Vahanian speaks. A secular age is rather marked by "a move from a society where belief in God is unchallenged and indeed, unproblematic, to one in which it is understood to be one option among others, and frequently not the easiest to embrace."[24] A secular age is thus backgrounded by what Taylor calls the "immanent frame," the sense that human experience and aspiration are now contained entirely within a natural order, such that human flourishing no longer requires a transcendent background against which its ideals need be measured. For the first time in human history, it becomes widely possible to imagine spiritual yearning without a transcendent referent. But this persistence of that yearning is evidenced by what Taylor calls "the nova effect," an explosion of spiritual possibilities that spawns "an ever-widening variety of moral/spiritual options, across the span of the thinkable and perhaps even beyond."[25] The enduring need for spiritual practice or commitment often requires "sacrifice" (of time, of rest, of entertainment) even when the practice is not traditionally religious. Seen within the context of the nova effect, the swapping of kneelers for NordicTracks may not indicate a fundamental change.

Within the immanent frame, the adherents of transcendent cosmologies find themselves under what Taylor describes as "cross pressure," the sense in which people are compelled to grope for a "third way" between the unsatisfying choices of traditional theisms and a disenchanted world.[26] The cross-pressured are those who feel pulled toward the transcendent even against the headwinds of the immanent. "The whole culture experiences cross pressures, between the draw of the narratives of closed immanence on one side, and the sense of their inadequacy on the other, strengthened by encounter with existing milieux of religious practice, or just by some intimations of the transcendent."[27] Cross pressure contributes to the nova effect as people begin to search for ways to put

8   PERSUASIONS OF GOD

expression to their intimations. As they try to express this sense of the transcendent, they will encounter the existing milieux of religious practice—including the commonplaces now abandoned by a diminished religious power, whose terminology has become theologically unmoored.

In other words, the dawning of a secular age occasions a rhetorical crisis. "Perhaps totally new words are needed; perhaps a decent silence about God should be observed; but ultimately, a new treatment of the idea [of God] and the word can be expected, however unexpected and surprising it may turn out to be."[28] Another religious scholar writes, "religious language had lost its meaning, or, even worse, the inherited meanings had grown perverse in the wake of a long list of modern atrocities."[29] Bruno Latour practices the same sort of anonymous theorhetorical theorizing, lamenting "the *torments* of religious speech," the agony of being trapped between dead and unborn languages.[30] For Latour, the seemingly moribund lexicon of Catholicism demands "flurries of 'mental reservations'" in order to be uttered. How can it still be possible to say things like, "Virgin Mary," "descended into hell," or "life everlasting"?[31] Latour feels the "temptation to purify" religious language of these older forms, but this solution seems equally unsatisfying.[32] Once you start smashing the old images, Latour argues, you will end up with

> the lowest common denominator of religions, something so bland and so versatile that it could be spread throughout the world without shocking anyone. A "moral ideal," a "feeling of the infinite," a "call to one's conscience," a "rich inner life," "access to the great all"? What a lot of poppycock that "God" is! A simple portmanteau of morality—as if morality needed the support of religion. Thanks to such purification, we've got rid of the useless dross, but there's nothing left that would allow us to address ourselves in words that bring life to someone who, on hearing them, would find themselves transformed.[33]

The choices seem appalling: either a traditionalism that calcifies into the reactionary or a progressivism that floats into the ether.

In 1961, Vahanian insisted that the death of God in the West demanded "either an almost inconceivable reconstruction of Christianity or the emancipation of Western culture from Christianity in its present condition."[34] Four decades later, Latour's remarks suggest that the crisis has only intensified. Given the radicalness of Vahanian's call—total reinvention or total emancipation—it is little wonder that "this question of the return of religion is transmitted not by theologians and/or religious leaders but by and through philosophers and cultural theorists who heretofore had little or no expressed interest in religious or theological questions."[35] Only in this transdisciplinary place, at the same time standing both inside and outside tradition, can we hope to invent new expression.

This book presupposes that rhetoricians are also given an assignment in response to this *kairos*. The search for new religious forms in a postsecular, post-Christian age presents an opportunity for rhetoricians to exercise their fundamental vocation, which John Poulakos memorably defined as "the art which seeks to capture in opportune moments that which is appropriate and attempts to suggest that which is possible."[36] (This is only one of the many plausible and useful definitions of rhetoric that we will revisit throughout the book.) It is clear that rhetoricians with religious interests find themselves in an opportune, even epochal moment; it is for them now to discern that which is appropriate and suggest that which is possible. Whatever those interventions may be, it seems clear that rhetoricians interested in religion need not confine themselves solely to the observation and description of rhetorical activity within religious spheres. Given the lingering power of the "religious," despite (or because of) the waning power of "religion," our task must include the discovery and creation of new religious expression, up to and including persuasions of God.

To be clear, my argument is not that Christian tradition represents the only possibility for theorhetorical invention. Rhetoricians can and should invent multiple rhetorics across multiple traditions. But the present study will confine itself to Christian tradition if only because its persuasions endure even in a post-Christian era. The crosses and Christian messages that marked the January 6 Capitol attack demonstrate this point, as does the overall problem of Christian nationalism in the United States. Paradoxically, Christian nationalism is often most intense in the *absence* of religious practice and theological literacy. So-called cowboy churches, untethered to any larger affiliation or theology, have become a breeding ground for this nationalistic, theology-free identity.[37] But even the theologically literate are not immune from the temptations of power. Leon Wieseltier has coined the term "Christianists" for those who see Christianity as a political program rather than a religious faith, particularly the Catholic "integralists" who aspire to institutional dominance rather than the free-range identity politics of the cowboy preachers. The integralists would correct the defects of liberalism through the institutional establishment of a blinkered vision of Catholic Social Teaching. This movement presents a problem for Catholics and other Christians but certainly not only for them. Wieseltier warns, "the programs and the fantasies of the Christianists bear upon the lives of citizens who are not Christians, who answer to other principles."[38]

These phenomena underscore Taylor's point that a "subtraction story" is too simplistic an explanation for the ongoing religious shift in US culture.[39] If the subtraction story is an unlikely vision of the future—and the rise of both the seeking nones and the identity-driven Christianists suggests that it is—then there is a responsibility for rhetoricians to observe the available means of more authentic Christian rhetorics that might challenge violent distortions of Christianity more decisively than any secular critique. What we need is not a subtraction story but a transformation story. That transformation story must include the invention of post-Christian persuasions of God—persuasions of God that speak to and within a moment in which Christianity is both tethered and unmoored from its theological traditions. The project of this book is to imagine a theorhetoric for this moment—an appropriate and possible post-Christian theorhetoric *that is not in rivalry with any other persuasions*. My aim is not to reassert "Christian culture" nor simply to revert to traditional Christian expression nor to reject all such expression. Instead, I hope to relieve the torments of post-Christian religious speech while also resisting the temptation to purify it.

As I pursue this project, my major interlocutor will be a thinker whose own cross-pressured position makes his work particularly useful for inventing a post-Christian theorhetoric: René Girard (1923–2015). Girard is perhaps best known for his insight into the dangers of the sacred, as explicated in his 1972 book *Violence and the Sacred*. But Girard's interest in religion extends beyond the origins of religion and into the Hebrew and Christian scriptures. Drawing on these sources, Girard presents a compelling case for an authentic reading of the Gospels against the misuses to which they have often been put. Through this reading, Girard presents what David Dawson calls "a Christian witness against Christendom," a phrase whose paradox captures the sense of cross pressure described by Taylor.[40] Girard is a thinker who considers the Gospels the text par excellence for decoding the problems of human culture but who is also sometimes credited as having formulated "*the* most formidable theory of the death of religion ever ventured."[41] That theory goes to the heart of Christian rhetorics of sacrifice, atonement, and the cross, all connected in the commonplace that "Jesus died for (y)our sins." Not surprisingly, many people both within and outside of Christian tradition find the prevalent expressions of this idea unpersuasive. Nick Flynn succinctly captures this rejection in his poem "Emptying Town": "My version of hell / is someone ripping open his / shirt & saying, / *look what I did for you.*"[42] This idea is also thoroughly critiqued by Kenneth Burke in *The Rhetoric of Religion*, where Satan himself is scandalized by the notion of a perfect sacrifice. As Burke argued in 1961, just a few years after Vahanian's *Death of God*, the connection between violence and reconciliation presents both rhetorical and political problems for Christians and non-Christians alike.

At the heart of the issue, argues Girard, lies the problem of rivalry. Because human subjects desire mimetically, their desires often converge on the same objects, including relationships, wealth, property, or prestige. That competition is very often resolved through the scapegoating of innocent third parties, scapegoating that is hidden by means of a sacralization. For Girard, however, the basic problem is not language but mimetic desire. Our ontology—or anthropology, as Girard prefers to call it—is structured through a constitutive mimesis that always threatens to descend into competition. This same sense of competition, and the violent form of resolution that accompanies it, has infected certain Christian theories of atonement (i.e., "Jesus died for [y]our sins"). The rhetorics around these theories are warped by the same impulse, as Burke observes. Yet *pace* Burke, this economy is not the only available understanding of what Christians take to be Jesus's sacrifice. As Girard reads them, the Gospels present a counternarrative in which an act of vulnerability becomes the means of exit from the violent economy of the sacred. The Crucifixion is not simply an iteration (and therefore confirmation) of that economy but rather the rejection of it. It is also a rejection of the sense of rivalry that animates the scapegoating process in the first place and has warped historical expressions of Christianity. This is what Dawson means by a "Christian witness against Christendom." The challenge for any post-Christian theorhetoric, therefore, is to invent a Christian rhetoric that is not shaped by an impulse toward rivalry, a rhetoric that refuses to begin from a place of competition.

Such an idea may seem antithetical to the nature of rhetoric, which is often understood to offer a means of managing rivalry and competition. Rhetoric finds its home, as Burke famously put it, within "the Scramble, the Wrangle of the Market Place, the flurries and flare-ups of the Human Barnyard, the Give and Take, the Logomachy."[43] In Burke's project, rhetoric becomes a means of observing the implications of identification and division, of cooperation and conflict. These are not merely opposites but rather mutually constitutive. Our fundamental need for "consubstantiality," for forming common ways of life, makes the tension between cooperation and conflict unavoidable.[44] Within this tension lurks the persistent danger of scapegoating, a danger particularly acute within religious forms of consubstantiality. "*Corruptio optimi pessima*," writes Burke, "'the corruption of the best is the worst.' And it is the corruptors of religion who are a major menace to the world today, in giving the profound patterns of religious thought a crude and sinister distortion."[45] Burke was writing about the "Hitlerite distortions" of Christianity that would contribute to the Nazi scapegoating and attempted genocide of European Jews. Seventy years later, we can look around and see new expressions of these crude and sinister distortions. One might reasonably wonder whether the patterns of religious thought are all that profound if they are so easily twisted. One might also wonder whether rhetoric's art of managing rivalries—through contrasting arguments, staging controversies, presenting options—can finally purify the Christian religious *eristic* with a more irenic *agon*.

Yet my argument does not deny these traditional agonistic rhetorical practices. If anything, my argument pursues these practices more intensely by imagining a theorhetorical *agon* that distinguishes rivalry from difference and even conflict. A post-Christian theorhetoric is one that should not be distorted by the impulse to competition, whether it is competition with other religious traditions or even with the absence of tradition. What we need now, perhaps more than ever, is a Christian religious rhetoric that refuses to see Christianity as a "team sport," to borrow a phrase from Jonathan Haidt. In *The Righteous Mind*, Haidt argues that, contrary to conventional assumptions, faith is primarily a matter of community building rather than belief. Religion is very good at enmeshing people in cooperative relationships, but that is also precisely what makes it "well suited to be the handmaiden of groupishness, tribalism, and nationalism."[46] My project is to image a theorhetoric that is post-Christian precisely insofar as it refuses groupishness, tribalism, and nationalism, all of which are formed by rivalry—the impulse to reduce one's perceived opponents to a mirror for our own reflection. Rivals, according to Girard, do not differ from each other; they imitate each other—that is, rivals imitate the very people to whom they believe they are opposed. This is the game that a post-Christian rhetoric must refuse to play. If rhetoric is the practice of the open hand proffered in friendship, a post-Christian theorhetoric must be the practice of the open hand raised in preemptive surrender.

I take this kind of nonrivalrous rhetoric to be the implied rhetorical goal of Girard's project (though it is not a goal Girard himself would have recognized). Girard argued that our historical period was marked as a transition from one expression of religion to another. In a late interview, he offered this read of the post-Christian situation: "If I'm right, we're only extricating ourselves from a certain kind of religion so as to enter another, one that's infinitely more demanding because it's deprived of sacrificial crutches. Our celebrated humanism will turn out to have been nothing but a brief intermission between two forms of religion."[47] The "sacrificial crutches" to which Girard refers are the habits of the violent sacred—the practice of exclusionary sacrifice that shores up group identity on the backs of victims. Though these sacrificial practices often unfold within religion, Girard insisted that authentic religion refuses victimage. In *Violence and the Sacred*, Girard initially defined religion as "another term for that obscurity that surrounds man's efforts to defend himself by curative or preventive means against his own violence."[48] In later work, however, he insisted that true religion seeks to uncover this obscurity and then to refuse participation in the purgative violence it hides. The central message of the Gospels—along with the Hebrew scriptures, without which the Gospels cannot stand—is a rejection of violent sacrifice as the touchstone of religion. This is how Girard's work can be understood as a "Christian witness against Christendom," which is a good shorthand for a post-Christian theorhetoric. Articulating this emergent rhetoric is the critical and inventive project of the present book. Its project of rhetorical criticism is to observe the rhetorical structure and implications of Girard's argument; its project of invention is to fashion a rhetoric that might speak about God without leaning on the violent sacred.

Method: Toward Theorhetoric

In *On the Modern Cult of the Factish Gods*, Latour opens a religious address with the following caveats: "I have no authority whatsoever to talk to you about religion and experience, since I am neither a preacher, nor a theologian, nor a philosopher of religion, nor even an especially pious person. Fortunately, religion might not be about authority and strength but exploration, hesitation, and weakness."[49] This statement captures both the transdisciplinary risks and aspirations of the present project. Exploration, hesitation, and weakness seem to be appropriate methodological starting points for the rhetorician embarking on a study of God, a project usually managed in theology. But the aspiration of theo-rhetoric is not to pursue theology in any professional sense; instead, it is to ask questions of a theological import and to answer them by rhetorical, transdisciplinary means. Theorhetoric does not, therefore, amount to practicing theology without a license. Yet the invention of the persuasion of God is "theological" in a broad sense, as the theologian Jens Zimmerman explains: "Whenever one reflects on the meaning of biblical texts or reasons about God, one is, in fact, doing theology."[50] By this standard, theorhetorical reflection is authorized.

It is particularly authorized by those theologians—and there have been many such theologians—who have felt authorized to draw on rhetorical scholarship. The theologian Elizabeth Johnson writes that she and her colleagues "ply their craft by marshaling reasons, laying out arguments, making a case the way a trial lawyer might do, seeking to present an intelligible and convincing scenario."[51] Even beyond the "big rhetoric" sense, contemporary theology has been self-consciously rhetorical. "Following the death of the God of theism," David Klemm writes, "theology seems not so much to lack a subject matter as to need new and persuasive ways of disclosing it."[52] Klemm's comments indicate a rhetorical turn that began in scripture studies in the 1960s, when theologians and scripture scholars began to turn to the "new rhetoric" for new available means.[53] By 1987, Wilhelm Wuellner observed the advancement of this approach beyond studies of formal structure and into larger questions about the way in which scriptural interpretation informs value, judgment, and community.[54] For these reasons, Wuellner would describe rhetoric, "whether the classical 'old' or the proposed 'new rhetoric,'" as "philosophy's archrival and religion's closest ally."[55]

The theologian and scripture scholar Elisabeth Schüssler Fiorenza goes even further than Wuellner, arguing that rhetoric does not only oppose the ethical, as the usual Platonic framing has it, but actually ensures the ethical. Rhetorical methods, Fiorenza insists, introduce an "ethics of accountability" by insisting that theologians acknowledge their own purposes, contexts, and audiences.[56] These rhetorical issues, Fiorenza insists, help to bring forward the social locations of both the theologian and the theology that is produced. This commitment to a kind of rhetorical transparency becomes especially important for feminist, womanist, and liberationist theologies, all of which insist that there is no "theology in general" but only theology that is produced at particular moments by particular people to respond to particular problems.

There is long-standing precedent, therefore, to pursue Christian theological reflection in a rhetorical key, a project undertaken by rhetoricians like George

Kennedy and James Kinneavy. As the theologian John Milbank notes—citing Kinneavy—Christianity "from the first qualified philosophy by rhetoric in contending that the Good and the True are those things of which we 'have a persuasion,' *pistis*, or 'faith.'"[57] "Faith," adds Kenneth Chase, "is rhetorically constructed, and this faith provides the basis for embracing rhetorical practice."[58] To imagine a Christian theorhetoric—even a post-Christian theorhetoric—is therefore hardly alien to Christian tradition. If anything, "Christian theorhetoric" is a pleonasm that reminds us of the centrality of rhetoric to whatever Christianity is and whatever post-Christianity may yet be.

Even rhetoricians who do not speak explicitly about religion or God have sensed the theological implications of rhetorical inquiry. In *Deep Rhetoric*, James Crosswhite insists that, contrary to conventional expectations, rhetoric is an appropriate means of asking ultimate questions. Rhetoric has not only a horizontal axis but also a vertical axis, "along which it generates ideals of freedom and reason and nonviolence and the human formation of human beings." These axes cannot of course be separated: "Every historical situation has its own verticality, its own imagination of what goes beyond the situation."[59] But the vertical axis suggests that rhetoric addresses questions beyond the immediately practical (even as it takes those questions seriously). Theorhetoric would seem to be naturally interested in the question of the vertical, not because of some quasi-Platonic notion of a sky-bound heaven but because rhetoric is ultimately "a way of being human, a way of educating human beings, a way of nonviolence, a way of reason and freedom, a political way . . . and more."[60] The aspirations of rhetoric—the "more"—allow for the aspirations of theology and, by extension, theorhetoric. Pursuing this project includes a more rhetorical understanding of argumentation that "rhetorical theory must work to retrieve from millennia of philosophical and theological reifications," which is to say that rhetorical theory needs "to translate philosophical terms into communicative ones, back into rhetoric, without losing the passion of philosophy for something more."[61] Those theological reifications include the idea that God is primarily or exclusively a metaphysical proposition question rather than a practical question.

Many theologians and philosophers of religion have already undertaken the work of rescuing God from theological reification. A theorhetoric will join this project, not initiate it. But in joining it, rhetoric will push the question of God toward the communicative, toward the persuasive, toward an invention that responds to the transcendence of both the other and the Wholly Other. "Since transcendence always moves toward something," Crosswhite writes, "and influence is always influence in some direction, the question of whether there is some overall purpose to rhetorical transcendence, some overall goal, will always arise, and so deep rhetoric will always generate formally 'theological' and teleological and ethical questions."[62] Just as theology cannot but rely on rhetoric to advance its claims, rhetoric cannot advance its claims without touching on theology. Though Crosswhite himself might be disinclined to speak primarily in those terms, he suggests that to be deeply rhetorical implies the possibility of being deeply theological.

As Crosswhite's broaching of the theological suggests, the book's method can be characterized by the phrase "complicit invention," an idea I borrow from Eric Charles White's *Kaironomia*. White reminds his readers that *kairos* indicates the possibility of new or surprising response to the world; without its timeliness and flexibility, response becomes habituated, rote, deadened. In other words, new situations would seem to demand a kairotic, rather than merely traditional, response. "How can one make sense of a world that is eternally new simply repeating the ready-made categories of tradition? Tradition must answer to the present, must be adapted to the new circumstances that may modify or even disrupt received knowledge."[63] This is the reason that the post-Christian represents a crisis as both emergency and opportunity. Traditional language and ideas no longer seem able to answer to the present; new permutations are needed.

But White's understanding of *kairos* reminds us that any rhetorical intervention will always be a permutation—that is, a reworking. This is true, argues White, even for the radical situatedness of Gorgias's sophistic rhetoric. White understands *kairos* to be in a paradoxically "complicit" relation with tradition, or *doxa*.[64] Only through such complicity can the insights shaped by *kairos* become communicable. "The desire that thought should continually innovate, so that rather than simply repeating, it would always posit alternatives to tradition, is accompanied by the recognition that *thinking must become complicit with tradition if it would communicate with an audience*."[65] No rhetorical invention can be entirely new; even the "unprecedented" depends on precedent to be described as unprecedented at all. *Kairos* can therefore promise no meaningful response or practical action without some measure of complicity with those traditions or habituated responses that might preclude kairotic response—hence White's term "kaironomia," which suggests a mutually constitutive relation between the singularity of *kairos* and the regularity of custom, or *nomos*.

The notion of complicity—of working through and by means of the tension between *kairos* and *nomos*—also resonates with John Muckelbauer's treatment of rhetorical invention in *The Future of Invention*. Too often, Muckelbauer argues, methods of invention and structures of thought assume the negative dialectic—that is, that "negation is the generative principle of transformation."[66] Any position is held in reaction to some other position, whether it a position for, against, or even a "third way" that somehow synthesizes and transcends the options. But all of these options are structured on negating. Despite what may seem like powerful postmodern critiques of conventional modes of argumentation our habits of discourse continue to be articulated through a dialectical form in which advocacy, critique, or synthesis are the only available positions. But there also seems to be no escape from this problem. To deny the gesture of negation—to be "against" it somehow—is to affirm the very gesture that one is trying to evade.

In response to this problem, Muckelbauer urges a movement *among* the three positions of advocacy, critique, and synthesis. Rather than "overcoming" the dialectic, which would simply repeat the action of negation, Muckelbauer urges what he calls an "an 'affirmative' sense of change," in which moving among or through positions creates the conditions in which new possibilities and insights might emerge. It is not a matter of whether one repeats but how one repeats.[67] Richard Lanham writes, "No synonymity is ever exactly synonymous. Each new variation can be read not as an opaque variation or an already determined reality but as a transparent glimpse into a new reality."[68] Invention does proceed through an absolute rejection but by traveling through available possibilities as a practice of "immersive responsiveness" in which the rhetor discerns "what [a position, an idea] can do."[69] These notions of repetitions and immersive responsiveness resonate with the idea of complicit invention that I am drawing from White. They also provide a particularly appropriate methodology for a post-Christian theorhetoric that must say something new even though it cannot jettison the old. A post-Christian theorhetoric is inherently "complicit" with Christian tradition, in all senses of that term. It is inextricably folded into (L. *com*, with + *plicare*, fold, twist) Christian tradition and implicated in what that tradition has sometimes wrought. I am not seeking to purify Christian discourse of appeals to meekness, sacrifice, atonement, or holiness. Nor do I wish to replace them, a move that might render unrecognizable what they represent. (Again, nothing can ever be utterly unprecedented.) Rather, my project is to reinvent these terms through complicity with the tradition that produced them. This reinvention begins by reconceiving these terms as topoi, which Wayne Booth once defined as "the almost-empty places-of-agreement where those who think they disagree can stand as they hammer out their disagreements."[70] Though the argument I present here goes beyond traditional notions of argument, Booth's notion of "almost-empty places" recalls that topoi are equipped with contour and shape. Put another way, they come with baggage, or what Burke might call "equipment for living," along with equipment that may make living harder than it need be. This equipment cannot simply be abandoned; it must instead be retooled, just as contour must be reshaped. My aim is therefore to reconfigure these topoi so that they generate appeals more appropriate and possible in a post-Christian moment.

An Alienated Ethos

Any complicit invention also includes the rhetor. White argues that when Gorgias describes Helen as being overcome by seduction, the sophist is also describing himself. The paradoxical position by which the seducer is also seduced "can be taken as the emblem for an ideal dynamic between a principle of intentionality (or the self that would repeat itself in the world) and a principle of spontaneity (or the unforeseen opportunity of the immediate occasion)."[71] This paradox resonates with Crosswhite's equally paradoxical notion of a "deep rhetoric," which he defines as "a way we open ourselves to the influence of what is beyond ourselves and become receptive, a way we participate in a larger world and become open to the lives of others, a way we learn and change."[72] The notion of opening, of being receptive, at once passive and active, vulnerable and intentional, speaks to the posture that is most appropriate for the persuasion of God, which implies both traditional persuasive activity and the ontological condition of persuadability, especially in response to the Wholly Other.

The dynamic between intention and spontaneity, between the activeness of opening and the passiveness of being open, also suggests something about the ethos from which and through which I offer these arguments. It is an ethos that stands somewhat at odds with the kind of "explicitly Christian theory or approach to the study of rhetoric" for which Martin Medhurst called in 2004. Medhurst asks, "Don't we need an explicitly Christian theory of rhetoric for the twenty-first century that does, in fact, engage the revealed Truths/truths of Christianity?"[73] In some ways, my project is an answer to Medhurst's question insofar as it draws on the sources that he insists are necessary to any putative Christian rhetoric: Christian scripture, Christian theology, and contemporary rhetorical theory. My project also engages questions of "the revealed Truth/truths of Christianity" that are appropriate and possible for the twenty-first century. But that chronological placement is also where my project begins to diverge from Medhurst's. The twenty-first-century context seems to me to call for something that accounts for Girard's notion that one form of Christian religion is giving way to another, a more demanding form that must stand without the sacrificial crutches on which it has too long leaned. This is how we might understand the idea of post-Christian rhetoric: a rhetoric that draws on the sources outlined by Medhurst but toward the project implied by Girard.

To imagine such a crutchless Christianity is to pursue something akin to Darrell Fasching's notion of "alienated theology," in which one asks theological questions "'as if' one were a stranger to one's own narrative traditions."[74] The present book may therefore be understood as a project of *alienated theorhetoric*, an attempt to refashion theological concepts as rhetorical topoi and to do so as if I were a stranger to the tradition that produced those concepts. The subjunctive is important here. The truth is that I am not a stranger to these traditions. As a Christian (of the cradle-and-still-practicing Catholic persuasion), I feel the persuasive force of the topoi of meekness, sacrifice, holiness, and especially atonement. I do not wish to evacuate this power, but I also want to imagine less coercive expressions of that power. I endorse Latour's stubborn refusal to purify the "useless dross" but also Nick Flynn's equally stubborn refusal to be guilted into gratitude. This is how I understand the alienated ethos that might produce an alienated theorhetoric (haunted, I haunt). I write from "my" tradition because it is the one I know but also because it is the one with which I identify. This identification makes me responsible for it—not solely or ultimately, of course, but responsible nonetheless. Fortunately, I have guides—including Girard, Latour, Catherine Keller, Richard Kearney, and Jacques Ellul, among many others—who also write from this sense of alienation and responsibility.

Any project of theorhetoric, no matter the tradition from which it springs, raises the question of the rhetorician's own position. The theologian Rudolph Bultmann writes that "it is not legitimate to speak about God in general statements, in universal truths which are valid without references to the concrete, existential position of the speaker." He adds, "It is as impossible to speak meaningfully about God as it is about *love*. Actually, one cannot speak *about* love at all unless the speaking about it is itself an act of love. Any other talk about love does not speak about *love*, for it stands outside love."[75] To speak *of* God is to engage in relationship *with* God, even if that relationship is articulated through alienation. As I seek to invent a theorhetoric-*about* in these pages, I am perforce expressing a theorhetoric-*to*, an imprecation to the God who I hope may be. That imprecation is inescapably rhetorical, for the religious word, as Ernesto Grassi writes, is always "expressed in rhetorical language, in that language that urges itself on us in our desperate and pathetic engagement, for with it the chief concern is the formation of human existence."[76] By these understandings, one cannot embark on a project of theorhetoric except from a place of desperate and pathetic engagement where the speaker is forming some human existence. This existential posture does not deny rigorous standards of scholarship, but it does admit the ultimate motivations of such scholarship.

The poet and memoirist Christian Wiman offers a useful rule of thumb for judging the kind of writing to which theorhetoric aspires: "trust no theory, no religious history or creed, in which the author's personal faith is not actively at risk."[77] My personal faith is very much at risk in these pages. My theological imagination has long been shaped by the ideas I take up here, both while I was raised in the church and even after I left it. These ideas have continued to claim my imagination since my return. Describing her own return after a period away, the poet and memoirist Kathleen Norris captures my own experience of reversion: "When I began attending church again after twenty years away," she writes, "I felt bombarded by the vocabulary of the Christian church." The familiar vocabulary of faith "seemed dauntingly abstract, . . . even vaguely threatening."[78] That sense of bombardment and threat hangs over the ideas of meekness, sacrifice, atonement, holiness. And yet, these notions cannot be simply erased. Who, then, would inherit the earth? How could we recognize generous self-sacrifice? Or genuine reconciliation and restitution? Or a divine encounter that requires no exclusionary violence? My study is therefore motivated by a very personal and profound hope that a different kind of theorhetoric might invent different persuasions of God.

Chapter Outline

The argument of this book proceeds through four chapters. Chapter 1, "The Meek Defense," begins the work of inventing a post-Christian theorhetoric by imagining a rhetoric of meekness, a rhetorical style or posture characterized by a refusal of rivalry. Though the Christian associations with meekness are familiar (Matt. 5:5), many of this book's audiences may balk at meekness as a rhetorical style or posture. For many non-Christians, meekness may sound like a dangerous moral approbation of unjust suffering. Indeed, even for Christians, meekness may sound like an overpronounced Christian humility that would silence Christianity altogether. For rhetoricians, finally, meekness may seem inimical to the productive agonism that characterizes rhetorical practice and exchange. Nevertheless, chapter 1 argues that the Christian idea of meekness resonates with current rhetorical theory, which has developed an understanding of rhetoric as an ontological reality, a way of being that characterizes all relations long before anyone attempts to "wield" any "art" of rhetoric. Rhetoric describes what we are as much as it describes what we might do. Within that stance of fundamental vulnerability, we can no longer speak of rhetoric only or even primarily as a technique that one might possess. Yet our constitutive vulnerability does not mean that one cannot practice a "style of engagement," to borrow another phrase from Muckelbauer.[79] Meekness is thus a style as well as a feature of our rhetorical ontology. It is a term that can be used descriptively as well as prescriptively. In the latter case, meek rhetoric seems most appropriate for a post-Christian theorhetoric that would invent from Christian tradition without placing that tradition in rivalry with other traditions.

Chapter 2, "Friendly Injustices," presents a rhetorically oriented overview of René Girard's study of religion. Though Girard's work has made the occasional appearance in rhetorical scholarship, his work has not attracted sustained attention.[80] Recent work in the rhetorical study of the sacred has begun to engage Girard, and chapter 2 extends that engagement.[81] This chapter's primary aim, however, is to observe the rhetorical implications of Girard's thought. Though Girard does not recognize those implications as rhetorical, he does acknowledge that his conclusions about religion demand new forms of religious expression within Christian tradition. That rhetorical demand in turn requires a reconfigured understanding of rhetoric, one that takes account of mimetic desire and its relation to the sacred. This reconfigured understanding resonates with the rhetorical theory outlined in chapter 1. The meek defense provides the most appropriate framework for a post-Christian rhetoric—a rhetoric that maintains a relationship to tradition even while problematizing it and a rhetoric that refuses rivalry. As we will see, the refusal of rivalry is yet another implication of Girard's thought that Girard himself does not recognize. In his discussions of Christianity, Girard sometimes falls into the very sort of competitive impulse that his theory is trying to critique. Despite this issue, Girard's thought provides a way to articulate an alienated theorhetoric. Chapter 2 accommodates Girard's ideas to rhetoric and rhetoric to Girard's ideas, thereby opening the way to the more explicitly transdisciplinary theorhetorical invention that follows in chapters 3 and 4.

Chapter 3, "Overcoming Christianity," elaborates a post-Christian style of engagement by tracing three Girardian encounters—with Kenneth Burke, Christian atonement theology, and the Italian philosopher Gianni Vattimo. Each of these encounters provides available means of inventing a post-Christian theorhetoric. In the case of Burke, Girard provides a challenge to the logology of *The Rhetoric of Religion*, which is premised on a particular Christian atonement theology. One of our field's foundational studies of religious rhetoric assumes a highly contestable notion of divine relation (despite the book's protestations to be strictly atheological). Girard's work, however, points toward an understanding of the atonement as a form of persuasion rather than punishment. That understanding of the atonement, which represents an alternative but still-orthodox Christian theological tradition, is best articulated through the kind of rhetorical style imagined by the meek defense. Finally, chapter 3 propels these theological questions into a series of debates between Girard and Gianni Vattimo. Vattimo is best known for his idea of "weak thought," which designates the thought that follows in the wake of the enfeeblement of Being. This postmodern project of radical hermeneutics seems, at least at first, radically at odds with Girard's self-described anthropological and empirical project. Despite these differences, Vattimo finds in Girard a religious confirmation of weak thought using a Heideggerian *Verwindung*, a distortion or twisting that maintains a relation to an original claim. *Verwindung* suggests a paradoxical relation to tradition that is at once a recovery and a recovery *from*. Girard, for his part, rejects these readings as too ludic a take on the harsh reality of the cross; the fundamental problem of mimetic desire means that there can be no Christian expression without the Crucifixion. Chapter 3 treats this argument as a kind of fundamental topos for inventing a post-Christian, alienated theorhetoric.

Chapter 4, "Uneasy Holiness," extends the theorhetorical inquiry into how "the sacred" and "the holy" have functioned within both religious studies and rhetorical studies. The chapter thus forwards an emerging inquiry into the role of rhetoric in what Rudolf Otto dubbed the "numinous" (L. *numen*, divine, divine majesty, deity), an experience or encounter with the otherworldly.[82] Within this inquiry, a debate is developing over whether "sacred" or "holy" represents the richest resource for theorhetorical invention. For some scholars, the "sacred" preserves the otherness of the Wholly Other, which Otto also called the "*mysterium tremendum*," the frightening mystery at the heart of divinity.[83] For others, including Girard, the "holy" suggests a divine relation free of violence. As rhetoricians engage in this argument, they will, naturally enough, turn to the literature of religious studies (e.g., Otto, Émile Durkheim, Mircea Eliade, and Giorgio Agamben, among others) to understand the function and meaning of these familiar terms. But this inquiry presents only further uncertainty. As one might expect in an inquiry into the ineffable, the available lexicon is often unequal to the task. Yet the paradox of ineffability is that it compels a rhetorical response, even when the response must draw on unstable terminology. As a case study of these issues, chapter 4 extends the theorhetorical reinvention of atonement to a case study of Pope Francis's *Gaudete et Exsultate* (2015), an "apostolic exhortation," or letter intended to move the faithful toward some desired aim. Though such a document may seem an odd resource for a post-Christian theorhetoric, the exhortation nevertheless bears the traits we will have developed throughout the book: a meek rhetoric that refuses rivalry, that presents a convalescence of tradition, and that aspires to holiness free of exclusionary violence.

1

The Meek Defense

Stripped to its bare minimum, rhetoric is a defense mechanism.
—George Kennedy, "A Hoot in the Dark"

In *The God Who May Be*, Richard Kearney imagines a God who can never be spoken about in absolute confidence. God, Kearney suggests, is only possible insofar as human persons respond to God's covenantal commitment and ethical mandate. The God-who-may-be is thus eschatological promise, made good for human persons in relation to their own response and only in the fullness of time. Kearney's notion is captured in God's cryptic naming/unnaming at the burning bush: "Ehyeh-Asher-Ehyeh" (Exod. 3:14), which can be translated as "I Am That I Am," "I Am Who I Am," and "I Will Be What I Will Be." The uncertainty of this translation leads Kearney to conclude that God must be understood not simply as enduring but also as emerging—as possibility as much as being.[1] God is thus construed neither as the "hyper-ascendant deity of mystical or negative theology" nor as "the consigning of the sacred to the domain of abyssal abjection," which both "share a common aversion to any mediating role for narrative imagination."[2] Against these extremes, Kearney urges us to "'muddle through' with the help of a certain judicious mix of phronetic understanding, narrative imagination and hermeneutic judgment," a triad that implies persuasion.[3]

Following Kearney, this chapter brings the resources of the rhetorical imagination to bear on the question of God. But in rhetorical fashion, I speak not of the God-who-may-be but rather the God-who-probably-is or, rather, the God-who-is-*probably*, the God who is known, insofar as God is ever known, through persuasion. Persuasion offers a way to make decisions, articulate commitments, and take action within conditions of uncertainty—to muddle through. "In the wreckage of modernist foundationalisms and totalizing metaphysics," writes Kenneth Chase, "the ancient legacy of contingent argumentations and situated ethico-aesthetic appeals deeply resonates with a contemporary age broken by shattered hopes and the specter of never-ending violence."[4] Persuasion becomes crucial for a post-Christian moment in which Christianity's own shattered hopes and moral failings have created the very conditions in which a naïve Christian theism no longer seems possible.

Researchers continue to reveal Christianity's complicity in antisemitism, colonialism, homophobia, patriarchy, segregation, slavery, and white supremacy. If Western culture finds itself at a post-Christian moment, it is in many ways because it has rejected the project of "Christendom," of the notion of moral and legal orders buttressed by explicit religious framework. In this context, to speak of the God-who-probably-is may sound like a last-ditch attempt to shore up a crumbling façade. By contrast, the God-who-is-*probably* is meant to speak of a God who reveals Godself through the uncertainty of persuasion. The God-who-is-probably is a God who "makes Godself vulnerable to the other, dependent on the other as to how the future will evolve, and in the vulnerability of divine obligation allows the other to affect who God may be in the future."[5] However God may be, God is probably.

I approach this probable God through a *rhetoric of meekness*, which I define as a rhetoric of nonrivalrous response. It is a rhetoric of compassionate agonism that refuses both a self-diminishing submission to and a mimetic mirroring of an opponent's antagonism. As such, a rhetoric of meekness is appropriate for a post-Christian theorhetoric. It draws on recent developments in rhetorical theory that have shifted our understanding of rhetoric away from an exclusive focus on rhetoric-as-art and toward rhetoric-as-ontology, and it emerges from a long conversation in rhetorical studies about the depth of rhetoric's role in social relations. This conversation includes Richard Lanham's famous critique of the "weak defense" of rhetoric, Richard Marback's challenge to the "strong defense" of rhetoric, and several other contemporary rhetoricians—including Michelle Ballif, James Crosswhite, Diane Davis, Bridie McGreavy, Kelly Pender, Nathaniel Rivers, and Nathan Stormer—who insist that we should not see rhetoric first and foremost as something unproblematically available for our use but rather as a kind of constitutive openness to the other. A rhetoric of meekness draws from these thinkers by imagining an orientation to rhetoric that recognizes that constitutive vulnerability but also preserves a practice of response within that vulnerability. If ontological notions of rhetoric rightly challenge our confidence in simplistic notions of purpose (along with intention, means, and ends), a rhetoric of meekness articulates a form of response that accounts for that challenge.

26   PERSUASIONS OF GOD

Meekness is not mere mildness or submissiveness. It is instead a profound power to respond to a situation without rivalry—that is, without mirroring the competitive or even malevolent instincts of others in a given situation. Meekness is not powerlessness, but its power is neither power *over* nor power *against*. Rather, it is the power to refuse—where appropriate—to be (de)formed by the collective feeling that has formed an emerging situation. René Girard calls this collective feeling "mimetic rivalry," the way in which mimetic desire can lead actors to mirror the feelings and actions of others, including one's purported opponents. Yet a rhetoric of meekness does not seek to evade confrontation altogether. It preserves the ability to confront in different terms than those that have been presented. Meekness thus presents a model for a post-Christian theorhetoric, and not simply because meekness recalls a familiar Christian virtue. More importantly, meekness offers an approach appropriate for speaking from a position of alienation within a tradition, which is to say a kind of constructive disloyalty appropriate for a post-Christian theorhetoric.

To pursue this argument, the chapter begins with an overview of another attempt to invent new ways of speaking *of* God *after* God: *theopoetics*, the tradition in which Kearney is writing when he imagines the God-who-may-be. Theopoetics is essentially the practice of theological reflection through the narrative or poetic imagination rather than the rational or argumentative imagination. Yet, while the timeline of contemporary theopoetics roughly parallels the recovery of rhetoric, there has been no parallel project of theologizing through the rhetorical imagination. The chapter then presents an account of the rhetorical imagination as a prolegomenon for the "meek defense." This presentation has two purposes: to offer a rationale for the meek defense and to introduce rhetorical theory to readers, particularly mimetic theorists, who might understandably be unfamiliar with contemporary developments in rhetoric. This section covers some ground that may be familiar to rhetoricians, but it quickly turns to a full articulation of a rhetoric of meekness, which conceives of rhetoric as the paradoxically active passivity of opening ourselves to the influence of others.[6] Its practice of invention pursues a process of affirmative, nonnegating rhetorical invention that evades rivalrous orientations.

A Theopoetic Prelude

Catherine Keller provides the most ambitious and the most succinct description of the project of theopoetics: "To make God: quite a project."[7] Since the early

1960s, a diverse group of writers from a range of fields and interests, both inside and outside the academy, have developed the idea of theopoetics as an alternative means of inventing God. Theopoetics sets out to remind us that the poetic, rather than the philosophical or theological, has been the primary vehicle of extrahuman communication.[8] The philosopher John Caputo writes, "Religion is served up to us in great Scriptural narratives, . . . the defining features of our life magnified in moving and unforgettable stories, in brilliant figures."[9] Poetics keeps in view that when we speak of God, we can only ever speak from a position of approximation, uncertainty, and tentativeness, salutary approaches for speaking about something as powerful and potentially dangerous as the *mysterium tremendum*. Kearney, meanwhile, insists that poetics can cultivate ethical response "by recalling the limits of human judgment and the unavoidable play of interpretations which attends every application of justice."[10] In addition to interrupting rote habits of response, hermeneutics also contributes to habits of hospitality and generosity insofar as it orients us toward difference.

Yet theopoetics is not simply a matter of expressing theological claims with renewed poetic flair. The theologian David Miller insists on a difference between what he calls "theopoetry" and theopoetics. "Theopoetry," he writes, "is just another way of expressing theology's eternal truth." Theopoetics, by contrast, is after something bigger than prettified assertion. Miller argues that theopoetics constitutes "a reflection on *poiesis*, a formal thinking about the nature of the making of meaning, which subverts the *-ology*, the nature of the logic, of theology."[11] Theopoetics assumes that artists may be better equipped than theologians to deliver theological insight. In this way, theopoetics goes beyond the representational; it recognizes that theological thinking results in embodied effects. Keller suggests that the basic aim of theopoetics is "that theology must risk a return *in style* to the heteroglossia of Scripture and the multimedia of liturgy, to the affective and aesthetic genres of the spiritual imaginations—if it is to stand a chance of postmodern rebirth."[12]

Richard Kearney and Matthew Clemente identify both ancient and modern lineages for theopoetics in "both the Hellenic and the Abrahamic traditions," where "*poiesis* is often understood as *theo-poiesis*—God made present in and through making."[13] Keller finds an ancestor of theopoetics in the ancient Greek notion of *theosis*, usually translated as "deification." The idea of deification is a common one among the church fathers; perhaps the most well-known statement is that of Athanasius: "For he [the Logos] became human that we might be made God."[14] At least one purpose of the Incarnation is not simply the divine descent to the human but the human ascent to the divine. "In other words," Keller adds, "the high Christology behind the Council of Nicaea was originally accompanied by a high anthropology. The glory of the Creator does not yet play the zero-sum game with the dignity of the creature."[15] The rejection of a zero-sum game anticipates arguments we will develop about the nonrivalrous nature of a meek rhetoric.

The contemporary emergence of theopoetics in the 1960s occurred as theologians and philosophers of religion began to grapple with a number of different cultural shifts, including the reverberating echoes of the death of God, the aftermath of the three disastrous decades of 1914–45, and, of course, the upheavals of the 1960s themselves.[16] These events contributed to what Keller calls a "boundary-discourse" that marks the moment that everything changed.[17] The very notion of "God," suggests Keller, has become so radioactive that it repels potential theological allies across areas of inquiry. "No matter how gracefully we transcribe, defer, mask, diversify, or humble our God-talk, does not 'God' obstruct the interdisciplinary, indeed transdisciplinary, coalescence we need?"[18] Calcified by assertion and proposition, "God" may become a stumbling block to inquiry and invention, which theopoetics seeks to revive through "the transdisciplinary conversations of the new materialism, of affect theory, of deconstructive theology, and of a speculative *aesthesis*."[19]

This project, insists Caputo, can produce only a "weak theology," by which he means not "something debilitated, ineffective, and anemic but a theology that abandons the mode of claiming and gives itself over to a prior being-claimed."[20] Weakness—which begins to introduce the meekness taken up later in the chapter—contains its own strength: the rigor of theopoetics is "*to sustain an exposure to the inbreaking of something.*"[21] Here, we can detect an echo of Crosswhite's notion of deep rhetoric as an active-passive movement of opening ourselves. The notion of weak theology also suggests the possibility of a post-Christian theological reflection. Caputo argues that theopoetics expresses the possibility of "religion without religion," the possibility of religious experience that is both enabled and unbound by the traditions, practices, and communities we normally refer to as "religion." Religion in this latter sense can never fully capture religion in the former sense, which is "that notion of life at the limit of the possible, on the verge of the impossible."[22] At the same time, sustaining our exposure to the edge does not mean eschewing traditional theology or theological texts altogether. "Where," Caputo asks, "would I be without my tradition, without my worn-out copy of the *Confessions?*"[23] Theopoetics is complicit with tradition insofar as it calls on and responds to what has come before. To speak of "religion after religion" is to speak of new permutations of old yearnings.

The return and renewal of faith after God, Kearney writes, is "not just a question of returning in time but also of returning in space. It involves a topos as well as a *kairos*."[24] These invocations of rhetorical language suggest the need for persuasion in the project of making God after God. Yet the possibility that rhetoric may be involved also seems fraught for thinkers who align themselves with the project of theopoetics. Kearney is at pains to insist to his interlocutors that he abhors "anything that smacks of evangelism or apologetics. I would hate to think I am trying to convert you now. God forbid. But I would say that in any meaningful exchange of narratives on religion, there might be some kind of mutual transformation."[25] Kearney's refusal to reduce the other to the same is appropriate and admirable. The Christian will-to-convert not only risks alienating the stranger but also can make interreligious dialogue impossible. Moreover, in the academic setting in which Kearney is operating, it would be inappropriate to seek conversion in anyone. Yet, at the same time, his admission that meaningful exchange always entails the possibility of mutual transformation acknowledges an irreducible rhetoricity. In other statements, meanwhile, rhetoric is reduced to a form of mereness. Miller, a student of Stanley Hopper, insists that theopoetics is not simply "an artful, imaginative, creative, beautiful, and *rhetorically compelling* manner of speaking and thinking concerning a theological knowledge that is and always has been in our possession and a part of our faith."[26] In this formulation, rhetoric might make the old more persuasive, but it cannot discover the new. With Keller, however, we pivot to "mereness" as mendacity. "Of course," she writes, "humanists might immediately be suspicious—I would be—that theopoetics is a *rhetorical sleight of hand*: a way to *disguise* good old God with an aesthetic aura, and then *sneak* Him back in under the *disarming guise* of metaphor."[27] Poetics mediates; rhetoric disguises. In these statement, theopoetic thinkers offload their discursive anxieties onto rhetoric, even while they continue to speak in unacknowledged rhetorical terms. Caputo argues that theopoetics does not rely on a "proud overarching ahistorical thing called pure 'Reason'" but rather the "humbler hermeneutical idea of 'good reasons,' in the plural and the lower case." Caputo goes on to develop this position in other familiar ways, including the idea that theopoetics might include *phronesis*.[28] I do not point out these tensions to catch out theopoetics in a failure or contradiction.

My argument is simply that the faith imagined by theopoetics also implies rhetorical matters of persuasion, influence, judgment, and decision. Moved by the insights and possibilities articulated in theopoetics, the rhetor may be prompted to ask how the fecundity of theopoetics can translate into congregation or whether its translation into congregation also relies on segregation. We have already seen the ways in which theopoetical speculation will still bear some of the familiar markers of small-*c* confession (recall Caputo's copy of Augustine's *Confessions*). Here, it is prudent to recall the etymology of religion: *re-ligare*, "to bind again," suggesting the ways in which religion binds us to the divine and to each other. These issues seem to push us into the territory of rhetoric; whatever else it may be, rhetoric is something that cannot be practiced alone. My argument is that a project of theorhetoric can extend the project of theopoetics by focusing the making of God more resolutely on the issue of relationality, particularly in (and even through) moments of conflict. I begin to take up these matters in the next section, which also introduces a more contemporary understanding of rhetoric that extends far beyond the idea of persuasive speech and into the most profound questions of human and nonhuman influence. This is what Crosswhite means by "deep rhetoric," the "human transcendence" through which "we participate in a larger world" and "learn and change."[29] Understood in this way, rhetoric designates the way we understand the problems and possibilities of being human—our fundamental orientation to the world, an orientation prior to any systematic, rationalized, instrumental understanding of persuasion. The idea of "opening ourselves" suggests that rhetoric is enacted through a paradoxical relation between control and vulnerability, a relation in which the most influential action one can take is to make oneself available to the influence of others, along with the Wholly Other.

I will develop these and other understandings of rhetoric as this chapter proceeds. A more immediate point is this: as in the case of religion, the definition of rhetoric is at stake every time the word is deployed. If rhetoric is a "field" at all, it may be a field formed by a persistent uncertainty about the precise nature of its subject.[30] As much as we must speak of a God-who-may-be, we also need to speak of a rhetoric-that-may-be. We thus enter an inquiry into the ultimate question of God, unsure of how we are equipped to address it, whether with art or tool or practice—or perhaps something that includes and exceeds all such conceptions. Sorting through these possibilities becomes a prolegomenon to any theorhetoric.

Complicit Rhetoric

Such preliminary work becomes all the more important given the persistence of the idea that rhetoric is "just a hired gun."[31] To preview chapter 2, the conventional distrust of rhetoric that worries theopoetics also shapes the thought of Girard. On the rare occasions he speaks of rhetoric, Girard tends to frame it in the conventional fashion, employing phrases such as "rhetorical legerdemain," "hackneyed rhetoric," "rhetorical flamboyance," and "a glimmering veil of rhetoric over the sordid realities of life."[32] Girardians, then, may come to the question of rhetoric under the assumption that rhetoric is nothing more than a way to make the unpalatable palatable. To counter this tenacious idea, the present section reviews arguments that, for rhetoricians at least, have become commonplace. Such a review is crucial for a transdisciplinary project like theorhetoric. If theopoetics enjoins a hermeneutical discipline that exercises our ethical muscles through the suspension of judgment, theorhetoric practices a relational discipline that exercises our ethical muscles through action. In fact, rhetoric demands not only that we exercise but that we play the game, even if, as Robert Wess argues about rhetoric, "changing the rules of the game is the only game in town."[33] These rules about changing rules apply equally to religious rhetoric. Writing about religious discourse, Latour insists that there is no magic formula, no surefire protocol for conjuring properly religious effects. "You have to run the same risk every time and it will be different every time."[34] The risk I run in this section is to ask the question, "What is rhetoric?"

We can begin to discern an answer by returning to Eric Charles White's notion of *kaironomia*, which, as discussed in the introduction, suggests the pull between *nomos* (tradition, custom, culture) and *kairos* (timeliness, surprise, novelty). For rhetoricians, *kairos* names the occasion and in some ways the art—or perhaps instinct—that characterizes what John Poulakos defines as recognizing "opportune moments" both the "appropriate" and the "possible," with special emphasis on that which may have previously seemed impossible.[35] Echoing Poulakos and anticipating Latour, White writes, "As a prescription concerning the basis on which thought can *begin* to intervene in the world, *kairos* is offered with the understanding . . . that thought must always be willing, as circumstances change, to begin *again*."[36] *Kairos* is meant to name the fact that situations require us to run risks and those risks will be different every time.

The problem, as White describes it, lies in the inherent contradiction of imagining an art or practice that can somehow anticipate surprise. "Since *kairos* stands for precisely the irrational novelty of the moment that escapes formalization, any science of 'kaironomy' would find itself incoherently promising foreknowledge of chance."[37] If one has some foreknowledge of *kairos*, then it would no longer seem to be kairotic, since the foreknowledge would allow rhetors to prepare their response in advance. In other words, to anticipate a moment as "opportune" is to render it ordinary. For White, the idea of *doxa*, or received opinion, represents the ordinary, or at least the familiar and conventional (e.g., rhetoric is a hired gun). The question of *kairos* then becomes, "How can one communicate the 'unheard of' in such a way that it is understandable but not immediately assimilable to the *doxa*?"[38] If an idea is entirely novel, then how can it even be heard? But if it can be heard, how can it ever be novel?

This conundrum means that rhetoric must forever operate within a tension between the novel and the hearable. "The desire that thought should continually innovate, so that rather than simply repeating, it would always posit alternatives to tradition, is accompanied by the recognition that thinking must become *complicit with tradition* if it would communicate with an audience."[39] The idea of "complicity" may once again recall that rhetoric is ethically suspect. But complicity in White's sense suggests that the timeliness of *kairos* requires a relation to *chronos* even to be recognized as "timely." Unless *chronos* is there to provide a contrast to *kairos*, there can be no *kairos*. This is what White means by "complicity," which entails being folded into the familiar in order to introduce the unfamiliar.

The idea of complicity has profound implications for understanding rhetoric. White writes, "At once a theory and a practice, [*kaironomia*] remains caught in an inevitable double bind between an intention to 'speak the truth' about the endlessness of interpretation and an awareness that every 'truth' (including the one that would posit 'no-truth') is historically determined."[40] To "speak the truth" within a maelstrom of interpretation is paradoxically to acknowledge the historicity of such "truth," an acknowledgment that at once enables and undermines the *kairotic* claim. There is no way out of this double bind, only alternative ways of inhabiting it. The double bind also mirrors the way in which White understands the position of rhetors themselves, who must enter situations deeply enough to themselves be affected (and even effected) by the situation. But this openness to being affected/effected is precisely what makes it possible for the rhetor to be effective/affective. "The seducer who is seduced by the occasion of seduction can be taken as the emblem for an ideal dynamic between a principle of intentionality (or the self that would repeat itself in the world) and a principle of spontaneity (or the unforeseen opportunity of the immediate occasion)."[41] To seduce is first to be opened to being seduced; the contingency of situation (in)forms the contingency of the rhetor's subjectivity.

Complicity also has profound implications for inventing a post-Christian rhetoric. Recall the project that Martin Medhurst outlined for a "twenty-first-century" Christian rhetoric, a rhetoric that would "engage the revealed Truth/truths of Christianity."[42] The formulation "Truth/truths" can be taken to suggest an oscillation between the permanent and the provisional, along with the persistent and paradoxical movement of *kaironomia*. Any absolute Truth must become complicit with contingent truth(s). At its heart, the contingent is that which touches (*con*, with + *tangere*, to touch) rather than that which is absolute (*ab*, from + *solvere*, to loosen). "*Christ is contingency,*" insists Christian Wiman: not absolute but touching, incarnated in the world.[43] For those Christians who have been raised on a sovereign, imperturbable God, the idea of this radical contingency may seem unsettling. "But what a relief it can be to befriend contingency; to meet God right here in the havoc of chance."[44] This idea is both rhetorically and theologically sound. Kenneth Chase notes that the Incarnation is often understood within Christian rhetorical theory as the most profound divine communication. Fully appreciating this, however, results in a revised notion of rhetoric, one that implies an idea of "adaptation" "more ethically radical and sophisticated than that which we typically find in Aristotelian rhetorics."[45] The Incarnation is not simply God adapting to the havoc of chance but fully entering into and surrendering to it.

The idea of a "seduced seducer," moreover, reminds us that persuasion always draws in the persuader as much as the audience. Michelle Ballif captures this idea succinctly, describing the conventional understanding of rhetorical agency as one built on "a presumption that 'we' exist independently of 'rhetoric,' and that rhetoric is perhaps a tool that 'we' use to do a variety of work—work of our choosing—and work that advantageously benefits us."[46] Ballif argues that this common understanding of rhetoric begs several questions about agency, intention, and purpose. But the largest begged question is the question of persuasion itself. Implied in Ballif's remark is the third idea of persuasion outlined in the introduction: persuasion as a tendency, orientation, character, or haunt, all suggested by the idea of dwelling rather than essence or assertion. This usage of persuasion rearranges the order of agent and effect into a more reciprocal relation. Agency, whatever it may be, is as much an effect of persuasion as a driver of it. Diane Davis has articulated the grounds for this rearrangement most compellingly in her *Inessential Solidarity*, where she observes what she calls an "originary (or preoriginary) rhetoricity," by which she means a condition in which human beings (though not exclusively human beings) are occasioned by an "affect*ability* or persuad*ability*."[47] By this understanding, rhetoric may be construed as a tool that we use to our advantage (and, one hopes, to the advantage of others). But long before a tool-rhetoric is available, there is a primordial rhetoric already operating: "For there to be any sharing of symbolic meaning, any construction of a common enemy or collective goal, any effective use of persuasive discourse at all, a more originary rhetoricity must already be operating, a constitutive persuadability and responsivity that testifies, first of all, to a fundamental structure of exposure. If rhetorical practices work by managing to have an effect on others, then an always prior openness to the other's affection is its first requirement."[48] It is important to note here that Davis does not altogether reject the goal of effective discourse. But effective discourse cannot encompass the full reach of rhetoric's activity, which is under way before we recognize its workings in something like the very notion of effective discourse. This idea likewise resonates with Crosswhite's deep rhetoric, which "seeks after the senses in which we *are* rhetorical even before and behind and in addition to whatever symbolic actions we *take*." This "rhetorical ontology," he adds, is not about the construction of a discrete, sovereign self; instead, it is concerned with "*the ability to be a self* and the different ways of being that involves. We *are* a capacity for receiving and giving our being to each other."[49]

Rhetoric, to echo Ballif, is therefore not simply a power we possess. Rhetoric equally possesses us—not simply in the conventional negative sense of being easily manipulated but in a much more profound sense of being formed through and by means of relations with others. This is what "complicity" (*com-*, together + *plectĕre, plex-*, to plait, twine) means: to be folded together, interwoven, intertwined, a form of relationality in which whatever a subject may be is entirely dependent on what the other may be. But the notion of complicity also suggests the ways in which older permutations of rhetoric—agency, intention, purpose, aim—can and must be folded in with the new permutations I have been sketching here—rhetoricity, ontology, relationality. The notions of persuasion sketched in the introduction encompass all of these possibilities. The seducer seduces, and the seducer is seduced. God persuades, God is persuaded, and God has a persuasion. There is no single positionality through which we can discern, once and for all, the persuasions of God. It is the movement among these positions that constitutes divine invention. Each makes way for the other, creating a space for invention.

Empty Rhetoric

Related to the idea of complicity is the idea of *capacity*, which, as Crosswhite aptly argues, suggests a paradoxical relation between control and vulnerability. We do not "have" a capacity for receiving and giving; we *are* a capacity, as much possessed as possessing. Nathan Stormer and Bridie McGreavy suggest that capacity allows for a more profound understanding of rhetoric's ontological and ecological character than the more familiar notion of "agency." If "agency" (L. *agens*, acting) connotes the exertion of power, "capacity" connotes a relation between power and a kind of powerlessness. The Latin verb *capere* (to take in or capture) is related to the adjective *capax* (large, spacious, roomy). This etymology suggests the paradoxical power of emptiness, in which power is enabled by making room for something. This idea offers an entirely new understanding of the familiar phrase "empty rhetoric," which usually designates disingenuousness or deceit, a gap between claim and action. But understood as an alternative to simplistic conceptions of agency, empty rhetoric indicates the ability to make oneself open, available, and even hospitable to the influence of others. Empty rhetoric seeks to make a space, to move over, to make room. "By shifting the focus from agency to capacity, we revise the commonplace for discussing qualities that empower rhetoricity, emphasizing the ecology of entanglements between entities over the abilities that are inherent to humans."[50] For Stormer and McGreavy, the central issue is to account for the full complexity of rhetoric's ecology, in which rhetorical capacity is not a human possession over and against materiality but rather an extension of it. Within this ecology, the rules of the game shift. Stormer and McGreavy argue that the "most general relational quality is struggle; rhetoric emerges from and for struggle. However, ecological struggle is striving pursued *with*, not contesting *against*, other things. It is struggle in dependence, not between 'independents.'"[51] It is a struggle of complicity. Stormer and McGreavy suggest that a flower on the edge of the desert can be said to struggle against the environment but also to be dependent on it. One might also say that a herd of deer struggles against a pack of wolves, but the wolves' hunting also ensures that the herd stays healthy.

The idea of empty rhetoric can be applied not only to materialist notions of rhetoric but also to the seemingly immaterial idea of theorhetoric. Scholars and practitioners of Buddhism will be immediately alert to the Buddhist resonances with this idea of empty rhetoric. But there are also Christian resonances,

36   PERSUASIONS OF GOD

particularly in the Christian idea of *kenosis*, or divine self-emptying. Kenosis appears in Paul's Letter to the Philippians: "Rather, [Jesus] emptied himself, taking the form of a slave, coming in human likeness; and found human in appearance, he humbled himself, becoming obedient to death, even death on a cross" (Phil. 2:7–8). Kenosis suggests the Christian theological idea that the Son exercises the capacity for emptiness, divesting himself of divine power in exchange for a radical sense of intimacy in the Incarnation.[52] Through emptying, God becomes flesh. "Incarnation," writes Elizabeth Johnson, "bespeaks a different form of divine presence marked by an unimaginable intensity of intimacy. It is presence in the flesh. The omnipresent God is now present in and as a living, breathing human being."[53] ("Christ *is* contingency.") In the Incarnation, the "immaterial" divine—already present throughout the materiality of creation—enters the material in a profound way. This entrance includes a fundamental sense of vulnerability (L. *vulnus*, wound), up to and including death by violence. In addition, this divine capaciousness is what makes possible the theopoiesis, the "god-making" of "deification." The paradoxical path to theopoeisis thus lies in what we might call an "anthropo-kenosis," a human self-emptying: "For whoever wishes to save his life will lose it, but whoever loses his life for my sake will find it" (Matt. 16:25). By the arguments offered by Davis, Crosswhite, and Stormer and McGreavy, these capacities are understood to be thoroughly rhetorical insofar as they both emanate from a prior rhetoricity and indicate some sense of intentionality. One *surrenders*, to contingency, incarnation, the other, or the Wholly Other.

This latter possibility risks extending a descriptive understanding of rhetoric into a prescriptive one by indicating an attitude one might adopt within the ontological and ecological condition of prior rhetoricity. The risk I mention here is a significant one, especially given the humanist ontology (and ontotheology) that can frame rhetoric as the kind of "tool rhetoric" described by Ballif. The challenge for any notion of rhetoric-as-capacity is how it might be articulated without reinscribing a merely "instrumental" idea of persuasion, as in, "here's a heuristic by which one may reliably empty oneself." There is certainly also a risk in the other direction: even an entirely descriptive account of empty rhetoric cannot help but have prescriptive import (otherwise, what is the motivation for producing a richer description of rhetoric in the first place?), and this prescriptive import seems to invite the possibility of heuristic, practice, or method.

The idea of rhetoric as capacity does not and should not evacuate rhetoric of its power to persuade in the ordinary sense of the term. Rhetoric may well be ontological, but it is also technical, and technical notions of rhetoric cannot be understood as reducible to instrumental rationality and predictable ends. As Kelly Pender explains, the full implications of the idea of *techne* reach far beyond such how-to notions. While *techne* may refer to handbook know-how, it also includes less instrumental notions such as "inventing new social possibilities," "producing resources," and "bringing-forth," the last of which recalls Heideggerian notions of working *with* the "standing reserve" to bring forth in a way that does not reduce some other reality to a resource.[54] For Heidegger, Pender writes, the difference between instrumental production and "bringing forth" can be exemplified through the difference between a windmill and a coal mine. The windmill relies on the wind to produce the resource of energy, whereas a coal mine fundamentally transforms the land, putting a permanent stamp on a landscape that has now been reduced to a resource.[55] These examples offer different notions of emptiness, one that suggests a capacity enacted through a kind of vulnerability to ecology, the other a void.

Yet though the windmill "brings forth," it is still an intervention that both is produced by a certain kind of technical know-how and makes available something for human use. Pender's complex understanding of *techne*, in other words, does not valorize simplistic notions of either the "natural" or the "artificial." The technical can also be creative, surprising, even enchanting, to use a word with special resonance in contemporary discussions of religion. Pender illustrates this point with reference to the French literary critic Jean Paulhan, who argues against antirhetorical aesthetics by citing the image of a handrail placed at the edge of an abyss. Though it is easy to assume that the handrail limits one's freedom, in reality "the hand-rail allows [one] to get closer to the abyss, and to see every nook and cranny."[56] This example teaches us that the ontological conception of rhetoric imagined by Davis, Crosswhite, and others does not preclude the interventions of rhetors within situations. Someone, after all, builds the handrail. But that technical intervention emerges from the situation rather than dominating it. This is crucial for a meek rhetoric that would respond to opponents without rivalry. The handrail is not the rival of the abyss. In fact, it is precisely its concession to the power of the abyss that creates the circumstances for the technical intervention. Nor does the handrail fill the emptiness or eliminate the risk. (Someone could always climb over.) But emptied of any

PERSUASIONS OF GOD

rivalrous intent, a generative constraint may create the possibility of edging closer, even to danger.

A Rhetoric of Meekness

As I begin presenting a rhetoric of meekness, I want to begin with what I take to be a current expression of its ethos before turning to its historical origins in rhetorical theory. What I am trying to capture here is suggested by the notion of "directed inaction," as Daniel Gross describes it in *Being-Moved*. Gross links the idea to Stoicism, Gandhi's *satyagraha*, and the act of conscientious objection—all of which can be understood as "inactions" that are directed to social or political ends that involve a certain level of confrontation.[57] Gross notes that conscientious objectors' refusal to "act" constitutes decisive action; it is a clear and definite "no." But it is also a paradoxically passive action, not just in the objectors' refusal to be caught up in the march to war but also in the objectors' positioning themselves to be imprisoned for the refusal. In a sense, the objectors turn themselves over to the very powers to which they object, witnessing against the system from within it.

It is this extreme openness that constitutes for Gross a kind of rhetorical listening, which he borrows from Krista Ratcliffe's influential book of that title. Ratcliffe has urged rhetoricians to consider listening as a coequal form of rhetorical practice, "a trope for interpretive invention and more particularly as a code of cross-cultural conduct." Rhetorical listening signifies "a stance of openness that a person may choose to assume" in order to "negotiate troubled identifications" and "facilitate cross-cultural communication," particularly around issues of gender and race.[58] At its most basic, a rhetoric of listening proceeds first by listening to the other before trying to persuade the other. Gross takes this idea further and imagines a rhetoric of listening that avoids assuming a distinction between active and passive.[59] Gross forwards listening as a kind of radical patience, captured in the paradoxical phrase "directed inaction," in which refusal of action is itself action, but action marked by passivity. Seeing a model for this kind of listening in sacred rhetoric, Gross likens his suggested approach to that of Mary, who responds to the angel Gabriel by saying, "May it be done to me according to your word" (Luke 1:38). Paradoxically, Mary exercises a passivity; like the conscientious objector, she gives herself over to the call she has heard. She clearly makes a decision—the presence of her assent in the text suggests that she could have said no—but it is a decision that results in an even greater vulnerability, as becomes clear when Simeon, alluding to the grief she will one day experience, tells her, "and you yourself a sword will pierce" (Luke 2:35). Yet that vulnerability is not simply passive, as indicated by the prayer Mary shares with her cousin Elizabeth, a prayer known popularly as "The Magnificat." "[The Mighty One] has shown might with his arm, / dispersed the arrogant of mind and heart. / He has thrown down the rulers from their thrones / but lifted up the lowly. / The hungry he has filled with good things; / the rich he has sent away empty" (Luke 1:51–53). If this is inaction, it is very much directed.

This productive tension between the active and passive indicates the tension through which a rhetoric of meekness may be invented. The "active" and "passive" need not become a dialectic through which one position somehow defeats the other, nor do they provide a springboard for some transcendent third option. Instead, these positions indicate the contours of what Muckelbauer calls *"immersive responsiveness."*[60] Conscientious objection circulates through the active and passive, the confrontative and irenic, the decision and the hesitation, thereby demonstrating *"what [a position, an idea] can do."*[61] Conscientious objectors indicate the way in which a stance of confrontation need not be trapped in a negative dialectic or an eristic contest. I describe this kind of response as a rhetoric of meekness, which I present as a way of managing the double risk of zeal and hesitation involved in theorizing an appropriate post-Christian theorhetoric.

I build the idea of a meek rhetoric on frameworks familiar in rhetorical studies. The first such intervention is Richard Lanham's ideas of the "strong" and "weak" defenses of rhetoric articulated in his essay "The 'Q' Question," so named for the Roman orator Quintilian, who defends his vision of the ideal orator with what Lanham calls "the weak defense." The weak defense holds that "there are two kinds of rhetoric, good and bad. The good kind is used in good causes, the bad kind in bad causes."[62] Rhetoric is good insofar as the person who uses rhetoric is good. This common apologia for rhetoric imagines persuasion as a tool and argues that misuse does not discredit the tool itself. But the problem with the argument is that it concedes the very claim it means to refute. If rhetoric is nothing more than a tool liable to misuse, then rhetoric has no role in determining proper use. To grant this claim, as Quintilian appears to when he addresses the question directly, is to grant the terms of the Platonic critique that has troubled rhetoric from its beginnings—namely, that proper use must be established in a setting safely removed from the struggles of discord and advantage-seeking. Thus, the ethics of rhetoric is guaranteed by some extrarhetorical guardrail.[63]

Against the weak defense, Lanham insists on the "strong defense," which "assumes that truth is determined by social dramas, some more formal than others but all man-made. Rhetoric in such a world is not ornamental but deter-minative, essentially creative."[64] According to the strong defense, rhetoric is not simply a surface-level reflection of some deeper substance. Instead, rhetorical exchange contributes to the making of whatever "substance" is available. The strong defense, therefore, suggests "a figure/ground shift between philosophy and rhetoric."[65] That shift means that where we once sought foundation, we will now find persuasion.[66] Lanham's argument is a form of what Robert Wess calls "rhetorical realism," by which he means a recognition that rhetoric is not just a game but a game of changing the rules of the game. "Try to change some rules, not as a deviant but as the bringer of new orthodoxy. If you meet no resistance, you're cold; your new orthodoxy doesn't change any rules that matter. If you meet stiff resistance, you're hot."[67] The hotness of another's response indicates that something real is being argued, something with actual effects in the world.

To a culture trained in the assumptions of the weak defense, the claims of the strong defense may seem disturbing. But they should not be: "there is as much truth as we need, maybe more, but argument is open-ended, more like kiting checks than balancing books." The strong defense suggests that truth is "referen-tial, as in legal precedent."[68] To say that truth is fungible is not to say that it does not exist; rather, it is to say that it is backed by history, reflection, and experi-ence. Though the strong defense means that we always have to begin again, it does not mean that we ever begin at zero. Lanham urges his readers to consider the possibility that a world made by these rhetorical means is a more secure and more just world insofar as it is a world made of greater creativity, possibility, and participation. Rhetorical dexterity becomes a source of generosity rather than threat, of hospitality rather than manipulation.[69]

The priority of rhetoric does not mean that we have no recourse to a lan-guage of virtue; it simply means that the language of virtue emerges *from* com-municative efforts at transcendence, as understood in Crosswhite's notion of deep rhetoric. As the phrase itself suggests, deep rhetoric does not entail "los-ing the passion of philosophy for something more, something that is not one more expression of an ideology."[70] Rhetoric is also after ultimate questions. But insofar as rhetoric affects transcendence from and toward the other in front of us, then rhetoric becomes not the servant of ideology but the best means of resisting it. That is to say, the particularities to which rhetoric is designed to attend make it less likely that it will be distorted by "philosophical and theological reifications."[71] In addition, the strong defense offers a further justification for seeing theological reflection as inherently rhetorical, and not simply in the "big rhetoric" sense implied when one says that theology is something akin to putting a case forward in court. Theological reflection is rhetorical in a deep rhetoric sense in that it emerges from "the concrete urgency of life."[72] Lanham's argument is thus a crucial intervention into rethinking the arrangements that have reduced rhetoric to derivative status.

Yet, as compelling as Lanham's argument is, it also suffers from two limitations that threaten its appropriateness as a framework for theorhetoric. The first limitation is that Lanham's argument concentrates solely on human actors, thus ignoring the effects of nonhuman influence. To take this influence into account is not to undermine Lanham's argument but to casuistically stretch it to include more actors. Paul Lynch and Nathaniel Rivers thus suggest updating the strong defense to the "strange defense," which would increase the number of participants.[73] "The truth is made," the strange defense would grant, "but not solely by humans."[74] In the agora of the strange defense, "*everything* is nervously loquacious."[75] Stranger than even a posthuman rhetoric is an extrahuman rhetoric, which imagines rhetoric beyond a framework of interpersonal communication operating from a "humanist ontotheology" that "consists of speaking to and about God as a being, the Supreme Being, and then thinking being itself on the basis of this superior or perfect divinity."[76] Steven Mailloux notes that this framework treats God as a sort of person, even if God is the greatest and highest of persons. This presents not only a philosophical problem but also a theological problem insofar as it reduces God to a version of ourselves. As Terry Eagleton has memorably put it, God is not "some kind of *chap*, however supersized."[77]

To move around this impasse, Mailloux describes a Heideggerian rhetorical hermeneutics that reimagines communication with the divine not as a matter of words formed into requests but rather as a comportment that disposes us toward being-in-the-world-with-others. From this perspective, God is not the summit of some great chain of being, a perfect entity outside both space and time and accessible only through abstract conceptualization, but "someone" with whom we are already in a relation of address. (Recall the argument of Rudolf Bultmann—a colleague of Martin Heidegger—who argues that one cannot speak "about God … without references to the concrete, existential position of the speaker."[78]) The relationality that both precedes rhetorical address and is made possible by rhetorical address precedes and enables any subsequent theological insight. Here, we might note Crosswhite's observation that the relationality of rhetorical ontology is not "something that connects distant entities that are what they are independently of that relation." Rather, relationality refers to "an entity's internal references to other entities that allow it to be *what it is*."[79] In other words, it is only through relations (with both the human and nonhuman) that human creatures can become human creatures at all. But this idea of relationality would also extend to God: whatever God may be for us, it is only through relations with us that God may come to be that which God probably is.

Yet Mailloux wonders whether this relation can be articulated in the world as *Dasein* experiences it. Where, he wonders, "does such prayer leave an extrahuman finite rhetoric understood as working with publics within Dasein's world?"[80] At this point in his argument, Mailloux calls upon the angels. Referring to Heidegger's notes from a 1929 debate with Ernst Cassirer, Mailloux notes that Heidegger wrote the word "angel" in the margins. For Mailloux, this becomes a starting point for imagining how extrahuman communication might proceed. An intermediary messenger (Gk. *angelos*, messengers), the angel might traverse the chasm between human finitude and divine alterity. If the notion of angels seems too fanciful, Mailloux reconnects it to Heidegger's call of conscience, which "has the character of an *appeal* to Dasein by calling it to its ownmost potentiality-for-Being-its-Self."[81] This call "comes *from* me and yet *from beyond and over me*."[82] The sense that we might be called from our "lostness in the 'they'" is a kind of extrahuman communication that we receive within everydayness.[83] Mailloux's hope is that a rhetoric "associated with noncorporeal, living beings" might move us past a humanist ontology and thus model a rhetoric "directed toward embodied animals and nonliving bodies," a rhetoric that can account for and enable extrahuman communication. Rather than being preoccupied with the otherworldliness of angels, we might see them as "mediators, catalysts, and reminders for intensifying and heightening our own being-in-the-world."[84] Thus, we can imagine a rhetoric that is at once worldly and extrahuman. Ultimately, the path of my project travels toward and through the Incarnation rather than angels. But the Incarnation also moves us toward a communication that cannot be reduced to humanist models; to speak to, for, and about a God emptied of divinity so as to become the poorest of the poor also requires its own strange defense of rhetoric.

The second problem with Lanham's strong defense is related to the first. In addition to excluding the nonhuman or the extrahuman, the strong defense also frames rhetorical exchange as primarily defensive. Not antagonistic, to be sure; Lanham is inviting his Platonic opponents to play a game rather than have a fight. To his credit, Lanham is primarily concerned with making sure that everyone (and, with Lynch and Rivers's casuistic stretch, every*thing*) is both invited and fully equipped to play. Lanham's crucial point—and it is a point as urgent now as when he wrote it in 1989—is that trying to establish a baseline sense of goodness prior to rhetorical exchange usually amounts to nothing more than a power play disguised as pious moralizing. Yes, the risk of rhetoric is always that virtuosity might not always result in virtue. The way to mitigate that risk, however, is not to define virtue at the outset but to dispute it. Lanham is compelling on all these points. Nevertheless, the strong defense inadvertently grants a basic claim of the weak defense, which is that rhetoric (whatever else it may be) is something to be guarded against or geared up for. Enamored by the game, Lanham does not spend much time acknowledging that there must be losers, nor does he contemplate the reality that we must all learn to lose the game if it is to continue.

"Losing" is a key issue taken up by Richard Marback in "A Meditation on Vulnerability in Rhetoric," an essay that deserves to be better known. Marback crystallizes the way in which Lanham's strong defense still operates on the central premise of the weak defense, which is that vulnerability is always the greatest danger. This is the assumption that Marback wants to call into question. Though he nowhere invokes Lanham's argument, Marback stages the argument in strikingly similar terms, posing "strong rhetoric" against "mere rhetoric," which is somewhat but not entirely similar to Lanham's "weak defense." Marback's ultimate claim is that "strong rhetoric," or the "strong defense," actually fails as an answer to "mere rhetoric."

Marback begins by granting the premise that rhetoric plays a constitutive, formative role in the ethical: "Rhetoric is a given; people cannot have relationships or communicate with each other except through their aspirations to appeal to, influence, inspire, or persuade each other."[85] This basic premise is still controversial; the way we often respond to influence that we do not like is by calling it "mere." But this familiar epithet "mere" surfaces a paradox by which rhetoric is at once dismissed as obviously manipulative while also being characterized as dangerously powerful.[86] In its attempt at diminishment, "mere" pays an ironic homage to a power that the epithet insists does not actually exist. The thing that the mere-wielders do not want to admit to themselves is that none of us is self-sufficient.

Strong rhetoric, or the strong defense, would seem at first hearing to embrace the pervasiveness of rhetoric. Strong rhetoric, argues Marback, counters the fear of insufficiency with "an audience's shared responsibility for meaningfulness and valuation."[87] Strong rhetoric, like the strong defense, insists on the centrality of rhetorical exchange and therefore construes the audience as a coequal participant in rhetorical exchange. This is the assumption that drives much of the classical pedagogical tradition that is also Lanham's concern. If more people are trained in rhetoric, more people can safely participate. But whether defensive or participatory, rhetoric is supposed to protect its users from being had. The primary fear that motivates both strong and mere rhetoric is the fear of vulnerability. The real issue, then, is why we are so bent on avoiding vulnerability in the first place. "What is it we fear in our concern over vulnerability to deception and beguilement specifically and to rhetorical influence more generally? What might it mean to understand rhetorical influence in terms of a different, more positive conception of our vulnerability?"[88] Such a conception would begin by recognizing that human beings are not discrete agents who happen to need to cooperate to get anything done. Rather, we—whatever we are, whatever subjectivity or agency we may possess—are the project of our interdependency. The notion of relationality that Marback assumes is the same one articulated by Crosswhite: relationality is what allows us to be who we are in the first place.[89] We become our "selves" through our relations and as a result of our relations. What that means, however, is that we are exposed to the risk of shame and hurt. The rewards of love, reconciliation, and forgiveness include the risks of hurt, shame, and humiliation. To sustain the necessary exposure for the inbreaking of the former includes the latter.

Yet, as Marback also suggests, we would not necessarily characterize such exposures as "weaknesses." If anything, the ability to sustain such exposure may be a sign of strength:

> There can be instances when we might want to say it is not a failure of rhetoric or a sign of weakness when appeals to such traits as forgiveness or guilt or loyalty risk either deception or disruption. We might want to say the vulnerabilities that attend forgiveness or guilt or loyalty are instead necessary for successes of rhetoric. Which is to say it is possible that at the same time we regret being deceived or disappointed, we do not regret allowing ourselves to be vulnerable to deceit or disappointment. We can put greater value on our availability to persuasion than we put on our aversion to deception because being available is itself an assertion of efficacy.[90]

Vulnerability thus becomes a sign of virtue. Marback here charts the risks of vulnerability that have always attended rhetoric but to which the field is becoming more and more attuned. One's intentions may be toppled by surprise, and rhetorical efficacy is a matter of sustaining exposure to that surprise. But Marback ups the ante by noting the depth of the risk to which this efficacy exposes us.

This risk must be carefully observed. Not all vulnerabilities are created equal, as Marback understands from his study of the South African Truth and Reconciliation Commission. Similarly, Judith Butler notes the danger of paternalism that follows upon designating certain individuals or groups as "vulnerable." The greatest ethical risk lies in the possibility that those who do the designating may, in the very act of designating, divest themselves of their own vulnerability. "Those of us who understand ourselves as responding to an ethical claim to safeguard life, even to protect life, may find ourselves subscribing to a social hierarchy in which, for ostensibly moral reasons, the vulnerable are distinct from the paternalistically powerful."[91] The call of the rhetoric imagined by Marback is that one that forgoes paternalism for solidarity.

This possibility lies within Marback's paradoxical notion of "being available" as an "assertion of efficacy," which is akin to Gross's notion of "directed inaction." There is a weakness to this sort of rhetoric, but it is not the weakness of the "weak defense," which remains embarrassed by the thought that persuasion might play a constitutive role in the ethical, the generous, the forgiving. There is instead a meekness to the sort of "directed" work required to risk the radical passivity, a passivity that may paradoxically constitute a confrontative gesture. Meek rhetoric need not shirk from persuasion because it more readily recognizes that the persuader is persuaded, that the alleged "seducer" is always seduced. There is also a strength to meekness in the effort to sustain the exposure to the inbreaking of something, most especially the potential inbreaking of the Wholly Other. One could imagine Mary both fearful and bewitched in the presence of Gabriel; despite these responses, she makes an affirmative choice, before also choosing to leave home, in "haste" (Luke 1:39), to see her cousin Elizabeth. If this is meekness, it involves some decisive choices.

Nevertheless, "meekness" is a risky term. In many situations, we might welcome attitudes of "humility" and "mildness," especially when religious assertions are being made. In other contexts, however, many might be understandably wary of ideas of "submissiveness" or "tameness" and especially alarmed by the ways in which meekness has so often been gendered. An obsolete meaning of meekness assigns it to a social superior, as in "merciful, compassionate, indulgent." But the term is more readily associated with social inferiors, as in "inclined to submit tamely to oppression or injury, easily imposed upon or cowed, timid, biddable" (*OED*). These connotations do not make meekness persuasive. The obsolete meaning implies an unacceptable level of social stratification; the latter, more familiar definition implies an equally unacceptable level of social submissiveness. This is all before we get to the term's use in scripture, the most famous instance of which is Jesus's claim that the meek shall inherit the earth (Matt. 5:5). The endorsement of meekness (Gk. *praus, praeia, prau*) has often been taken as a soothing promise to the poor: suffer now, and you won't later.[92] Construed as a term of political theology, meekness might anesthetize the aspirations of the *anawim*.

Yet the context of Jesus's announcement suggests something far more assertive than is often understood. When Jesus assures his audience that the meek shall inherit the earth, he invokes Psalm 37, which claims that "the lowly shall possess the land" (Ps. 37:11), an echo of God's promise to Abraham. Jesus's announcement is thus a statement not only of how things may be someday but of how things ought to be now.[93] In Jesus's thinking, meekness is actually much closer to the notions of directed inaction or *satyagraha* discussed by Gross. The theologian Walter Wink confirms this connection. Wink explains that Jesus's famous injunctions—to turn the other cheek, to give your cloak when your coat has been demanded, to go the extra mile when only one has been imposed—are species of resistance rather than acquiescence. We mistake these injunctions for masochism, Wink argues, when we forget to pay attention to Jesus's rhetorical situation, particularly his audience. "Jesus's listeners are not those who strike, initiate lawsuits, or impose forced labor, but their victims." His audiences include those who are "forced to stifle outrage at their dehumanizing treatment by the hierarchical system of class, race, gender, age, and status, and as a result of imperial occupation."[94] For these listeners, to be struck on the right cheek was to be humiliated by a social superior, the kind of person who would strike with the left hand (used for unclean tasks) or the back of the right hand, which would also add insult to injury. In this context, turning the cheek would not be an act of deference but of defiance. Similarly, in a culture in which nakedness was a greater shame for the viewer than the viewed, to offer one's last stitch of clothing was to ask, "You want this, too?" The same was true for carrying the pack the extra mile. Because Roman soldiers could legally order someone to carry their pack for one mile and one mile only, offering to carry it for a second would focus attention on the initial injustice: if you want to take advantage of me, then let's really do it. Such an offer, Wink insists, would be "no way to *avoid* conflict!"[95] "Do not think," warns Jesus, "that I have come to bring peace upon the earth. I have come to bring not peace but the sword" (Matt. 10:34).

Judith Butler observes a contemporary version of the ironic rhetoric of the meek defense in the "standing man" protest that took place in Taksim Square in Turkey in 2013. In response to a government edict banning public assembly, the performance artist Erdem Gündüz arranged a protest in which individuals stood silently at the mandated distance from one another. Technically they did not violate the terms of the edict. "What they did," writes Butler, "was to perform compliance perfectly."[96] Their form of protest managed both to demonstrate and to demonstrate against the ban. "The performance thus both submitted to and defied the interdiction, in and through the same action. It shows the knotted position of the subjugated subject by at once exposing and opposing its own subjugation."[97] In this case, the protest at once mirrors and refuses to mirror the government's action. By mirroring the edict exactly—by complying with it exactly—the protesters hold up a mirror to the government, but without imitating the government's repression.

This last aspect of the complicit protest is the most important for arguments I am developing. Meekness imagines the possibility of confrontation without rivalry—without, that is, the imitation of the opponent. Meekness confronts, but not by mirroring. The Italian philosopher Norberto Bobbio insists that meekness is not the same thing as mildness, passivity, or what we might call "undirected inaction." Meek persons do not avoid action. Rather, they "refrain from exercising the spirit of contest, competition, or rivalry, and therefore also of winning."[98] Meekness is not against winning per se—winning new rights, liberties, and so on. But it avoids defining winning exclusively in terms of the opponent's defeat. To anticipate the arguments we will pursue in chapter 2, Girard's basic argument is that rivalry is a product of mimetic desire: we converge on the same objects and find ourselves in competition. Those who are in some kind of contest are thus prone to mirror each other, to return like for like. Think of the old *Spy vs. Spy* comic from *Mad* magazine: two spies trying to outdo each other. One is white, the other black, but they are otherwise identical, which means that both their bodies and their actions are perfect mirrors of their enemies. Visually, each requires the other as background in order for their own actions to be visible. Bobbio's comment, read through Girard, indicates that the meek person *does not imitate or mirror the desires of the opponent*. This is a crucial

48   PERSUASIONS OF GOD

distinction. The meek person may certainly occasion confrontation but not rivalry, because the meek person is refusing to play the game as it has been designed. The refusal that constitutes meekness is deeply rhetorical in the sense of rhetorical realism outlined by Wess. Rhetorical realism "does not theorize in advance where to expect the lines in the sand to be drawn" but rather "prepares us to be ready for anything."[99] When the meek person is playing, we may not know what the game is.

Crucially, Bobbio distinguishes meekness from mildness on the grounds that meekness is a social virtue whereas mildness is a personal virtue.[100] Meekness is thus manifested in relations with others, including those others who see social relations primarily through contest and rivalry. Meekness may well be the highest social virtue in that it offers others, especially hostile others, a vision of something better. "A meek person is someone needed by others to help them defeat the evil within themselves."[101] That is to say, the meek person dramatizes a different world, one not driven primarily by rivalry, competition, and one-upmanship. Mildness may be fine as a personal attitude, but meekness more clearly involves relations to others. Mildness also has its shadow side, as Kenneth Burke suggests in his approach to "meekness," which he sees as a species of "blandness," a kind of rhetorical passive-aggressiveness, a hiding of one's true motives under the veneer of "goodwill." Miss Prone, imagines Burke, recalls to Miss Preen a lovely visit she had at Miss Preen's home. Miss Preen takes advantage of this moment of vulnerability to say that she cannot recall the occasion. "The implication was, blandly, that Miss Prone's life must have been a starved one, in comparison with Miss Preen's, if Miss Prone thus cherished as a rich memory an occasion that Miss Preen had quite forgot."[102] Miss Preen gains a social advantage without ever having to admit her desire for such advantage. Maybe Miss Preen really did forget; maybe she has a bad memory even though she loves Miss Prone. Or maybe she was trying to communicate to Miss Prone, "I never think about you at all." Blandness, writes Burke, is "irony *that never quite shows its hand*; hence there is always the possibility that the surface meaning is the true one."[103] Blandness describes an inquiry into another's welfare that is actually an assertion of one's own superiority; it describes an act of generosity that is actually an expression of one's own riches. Miss Prone can never fully know whether she should be offended, hurt, insulted, or none of the above.

Burke finds another example of such bland "meekness" in colonization. Colonists will be the soul of a kind of meekness—mere settlers—as long as they depend on the Indigenous population to survive. After that, the newcomers will quickly trade meekness for strength. This irony does show its hand but only when it is too late. As Burke sees it, meekness will almost always devolve into a "Machiavellian gesture" unless animated by "the most sophisticated and exacting religious scruples (as in the Desert Movement of the fourth century)."[104] As is frequently the case, Burke here entertains the possibility of an authentic religion, true to its professed principles. But he is much more attuned to the lies that all—including and especially the religious—can tell themselves and by the very means that should have kept them honest. Yet Burke also insists that honesty is possible. "*Insofar as there are no deceptions involved*, any constructive-destructive act undertaken for the good of men is to be interpreted as constructive (as being infused with the spirit of purpose)."[105] The situations described by Wink and Butler, in which there are no deceptions involved, show how meekness is constructive.

"The essential rhetorical situation," insists Burke, "resides in this *constancy of the invitation to war*."[106] That invitation can lurk even in "the peacefulness and prayerfulness of heavenly intent," which can become "weapons in the war of words."[107] Burke rightly identifies the most powerful and perverse urge to combat hidden in religious language. So constant is this invitation that any refusal of it—even on religious grounds—may seem perverse. But in a recent study of apathy, Nathaniel Rivers observes the rhetorical powers of this sort of perverse refusal. Like meekness, apathy might initially strike the reader as both unrhetorical and unwelcome, a destructive disengagement that calls out for correction. Against these notions, Rivers defines apathy as "a rhetorical capacity—a disposition—to disengage from the often-arresting confines of an exigence terminally shaped by shared feeling."[108] By this understanding, turning the other cheek is not an expression of codependent dysfunction. Rather, it is a refusal to be dragged into the slapper's anger, a refusal to mirror the same violence. The meek person thus practices apathy as Rivers understands it. Apathy is not the same thing as antipathy. To be *a*pathetic is to refuse the feeling that others might impose; to be *anti*pathetic, by contrast, is to return a feeling of opposition. It is to mirror the other's feelings, to slap back, to allow the opponent to determine the rules of the game.

As an example, Rivers thinks through the 1983 film *War Games*, in which a teenaged hacker finds his way into the United States' nuclear missile systems as those systems begin to prepare for a self-initiated launch. Because the systems have been designed to exclude humans (whose capacity for sympathy, empathy, and indeed apathy makes them unreliable participants), the technicians cannot stop the computer from launching. As a Hail Mary, the computer is ordered to play tic-tac-toe and set the number of players to "zero." In other words, humans invite the computer to play a game, but not according to the usual rivalrous rules. Rivers writes, "Apathy doesn't introduce a new side, a third player, but zeroes out the game, which, nevertheless, must still be played. . . . The computer must encounter the futility of tic-tac-toe over and over and over again."[109] After repeated and futile attempts to win, the computer finally concludes that with some games, "the only winning move is not to play." In this case, however, the only way to come to that conclusion is through the game itself. "Apathy is an interruption emerging from within rather than without an intensely bounded rhetorical situation—apathy creeps within."[110] There is no new side or third player, but there is also no refusal to play. Rather, there is only a refusal to play the game according to the rules as they have been set out. Apathy, like meekness, is entirely rhetorical; it proceeds from the assumption that "changing the rules of the game is the only game in town."[111]

In this response, an exposure is being sustained. Like the apathetic person, the meek person "stands apart but never completely away from—always drawn, tending toward what they might leave. Apathy is still a species of *with-ness*."[112] But this vulnerability is not mere submissiveness. Rather, it is a vulnerability articulated through a refusal to mirror or imitate. This refusal is what ultimately distinguishes meekness from self-diminishment. That distinction is crucial to make, especially given the gender and class connotations of meekness. Meekness does not require that the victimized participate in their victimization. This is an especially important point in the discussion of any post-Christian theorhetoric, given that Christian rhetorics have often been articulated through distorted ideas of redemptive suffering. Many feminist theologians have challenged these myths. For example, Rita Nakashima Brock and Rebecca Ann Parker examine the way these myths can operate in women's experience of Christian faith. Each recounts personal experiences in which rhetorics of sacrifice expose victims to further suffering. In one such experience, Brock relates a harrowing story in which her father attempts to spank her. Spanking had been a common form of discipline in her childhood; in this instance, however, Brock is a twenty-year-old college student. Brock refuses to submit to this degrading violence. When her father attempts to force her, she fights back as she would against any attacker, even going so far as to kick his groin. She succeeds in ending the encounter, and he slinks away defeated.[113]

A superficial reading of this scene might lead one to conclude that Brock (however much we might endorse her actions) has not displayed meekness. Nor has she seemed to display apathy. Nor, finally, has she appeared to enact the kind of nonviolent response envisioned by Jesus. Indeed, a certain idea of nonviolence is the very notion that she and her coauthor are calling into question on the grounds that nonviolence can often lead simply to further victimization. But while she has used physical power to repel her assailant, she has not mirrored his emotions or motivations. That is the crucial distinction. Contrary to her father, her purpose is neither to hurt or to humiliate but simply to fend off. It also has the rhetorical effect of communicating that this kind of "discipline" is unacceptable. Her "violence," if it can be called that, is not an imitation of his. Rhetorically speaking, she has changed the rules of the game.

We will revisit Brock and Parker in chapter 3 in an examination of feminist critiques of traditional atonement theologies. My point here is simply that meekness does not entail taking whatever gets dished out. Meekness is instead characterized by the refusal to return like for like. As a public rhetorical strategy, meekness is not a refusal of conflict but rather a refusal of reflexive imitation. As an understanding of rhetoric itself—as we return to the fundamental uncertainty of what rhetoric may be—meekness imagines rhetoric as similarly nonrivalrous. If rhetoric is generally understood as the game of changing the rules of the game, then a rhetoric of meekness is one that changes the rules so as not to reactively mirror the desires of one's opponents. Certainly, there may be situations in which mirroring is appropriate; one can imagine situations of hermeneutic uncertainty in which imitation might be offered as a gesture of hospitality. But meek rhetoric preserves the idea that confrontation can occur without rivalry. The apathetic gesture as described by Rivers is a confrontative gesture, but it is confrontative precisely because it refuses to play the other's game, even when one is drawn, as we always are, into rhetorical situations not of our own making. Meek rhetoric articulates an understanding of rhetoric as directed inaction.

Most importantly for the present argument, rhetorical meekness is the most appropriate for the invention of a post-Christian theorhetoric. This appropriateness is not just a matter of the Christian endorsement of meekness. (Besides, the references to *satyagraha* should suggest that the kind of meekness I am describing here is not exclusively Christian.) But the paradoxical understanding of meekness suggested by the Christian scriptures indicates an appropriate approach for inventing with and through tensions between the rhetoric of strength and the rhetoric of weakness, the latter of which is a paradoxical rhetorical value for the Christian scriptures: "If I must boast," writes Paul, "I will boast of the things that show my weakness" (2 Cor. 11:30). Similarly, a meek rhetoric takes traditions seriously enough to recognize alienation from tradition; it is a rhetoric that attends to the uncertainty of saying who God *may* be while also recognizing the urgency of saying who God *probably* is. A meek rhetoric suggests both an ethos and a norm for a post-Christian theorhetoric. Though it may offer alternatives to other positions, it does not enter into rivalry with other positions. This refusal is crucial for any post-Christian rhetoric that would express Christian Truth/truths without the kind of absolutist, exclusivist, or competitive stance that may distort the Gospel into a vehicle for domination. Recalling Jonathan Haidt's *The Righteous Mind*, a meek, post-Christian rhetoric refuses to see religion as a team sport.[114] As we will discuss in chapter 2, this refusal is a key implication of Girard's idea of a "non-sacrificial Christianity."

Conclusion

Meek rhetoric articulates a stance of intentional openness and directed inaction— a rhetoric that refuses rivalry. The complicit and kenotic approach I mean to follow here is one that tries to avoid being trapped by the negative dialectic that, to recall Muckelbauer, assumes that "negation is the generative principle of transformation."[115] The generative negative assumes that every position is somehow a position against, a position that, in Girard's terms, is ultimately locked in rivalry with other positions: for, against, or above and beyond. But all three positions remain forms of rivalry in that one position is ultimately meant to "win" at the expense of the others. The vexing problem with dialectical negation as a habit of thought is that one cannot really escape it: to deny the gesture is to repeat the gesture; to be "against" dialectical negation is paradoxically to affirm it.

A rhetoric of meekness sidesteps this trap. For example, it does not seek the defeat of either Lanham's notion of the strong defense or Marback's notion of strong rhetoric. Rather, it is intended as an extension or complement working with and within the terms set by these earlier arguments, thus preserving the possibility of necessary and even salutary conflict, but without mimetic rivalry. The rhetorical notion of meekness suggests that refusal does not necessarily constitute denial. Apathy is not antipathy. In this way, a rhetoric of meekness is a product of what Muckelbauer calls a "singular rhythm." A singular rhythm "indicate[s] an unidentifiable and unrecognizable dimension of repetition that circulates within the identifiable and recognizable movement of dialectical negation."[116] The notion of a singular rhythm suggests that the issue is not whether one repeats but how.[117] The possibility it seeks is the "extraction of variation," which does not seek to reduce the other to a version of the same but instead inclines toward the possibility of difference.[118] The rhetor can extract these variations through an immersive responsiveness, the sort that invents the meekness of turning the other cheek. Only by immersing oneself—only by becoming complicit, even in the opponent's superior-inferior framing—is meek rhetoric able to challenge that framing. The meek rhetorician who turns the other cheek invents through the initial hostility that would reduce the rhetor to an object for the attacker's ire while also inventing through a variation that might see the attacker as a prisoner to his own violence.

At this point, a larger question emerges, one that can be articulated by recalling John Caputo's language: How does a rhetoric of meekness sustain an exposure to the inbreaking of something—especially the other and especially in situations of conflict? The meek defense may describe and even prescribe an appropriate rhetorical stance for acknowledging and maintaining relations within conflict. But that still leaves the hardest part ahead. To put the question in Gross's terms: How do we keep listening when the voice we hear is dangerous, either because it is the voice of a hostile other who threatens diminishment or violence or because it is the voice of the Wholly Other, who threatens to upend one's very sense of self? Not all vulnerabilities are created equal. It is one thing to say that we are always already exposed by means of a prior rhetoricity; it is another to ask how one responds within that situation of exposure. To the question of the hostile other, the meek defense answers by refusing to imitate the other, a refusal that in and of itself may constitute confrontation. But the defense remains meek insofar as some exposure is maintained. The refusal is not of the other but the refusal of the imitation of the other. But that still leaves the question of sacred rhetorics, in which the exposure is to the Wholly Other. Such encounters may indeed invite the kind of complex agency that oscillates between the active and passive, but that is no guarantee that one will heed the voice "through which we are spoken."[119] The refusal may be a rhetorical act, made possible by a prior rhetoricity. But the refusal still has consequences for the relationship.

These are fundamental questions, both for rhetoric in general and for a post-Christian theorhetoric in particular. I will return to the rhetorical issue of sustaining the exposure to the Wholly Other in chapter 4 and the postscript. The more immediate task is to present foundations of the meek defense within the thought of René Girard. Because his work goes to the heart of religion in the form of the "sacred," Girard is especially important for the invention of a post-Christian rhetoric, the persuasions of God after God, who no longer needs to lean on the sacrificial crutches of the violent sacred—the practice of exclusionary sacrifice that shores up group identity on the back of victims. Religion, Girard argues, has often been nothing more than "another term for that obscurity that surrounds man's efforts to defend himself by curative or preventive means against his own violence."[120] Yet he also concludes that the Jewish and Christian scriptures are the texts par excellence for revealing and thus recognizing this violent machinery.[121] In the wake of this revelation, institutional-historical Christianity, at least in theory, is deprived of this crutch and will now have to live up to its highest aspirations. Articulating this coming form of religion is an essentially rhetorical task.

2

Friendly Injustices

Your extreme rhetorical dexterity sometimes makes me a little uneasy.
—Michel Treguer to René Girard, *When These Things Begin*

In chapter 1, I outlined a rhetoric of meekness, an approach both timely and appropriate for a post-Christian theorhetoric. A meek rhetoric draws on a set of ideas already circulating in rhetorical studies: invention as a practice of complicity, rhetoric as a constitutive vulnerability, and the strange intervention of apathy or directed inaction. A rhetoric of meekness emerges as an encounter without rivalry, capable of distinguishing between productive and necessary confrontation and the reactive mirroring of another's desire. It imagines a kind of paradoxically unintentional intentionality, in which the intentional refusal of rivalry is only possible by means of a prior vulnerability (beyond intention) to a given exigence. A meek rhetoric thus accounts for the prior rhetoricity that makes persuasion possible while at the same time allowing for a rhetorical practice that seeks persuasion. This paradoxical orientation makes a meek rhetoric especially appropriate for post-Christian persuasion, a persuasion suitable for a time in which familiar Christian warrants are unavailable and even unwelcome.

The project of this chapter is to further develop this rhetoric through an engagement with René Girard (1923–2015). As rhetoricians take up the study of the sacred, a deeper study of Girard's work becomes urgent. Perhaps no thinker since Kenneth Burke has more resolutely focused his attention on the relation between religious order and sacred violence. From his lifelong study of literature, anthropology, and scripture, Girard claims that the sacred is occasioned by violence; to this argument, he adds the counterintuitive and untimely claim that the stories recounted in the Christian Bible indicate the best means of unmasking the sources of that violence. These claims have led one scholar to offer the paradoxical argument that Girard has presented both "the most formidable theory of the death of religion ever ventured" and "a Christian witness

56 PERSUASIONS OF GOD

against Christendom."[1] It is from this complex case that I observe the available means of a post-Christian theorhetoric, which would acknowledge that the passing away of "Christian culture" may represent a form of progress insofar as it rejects Christianity's sacrificial crutches. In addition, Girard's claim that we are simply in "a brief intermission between two forms of religion" indicates that the post-Christian era must be construed as a call for invention as much as critique.[2] Defending this claim and discerning its implications constitute the project of the present chapter.

The chapter begins with a basic presentation of Girard's thought before offering brief studies of his five basic keywords: desire, sacred, scapegoating, myth, and sacrifice. Through this lexicon, I present a case for Girard's work as a resource for the post-Christian theorhetorical persuasion of God. This presentation is followed by an examination of the most persistent criticisms of Girard's project, criticisms that have been expressed in both implicitly and explicitly rhetorical terms. These critiques challenge Girard on the grounds of his own anthropology of desire. They remind Girard that, according to his own theory, the revelation of the violent sacred cannot be construed simply as a piece of knowledge. In noting some of the limits of Girard's claims, however, these critiques paradoxically advance them. They offer what Burke calls "a kind of friendly injustice, in not requiring of a given debtor the full amount of his debt."[3] My approach here is to practice a similar kind of friendly injustice, in which I argue that Girard's revelation is also an invitation to persuasion.

Someone Has to Have a Thrashing

The 1989 film *Scandal* tells the story of the 1961 Profumo Affair in Great Britain. The basic facts are these: British war secretary John Profumo carried on an extramarital relationship with nineteen-year-old Christine Keeler, a model and aspiring actress. At the same time, Keeler was also having an affair with Yevgeny Ivanov, an attaché at the Soviet embassy. When these dual liaisons were revealed, Profumo's political career was ended, along with Harold Macmillan's conservative government. But the only person who was ever formally charged with any crime was Stephen Ward, an osteopath and society bon vivant who had first introduced Keeler to Profumo. Because Keeler had sometimes accepted money in exchange for sex and because Ward had sometimes financially supported her, he was painted as a pimp and prosecuted for living off immoral earnings.

He was quickly abandoned by his society friends, a fact the presiding judge cited as evidence of Ward's guilt.[4] Just before his trial ended, Ward took his own life. Since these events, the idea that Ward was scapegoated has become widely accepted.[5] The entry on Ward in the *Oxford Dictionary of National Biography*, for example, lists him as "osteopath and scapegoat" and further reads, "Ward was in fact incidental to the Profumo episode: he was a sacrificial offering."[6] Ward himself described what was happening in similar terms. "This is a political revenge trial," he complained. "Someone had to be sacrificed and that someone was me."[7]

This is also the position the film takes, as made plain in a scene near its conclusion. Ward (played by John Hurt) and Keeler (played by Joanne Whalley-Kilmer) sit together in Ward's darkened apartment at the end of one of his trial days. Ward recounts an incident from his boarding-school days in which a boy named Follett was assaulted for snoring in the dormitory. Because the school administration could not get anyone to confess, they decided to punish Ward, whose bed was nearest to Follett's. Years later, encountering his housemaster at a classmate's wedding, Ward asks whether he knew that Ward was innocent. Of course the housemaster knew. "Someone had to have a thrashing, Ward. It just happened to be you."

This chilling line sound-bites the primary concerns of René Girard, who pursued a lifelong study of the persistent human sense that someone has to have a thrashing. Ward, both as a secondary-school student and as an adult, becomes the surrogate victim whose punishment safeguards cultural structures. The foundational connection between surrogate victimage and cultural and religious order is the central insight of Girard's religious thought. In the case of Ward, the order to be protected may not appear conventionally or explicitly religious (though it is easy to imagine how institutional religion played a role in fomenting moral outrage). But it is most certainly *sacred*, which in Girard's view is tantamount to saying that a community is willing to dole out violence so that order will be maintained. This is what Girard means when he writes, "Violence is the heart and secret soul of the sacred."[8]

Girard's basic ideas can be quickly summarized. Human desire is mimetic; when we desire, we desire according to the desires of the people around us. The desire of those others, whom Girard dubs "mediators," both occasion and shape our desires, which are therefore never really ours in an absolute (i.e., noncontingent) sense. Our desires are always borrowed. The imitative nature of desire is ultimately a good thing, since it can indicate that which is good to desire. A PhD student, for example, models her desires on her mentor, whose career serves as a motivating example for her own. Such borrowed desires can be generative, but they can also become destructive, particularly when we find ourselves desiring the very same things as our mediators. When the student becomes a PhD and begins competing for the same venues, prizes, and grants as her mentor, their relationship may sour.

When such rivalry emerges, subjects and mediators may resolve their conflicts by scapegoating some third party. Rather than confronting the true nature of their conflict, they may malign or exclude some other person in a way that reinforces their buckling relationship. This kind of scapegoating phenomenon can also happen at a communal level. When it does—when a community reinforces its own fracturing unity by inflicting violence on some "other" (e.g., racial, ethnic, sexual, or religious minorities)—the community will not only justify their violence but "sacralize" it. In the case of Stephen Ward, his persecution reassures everyone that good order abides and that there is no wider corruption. In the case of wider economic insecurity, minorities or immigrants might become the scapegoat whose expulsion will restore "identity," "harmony," "prosperity," all terms with sacral resonance.

In the case of Stephen Ward, there may have been many reasons that he was particularly vulnerable to scapegoating: perhaps it was his marginal place relative to upper-class circles in which he moved, perhaps it was his seemingly dubious relationship to Ivanov, perhaps it was simply that his relationship with Keeler was unconventional. In both these cases, the chosen "others" already bear signs of difference that make them vulnerable to being targeted. In other cases, racial, cultural, religious, linguistic, and national differences suffice to attract the mob's attention. In Girard's estimation, the victim usually already is marked by some difference that acts as a magnet for the mob's attention. The mark of the scapegoat is also observed in the scene recounted earlier. As Ward explains to Keeler in the film, Follett snored because he had "asthma or something." It is easy to imagine how this weakness might have attracted unwanted attention at an English boarding school. So powerful is the obfuscation of scapegoating that Ward still cannot see what was happening to his asthmatic classmate. "He [i.e., the actual perpetrator] didn't hit him hard," insists Ward. "He just slapped him across the face, but unfortunately, he fractured his skull. He had a weak skull, Follett." Even as he is being dragged to the altar of his own victimization, Ward repeats the lie they have been telling themselves all this time.

At its ugliest, scapegoating kills. Burke reminds us that order is maintained through the "cult of the kill."[9] This is the link between the violent and the sacred, a link that lends its name to Girard's *Violence and the Sacred*. Unlike Burke, however, Girard does not see Christian theology as hopelessly malformed by this violent structure. Girard reads the Jewish and Christian scriptures that make up the Christian Bible as the most reliable means of revealing and therefore rejecting the cult of the kill. Because those scriptures repeatedly reveal the victims as victims, the illusion required for scapegoating cannot be maintained.

That is "Girardianism" in a nutshell, and it has attracted equal measures of admiration and criticism. Those who are sympathetic to it describe Girard as "one of the last of that race of Titans who dominated the human sciences in the nineteenth and twentieth centuries with their grand, synthetic theories."[10] Those less sympathetic criticize Girard for offering "a portentous 'theory of everything,' . . . a Casaubon-like key to all mythologies."[11] The singularity of Girard's obsessions has encouraged the idea that he is "the last of the hedgehogs," obsessed with the "one big thing" of mimetic desire as the ultimate source of resentment, identity and *community* formation, and the violent sacred.[12] Even admiring colleagues observed that Girard was sometimes "slapdash" and "disinterested in the critical questions his work raised."[13] Girard has also been critiqued for privileging the human at the expense of the nonhuman.[14] In addition, his understanding of the human seems to rely on a hopelessly reductive assertion of an intractable nature (de)formed solely by mimetic desire. This seeming reductiveness seems matched by Girard's sometimes reactionary cultural and religious instincts: "What," he asks at one particularly intemperate moment, "would Dostoyevsky say about our 'multicultural' universities, our dismal sexual 'liberations,' our radical feminists forcing their 'all-inclusive' versions of the Bible down the throat of meekly submissive Christian churches?"[15] Comments like these make it hard to imagine that Girard's presentation of Christian insight could be anything other than a revanchist *cri de coeur* against liquid modernity.

Yet Girard's thinking also anticipates ideas that have become commonplace in contemporary rhetorical studies. His notion of subjectivity, for example, rejects the discrete individual of liberal or modern humanism. Mimetic desire makes human subjectivity ontologically relational. Girard's implicit call for new religious expression is born of a skepticism that, if not exactly posthumanist, shares posthumanism's wariness of humanist overconfidence in self-enlightenment. When Girard dismisses "our celebrated humanism" as nothing more than an interval between religions, he means to caution anyone who would celebrate the exit from religion on humanist grounds: "I wouldn't wait around for it [the exit] to set us down gently in the dainty flower beds of a consumer society that's been tended and prettified by 'Christian values.'"[16] Without intervention, the sacred that will emerge from the end of humanism may be as brutal as that which preceded it. If, as the scripture scholar N. T. Wright has said, "the role of postmodernity has been to announce the doctrine of the fall to arrogant modernity," then Girard (despite his pronounced antipathy to postmodernism) is one of that announcement's leading prophets.[17]

My approach therefore treats Girard primarily as a theorist of the sacred offering a critique of religion. I am guided here by the thought of Otto Kallscheuer, who argues for engaging "Girardianism" less as a "testable anthropological or social-scientific theory" and more as a "metascientific challenge" to religion.[18] That is to say, my primary interest is not whether Girard is absolutely correct in the strongest expressions of his ideas (e.g., *all* desire is mimetic; *all* myths are myths of the hidden scapegoat; *all* sacrifice is violent at heart). Rather, I am interested in the implications of Girard's insights for post-Christian theorhetoric. Robert Manning has argued that Girard is best understood as speaking to his audience "powerfully from the spiritual and intellectual depths of Christianity."[19] This position shifts the ultimate import of Girard's claims away from purely academic arguments and toward an appeal that approaches the prophetic. It is this latter form of address that occasions the demand for new theorhetorical invention.

In exposing the sacred, however, Girard appears to undermine the foundations of religion, particularly the Christianity that has dominated Western culture. Though Girard would reject this characterization of his work, there is also no doubt that his thought animates a powerful critique of Christianity.[20] But it is a critique that comes from within Christianity rather than outside it. Girard's project, writes Jeremiah Alberg, "allows one to see that very thing that Christianity was meant to expose as false runs through Christianity itself. The theory is, in modern jargon, self-implicating."[21] The self-implicating (we might say "self-emptying") nature of this critique indicates that Girard's claims for Christianity do not amount to some reactionary reestablishment of "Christian values" or "Christian culture." In fact, one of Girard's most radical claims is that Christianity should never have founded any culture since cultures are founded on the very sort of victimage the Gospels seek to expose.[22] Instead, Girard's arguments make a theorhetorical demand for reinventing the persuasion of God, a rhetoric whose complicity with Christian tradition is radical enough to challenge the sclerotic stiffening of that tradition into sacrificial habits. My aim here, then, is to offer twin arguments: one for Girardians, the other for rhetoricians. For Girardians, I argue for the rhetorical implications of Girard's thinking; for rhetoricians, I argue for the ways in which Girard's insights can advance our understanding of sacred and religious rhetoric.

To lay the groundwork for this effort, I now turn to a critical *lexicon Girardiae* of the five basic keywords of Girard's thought: desire, sacred, scapegoating, myth, and sacrifice. As we will see, Girard often used these terms in idiosyncratic ways, running up various explanatory and rhetorical problems. In *Rejoicing*, Latour refers to such problems as "translation arrears," the debts run up because the "meagre funds" of traditional religious lexica have been seriously depleted by a failure to translate for new situations. "*In ceasing to translate*," writes Latour, "*we have ceased to preserve*, and this is what has thrown the word mill ... out of gear. This is what we need to return to, this particular mishap, to see if we can't repair the machine, the machine for grinding out religion."[23] This scarcity caused by this broken machinery forces Latour to run up massive "translation debts" as he tries to make traditional religious language speak to present reality. Girard, in his own effort to keep grinding out religion, runs up the same kind of debts, leaving his readers to cover the arrears. But paying off those debts, Girard's interpreters have extended and strengthened his claims. As my use of this Latourian metaphor suggests, my presentation of Girard's thought is critical rather than doctrinaire; the overview I present here observes the available means of Girard's religious critique while also acknowledging that critique's limitations.[24] Most distinctively, it is a rhetorical assessment of Girard's thought, an assessment that reveals resources for managing the exit from one kind of religion and the entrance into another.

Translation Debt 1: Desire

Though Girard is credited with founding "mimetic theory," Girard resisted the idea that he had concocted anything so grand as a theory. "There's no 'Girardian system," he insisted. "I'm teasing out a single, extremely dense insight."[25] That insight is mimetic desire. When human beings desire, Girard argues, we desire according to the desire of the other (*la désir selon l'Autre*) rather than ourselves (*la désir selon soi*). Our desires do not emanate from us and directly toward the "object" (item, person, honor, status) in question. Rather, our desires

62 PERSUASIONS OF GOD

are occasioned and mediated by the other. The presence of the mediator is the key to Girard's relational understanding of human subjectivity. There is not a discrete subject who then desires; rather, human subjectivity is called forth by the desires of others. For this reason, Girard speaks of the "interdividual" rather than the individual. Whatever else interdividuals may be, their structure is intersubjective, which is to say, dependent on mediators as models.[26] "Subjectivisms and objectivisms, romanticisms and realisms, individualisms and scientisms, idealisms and positivisms appear to be in opposition but are secretly in agreement to conceal the presence of the mediator."[27] As a result, desire has both a triangular and a recursive shape. Girard also construes desire as acquisitive rather than representational. Mimesis is not simply about imitating "types of behaviour, manners, individual or collective habit . . . words, phrases, and ways of speaking."[28] Rather, it is about acquiring things—money, property, prestige, and so on. This is why Girard prefers "mimesis" to "imitation."[29] If imitation implies conscious or intention mimicking, mimesis is meant to imply a primary force that is unconscious and unintentional.

Because the interdividual's desires are always mediated, they will inevitably alight on objects already desired by their mediators. Sometimes, this is not a problem. If my neighbor Jones has a new car in the driveway, I may acquire a similar car, all the while believing that my desires are original. If, however, my neighbor Jones has a new spouse, I face a different problem. When desires converge on the same person or object, interdividuals find themselves in the double bind of mimicking a mediator who is also a rival. This is the source of the peculiar nature of resentment: interdividuals resent the models whose desires have taught them what to want.

Here we encounter the first translation problem. Early in his work, Girard focuses exclusively on the destruction wrought by mimetic desire, whether Don Quixote's madness, the Karamazov love triangles, or the fancies of Emma Bovary.[30] Human beings are locked into mimetic structures that seem to condemn them to rivalry, resentment, and violence. Later in his career, however, Girard would acknowledge that mimetic desire must also be constructive. In a 1993 interview, Rebecca Adams puts this question to Girard: If mimetic desire is inherently rivalrous, then how can Girard recommend "good" mimesis as an alternative? Is mimesis not inherently and inevitably destructive? Girard recognizes the problem and, as though to confirm reservations about how he presents his ideas, admits to a certain carelessness with language: "occasionally I say 'mimetic desire' when I really mean only the type of mimetic desire that generates mimetic rivalry, and, in turn, is generated by it."[31] Girard adds, "I hear this question all the time: 'Is all desire mimetic?' Not in the bad, conflictual sense."[32] Here, the translation arrears begin to be paid off by Adams.[33] In contrast to his general claim that violence is the foundation of all culture, Girard here recognizes the role that a "positive" mimesis must also play in the formation of culture and interdividuals.

Eventually, scholars of Girard describe a "loving mimesis," which Adams understands as mimesis *on behalf of* the other.[34] Adams imagines subjectivity as both deeply relational and capable of choice. Mimesis can be loving when it is meant to cultivate the interdividual's freedom, even if that freedom does not depend on the idea of a discrete subject who can somehow stand utterly independent of all influence. The interdividual is by definition animated by mimetic desire and therefore permanently at risk of rivalrous desire, but the interdividual has some capacity to choose more ethical models and therefore more ethical behavior. Moreover, as Adams notes, Girard does not offer a fully fleshed account of desire-on-behalf, a model of which would seem to be crucial not only for a full understanding of mimetic desire but especially for the feminist understanding that Adams seeks to articulate. One can imagine a mimetic desire that is constructive rather than distorting. The way to manage the problem of mimesis is not to "unplug" from it somehow but rather to plug into better forms of desire.

In the terms we have been developing in the book so far, we might say that all desire is complicit. It is always animated and directed by others, even before there is a putatively discrete self who desires. In this way, Girard's understanding of mimetic desire resembles Diane Davis's notion of prior rhetoricity: desire precedes the "I" who might say, "I desire." The challenge of practicing a meek rhetoric, then, is not simply to refuse to imitate the desire of one's adversary (as in the *Spy vs. Spy* comic), though it is that. It is also the pursuit of more constructive desire, which is to say the recognition of more constructive models. For Girard, the central imitative practice is the *imitatio Christi*; other traditions suggest different models. But whatever the model, a salutary *imitatio* orients the "interdividual" away from direct rivalrous mirroring in a given situation. The meek defense not only asks a rhetor to be complicit in a situation, as described in chapter 1, but also asks the meek rhetor to be complicit—to fold their desires—into the desires of another who calls the rhetor to some possibility or hope beyond the immediate situation. Such transcendent hope is powerful, and dangerous insofar as it is powerful. For Girard, desire is at its most dangerous when it is articulated through the sacred.

Translation Debt 2: The Sacred

The darker side of mimetic desire is what originally interests Girard, and it is this more ominous expression that leads to his insights into the sacred. The ever-present risk of mimetic desire, Girard argues, is that it may lead to a double bind in which the model of one's desire becomes the obstacle to the achievement of one's desire. This circumstance sets the conditions for rivalry and eventually violence. Drawing from the classical Athenian literature that is also decisive for Girard, we might consider Antigone's brothers, Polynices and Eteocles, each of whom desires sole possession of the Athenian throne, each of whom is prevented by the other from achieving his desire. Their war on each other suggests the double bind of mimetic desire, along with what Girard calls a "sacrificial crisis," which Girard defines as "a crisis of distinctions—that is, a crisis affecting the cultural order. This cultural order is nothing more than a regulated system of distinctions in which the differences among individuals are used to establish their 'identity' and their mutual relationships."[35] When this crisis of distinctions begins to emerge—when the regulated systems of distinctions begin to collapse—the need for the sacred will soon follow.

According to Girard, the sacred is always first and foremost a response to a threat to order. "As long as meaning is healthy," Girard writes, "the sacred is absent."[36] The rhetorician Jean Bessette puts a rhetorical gloss on this statement: "as long as the meaning of kairos is 'unhealthy,' the sacred is present."[37] In this provocative formulation, the sacred's ritualized procedures are construed as formulaic and therefore rhetorically inappropriate responses to situations of conflict created by the contagious resentment of mimetic desire. The sacred is a response to a community whose "meaning" (i.e., the order of things) is somehow under threat. This threat may devolve into intracommunity violence unless some other target can be found. "Violence is not to be denied, but it can be diverted to another object, something it can sink its teeth into."[38] This "something" is the surrogate victim on which a community may discharge the vitriol they might have otherwise discharged on each other. Instead of confronting genuine sources of conflict, riven communities "deflect upon a relatively indifferent victim, a 'sacrificeable' victim, the violence that would otherwise be vented on its own members, the people it most desires to protect."[39] The ultimate function of this victimage, and indeed all "sacrifice," as Girard designates it, is "to reinforce the social fabric."[40] By discharging violence to the surrogate victim, a community manages to protect itself from more generalized violence.

Crucially, these communities do not realize what they are doing. Lynn Worsham notes, "there is always an element of delusion in scapegoating: we do not consciously know that the claim to virtue is a rationalization and that we are engaging in the kind of *deflection* enacted in *scapegoating* or *false witness*."[41] The surrogate victimage that reunites a community is not recognized as victimage by the community. Inside a community, all violence is moral. This is the central point that Alan Page Fiske and Tage Shakti Rai make in their *Virtuous Violence*. "When we posit that most violence is *morally motivated*, we mean that the person doing the violence subjectively feels that what she is doing is right."[42] Here, "moral" refers to the "evaluation of action, attitudes, motives, or intentions with reference to an ideal model of how to relate."[43] That is to say, "moral" refers to values operating within a given culture, values that might seem strange and alien outside of the culture. In addition, Fiske and Rai's invocation of an "ideal model" suggests something akin to Girard's notion of mimetic desire. Depending on the culture, an ideal model may be one that inflicts violence.

Most importantly, Fiske and Rai also recognize that the perversity of violence is that it works: violence redirected onto the surrogate victim succeeds in preventing an outbreak of more generalized violence. Because victims serve this function so well, Girard suggests, acts of violence will often result in a surprising change of attitude. Once peace seems to return in the wake of victimage, the one who was demonized will be lionized as the source of irenic "healing." "Thus the foundational victim becomes a transcendental being who sometimes rewards and sometimes punishes. Such is the mimetic genesis of divine ancestors, sacred legislators, full-fledged divinities."[44] Here rhetoricians are likely to hear echoes of Burke's notion of the victim who becomes the redeemer: "Guilt Needs Redemption / (for who would not be cleansed!) / Redemption needs Redeemer / (which is to say, a Victim!)."[45] Girard explains this seemingly strange connection between victim and redeemer in this way: "The peoples of the world do not invent their gods. They deify their victims."[46] Victims are sacralized because victimage "works." The sacred acts as a kind of inoculation against the disease of generalized violence through the introduction of a more manageable dose of the disease itself. (Though the dose works only for a short time; regular boosters will be required.) For this reason, the violent and the sacred "are inseparable."[47] Religion, Girard writes in *Violence and the Sacred*, is nothing more than "another term for that obscurity that surrounds man's efforts to defend himself by curative or preventative means against his own violence."[48] The sacred "is necessarily and inversely proportional to the understanding of the mechanisms that

66 PERSUASIONS OF GOD

produce it."[49] Again, as Worsham notes, the sacred works because those who participate in it do not recognize what is happening. When the Gospel records Jesus as saying, "Father, forgive them, they know not what they do" (Luke 23:34), the text is not only depicting Jesus's forbearance but is also making anthropological comment about the essential misrecognition that founds the sacred.

In this way, Girard begins to reconfigure the terms he has inherited from the sociology of religion, including ideas like Émile Durkheim's "ambiguity" of the sacred and Rudolf Otto's idea of the "numinous" as a *mysterium* both *tremendum et fascinans*. The sacred is a source of both terror and wonder because the sacred is at once the location, the motivation, the process, and the result of scapegoating. For Girard, the sacred remains primarily a function of an incipient mob expiating its violence in a way that avoids a further spiral of violence. To paraphrase Burke, the sacred is the ultimate disease of cooperation. It is born out of what John Caruana felicitously calls "the perils of participation," that is, the danger that follows when belonging turns bad.[50] (Here, we might recall the importance of apathy as understood by Rivers.)

Girard's critique of "religion" is actually a critique of the *sacred* and the way it still functions in religion.[51] There are a couple of translation problems with apprehending Girard's critique of the sacred. The first is simply Girard's particular use of the term, which focuses primarily on those rites that depend on exclusion. This usage, however, should not be taken to impugn ordinary usage of the term, as in "this object is sacred to me" or "this land is sacred to its Indigenous inhabitants." When Girard refers to the sacred, he is specifically referring to sacralized violence and its effects. A second problem is that Girard sometimes uses "sacred" and "sacrifice" in ways that blur distinctions. As a result, when Girard speaks of a Christianity without "sacrificial crutches," his meaning may not be immediately clear. He does not mean a Christianity that forgoes self-sacrifice; rather, he means a Christianity that recognizes that God totally rejects sacred violence as means of propping up community or order. ("Sacred crutches" might have been a better phrase.) Because the Gospels make clear that Jesus is innocent, Girard argues, they reveal the chronic misrecognition that animates the sacred. To read the Gospels—and the Hebrew scriptures that are the Gospels' central influence—is finally to recognize that order is maintained on the backs of innocents, a circumstance that authentic religion can no longer abide. But that refusal does not preclude "sacrifice" in other forms; it does not, for example, impugn all self-sacrifice as self-abasement or all martyrdom as a distorted desire for heroism. The sacred to which Girard objects is the sacred occasioned through the violence of scapegoating.

Translation Debt 3: Scapegoating

To the modern, the meaning of the word "scapegoat" seems clear enough: a scapegoat is someone unfairly blamed for a community's own wrongs, an innocent target whose expulsion allows a community to look away from its own failings. For rhetoricians, the great theorist of scapegoating is Kenneth Burke, who made scapegoating a fundamental concept of rhetorical criticism. In Burke's early work, the question of scapegoating centers on the most pressing political issues of his day, including the Jim Crow South and the Nazi genocide; later in his work, it founds the political theology that Burke lays out in his *Rhetoric of Religion*. Like the later Burke, Girard sees scapegoating as fundamental not only to the foundation of the sacred but to culture itself. The sacred is that which props up order, particularly when order is under stress. Sacred rituals, Girard argues, provide a kind of regular maintenance for order through repetition. But Girard suggests that they also reflect some originary act of victimage whose apparent success occasions the subsequent sacral repetition. In making this claim, Girard ventures into the speculative realm of the origins of human culture and religion, the same realm broached by Freud in *Totem and Taboo*. Girard follows Freud by speculating on the idea of a founding murder, a killing around which an archaic community coalesces.[52] From that original killing, some order begins to emerge, an order that is sacralized in such a way that the ritual process might substitute for actual violence. Ritual acts of sacrifice are "a way of expressing a circumstance that has actually taken place at the threshold of human culture."[53] The sacred order precedes and founds culture: culture is a product of religion, not the other way around, and we are therefore "the children of religion."[54] The sacred and its order-sustaining violence makes culture possible, whether or not a given individual claims to be "religious" (i.e., belongs to an identifiable tradition, institution, or denomination). Such arguments about human origins seem like the kind of venture that Robert Pogue Harrison has in mind when he describes Girard as "one of the last of that race of Titans who dominated the nineteenth and twentieth centuries with their grand, synthetic theories."[55] But even if such capital-M metanarratives can only ever be speculative,

68 PERSUASIONS OF GOD

"what is not speculative is the way in which scapegoating has in fact operated in communities throughout the world."[56]

Yet there are problems with Girard's seemingly elastic use of "scapegoating," a word that, in our day at least, encompasses both arbitrary victimage and the misrecognition of false witness. This meaning for scapegoating is the product of a long process of development and, as always with religious language, mistranslation. The idea of the "scapegoat" has its ultimate origins in Leviticus 16, which prescribes procedures for the Day of Atonement, procedures that include a goat that is chosen by lot to carry the sins of the people out into the wilderness. The English word "scapegoat" first appears in William Tyndale's sixteenth-century translation of the Latin phrase *caper emissarius* (literally, "the goat who escapes").[57] In the Day of Atonement rite, however, there is not the full sense of scapegoating as we use the word today. The goat has been arbitrarily but intentionally chosen, so there is no misrecognition or blame. The goat is a sin-bearer only in a functional sense; it is not considered guilty. By contrast, Stephen Ward is a scapegoat in the contemporary sense that the community believes him to be the source of their trouble. By expelling him through a prosecution, the community seeks to tell itself that a contagion has been expelled and that wholesomeness will return. That is not, however, what is happening in the Day of Atonement ritual.

By the time Girard uses the word to analyze pre-Axial religious practices, two millennia of Christian typology have effectively grafted the Greek idea of the *pharmakos* onto Hebrew ideas of sacrifice, which was not originally tainted by any sense of misrecognition. The fruit of this grafting is the critical term "scapegoating" as we now use it today—that is, to refer to a process of victimization that relieves the accusers of having to face their own complicity in the problem for which they blame the victim. In Girard's view, the absence of misrecognition in the Hebrew Bible is precisely what makes it so critical to the process of revealing the ugliness of the sacred.[58]

The more pressing question, at least for the consistency of Girard's theory, is whether a passage like Leviticus 16 also represents an instance of the Hebrew Bible's orientation toward victims. In the context of the Day of Atonement, the use of the word "scapegoating" may distort our understanding by imposing a modern, critical term on a ritual that has nothing to do with the unknowing sacrifice of an innocent. Leviticus is not a scapegoating ritual as the goat is not formally a scapegoat. If this is the case, then can Girard say that it is actually an implicit response to some category of scapegoating rituals? If not, then it would seem to be far more difficult to maintain the claim for the decisiveness of the Bible as a rejection of scapegoating and the sacred. At the same time, the "secularization" (i.e., general dissemination) of the word "scapegoat" offers evidence for Girard's thesis that the Jewish and Christian scriptures have offered an essential insight into human violence. The very idea of the scapegoat is a product of these writings.

We seem to have encountered yet another translation arrears, one built into the very term at issue. In an overview of the lexical history of the "scapegoat," from its appearance in Leviticus to its contemporary use, David Dawson acknowledges that Girard's use of the term can obscure his central insight, an insight that casts a bright light on the problem of arbitrary, surrogate victimage that produces and reinforces the sacred.[59] This is how Girard manages to use the word "scapegoat" to refer to what is both a spontaneous act and ritual practice.[60] Within those rituals that might be retrospectively and therefore incorrectly called "scapegoat rituals," Girard observes "the universal human tendency to transfer anxiety and conflict on to arbitrary victims."[61] This tendency often results in the abuse of an innocent, such as Stephen Ward. The signal contribution of the Hebrew scriptures is to turn this grammar on its head by making clear that the victims are innocent; those scriptures also make way for salutary forms of sacrifice. Over time—and, crucially, under the influence of the biblical witness—the term "scapegoat" comes to express "a preferential connotation in favor of the victim it names, an ineradicable bias that is also an implicit judgment of his accusers."[62] Girard finds in that witness a lens through which to see the role victimage plays in the sacred. It may be that Girard wields an ax rather than a scalpel when he speaks of the scapegoat, but the ax manages to separate violence and the sacred.

Most importantly, this witness emanates directly from the Hebrew scriptures, which, in Girard's estimation, begin the process of "desacralizing religion," the process of extracting religious feeling and practice from the feelings and practices of arbitrary victimage. The story of Joseph is just one example of the Hebrew Bible telling a story from the perspective of the victim, but the insight emerges as early as Cain and Abel, in which mimetic rivalry results in violence that God explicitly rejects. Girard writes, "these texts are the first in human history to allow those who would simply become silent victims in the world of myth to voice their complaint as hysterical crowds besiege them."[63] This is how Girard can come to the paradoxical conclusion that "religion" is both the source of our trouble and its surest remedy. More precisely, Girard sees the sacred as

70   PERSUASIONS OF GOD

our trouble insofar as it is occasioned by acts of scapegoating violence, and he sees the Hebrew and then Christian scriptures as possessing a singular insight into the connection of violence to the sacred. This desacralizing tendency is founded on what Girard takes to be the Bible's rejection of myth.

Translation Debt 4: Myth

For Girard, the notion of the scapegoat is the key to understanding the difference between "myth" and what, for lack of a better term, we might call "anti-myth." Like the word "scapegoat," Girard uses the term "myth" in the ordinary critical way: when we say that something is a "myth," we are usually referring to a lie that has taken hold of the collective imagination. A myth is by definition that which is not true but which nonetheless has powerful rhetorical effects. As Sharon Crowley puts it, citing Girard, myths provide "'psychosocial meaning' . . . for groups of people who may or may not have forgotten the historical event around which it coalesced."[64] For Girard, the falseness of myths pertains primarily to the way they serve to disguise violence from the communities that perpetrate it.[65] This is how the massacre at Wounded Knee becomes the "Battle" of Wounded Knee or how the racist attack on Tulsa's Black Wall Street becomes a "race riot." If surrogate victimage is the first piece of Girard's critique of religion, his understanding of myth is the second. "I tend to reserve the word 'myth' for those texts that begin with a crisis then have a collective murder where the victim of that collective murder is regarded as guilty."[66] Myths function first and foremost as means of obscuring the violence that founds community or reaffirms identity.

Myths "are invariably told from the *persecutors' perspective*."[67] Girard calls them "texts of persecution," texts in which "accounts of real violence, often collective," are "told from the perspective of the persecutors, and therefore influenced by characteristic distortions."[68] Girard locates a key representative example of such a text in the *Judgment of the King of Navarre*, a fourteenth-century disaster narrative of the Black Death and an anti-Jewish persecution. The narrative speaks of both fantastic events—rains of stones, cities destroyed by lightning, portents in the sky—and ordinary events, including widespread plague death. The author quickly assigns blame to the Jews, and revenge is not long in coming. "Every Jew was destroyed, some hanged, others burned; some were drowned, others beheaded with an ax or sword."[69] Reading this text, equipped with an understanding of scapegoating that is itself drawn from Jewish thought, the modern reader immediately discriminates the plausible from the implausible. Readers discard both the fantastic elements and the author's rationale for blaming the Jews, even as they recognize that Jews were actually scapegoated in this event. They realize that they are reading "a real persecution described from the perspective of the persecutors."[70] That is to say, "there is always a historical victim or victims toward whom community violence was once directed."[71] The author's persecutory perspective can be viewed as a kind of photo negative through which actual violence against a surrogate victim can be spied.

By contrast, a story is not a myth if it is told from the perspective of the victims. According to Girard's view, therefore, the film *Scandal* is not a myth because we are meant to see that Ward does not deserve what is being inflicted on him. *Scandal* is thus an "antimyth," a story that, by seeing things from the victim's perspective, loosens the hold of the sacred imaginary. Girard writes, "A society that replaces myth by an awareness of persecution is a society in the process of desacralization."[72] The awareness of persecution is why Girard considers the Tanakh and the Gospels desacralizing texts. Because these texts repeatedly take the side of the victims, these texts are antimyths in Girard's sense. Writing of the book of Job, for example, Girard argues that were Job a myth, "we would only have the viewpoint of the friends."[73] The story would endorse the argument made by Job's friends that he has done something to deserve his suffering. A myth would convince us that Job was guilty. It would also convince Job himself. The fact that he remains steadfast in his protestation of innocence once again indicates the desacralizing effect of the Hebrew scriptures.

Again, however, we run into a translation problem with Girard's definition of myth, a definition whose idiosyncrasy risks distorting his insight. Like Rebecca Adams, Richard Kearney articulates an important and refining challenge for Girard. Though he endorses Girard's hermeneutical suspicion, along with his insistence that myth must be answerable to ethics, Kearney resists Girard's claim that all myths should be understood as nothing more than ideological masks for some originary act of violence. Kearney notes Girard's argument that biblical texts introduce an ethical judgment on behalf of victims, a judgment that then provides grounds for the critique of "myth." "But," asks Kearney, "if

Girard is prepared to make an exception for biblical myths, why not also for some non-biblical myths?"[74] For Girard, the Christian Bible is the text par excellence for the ethical critique of scapegoating myth. But does that mean that no other "sacred" texts may serve a similar function? Insofar as Girard would exclude all nonbiblical myth, Kearney argues, he seems to have committed the very sort of "purificatory exclusion" that his entire theory is meant to condemn.[75] Kearney makes a similar observation when he argues that Girard leaves it up to the reader to make the "hermeneutic wager" of deciding which criterion of justification is most important. Is it an empirical argument? A typological argument? A pragmatic argument? An essentially religious argument?[76] Because Girard does not prioritize these criteria, readers are left to decide for themselves. In and of itself, there is nothing wrong with such a wager, though it does seem to undermine Girard's insistence on doing empirical work.

Ultimately, the matter is not simply one of categorization, which could be solved by fashioning a new term (e.g., antimyth). The issue, as Kearney suggests, is one of poetics. Girard tends to see poetics as having primarily an obfuscatory effect, and his ethical commitment against victimization compels his own suspicious hermeneutics. But, as presented in chapter 1, poetics can also serve ethics "by recalling the limits of human judgment and the unavoidable play of interpretations which attends every application of justice."[77] The indeterminacy of poetical form and the practices of hermeneutics required to observe such form may have the effect of delaying judgment, a delay that, in Girardian terms, becomes crucial for defusing incipient mob violence. Girard should therefore not be so quick to dismiss the uses of myth, or of narrative qua narrative. Kearney's argument, with the word "rhetoric" swapped for "poetics," offers another justification for the present project: the exclusion of rhetoric from Girard's theory ultimately ignores the anthropology on which the entire theory is based. That anthropology frames the human creature as one made first of desire and only second of rationality or intellection. To be a creature of desire, particularly intersubjective desire, is to be a creature prone to influence, and rhetoric can be reasonably defined as the formal study (*rhetorica docens*) and practice (*rhetorica utens*) of influence. The biblical texts on which Girard bases his key religious insights are both poetic and rhetorical. They do not simply inform; they have effects. But the central effect is to reveal the source and the persistence of sacred violence, both of which are hidden by certain self-exculpating myths.

Translation Debt 5: Sacrifice

We thus arrive at Girard's most expensive translation debt, which centers on the word "sacrifice." In his early work, Girard rejects the idea of sacrifice as thoroughly unbiblical. Yet this stance seems to abandon positive notions of sacrifice, including commonplace ideas of Jesus's death. Speaking theorhetorically, the problem is that we are left with one word for two entirely separate phenomena. This problem can be observed even in everyday usage. "Sacrifice" denotes both generosity ("she sacrificed so much of her time for the good of the community") and hypocrisy ("he sacrificed so much personal integrity to achieve power"). For the marginalized or oppressed, the notion of sacrifice is particularly fraught. Women can be lauded for self-diminishment ("she sacrificed her ambitions for those of her husband"), while the suffering of people of color can be papered over ("they sacrificed so much to build this nation"). The idea of sacrifice can ennoble and debase.

As Chaim Perelman and Lucy Olbrechts-Tyteca observe in *The New Rhetoric*, "the term of reference has no fixed value, but interacts constantly with the other elements."[78] Though "sacrifice" attempts to measure the worth of something, the standards in question constantly shift. Moreover, the value of sacrifice "is likewise modified during the action by the very sacrifices themselves."[79] The degree of difficulty can change our evaluation of a sacrifice, as when sunk costs motivate us to incur further losses or when the fallacy leads us to cut losses that actually should be commitments. Perelman and Olbrechts-Tyteca also speak of the "pathos of useless sacrifice," in which one sees that a tremendous sacrifice has gone for naught, a failure that "often leads to the disrepute of those who have made it."[80] A single sentence can indicate an object's value ("I sacrificed my youth to get this PhD") or worthlessness ("I sacrificed my youth to get this PhD"). "So . . . did you ever finish that PhD you were working on? You were at it for a long time, no?" Sacrifice can make us want to look away.

Within the ethnological framework within which Girard is working, there is even less clarity. Sacrifice remains "a polythetic term, encompassing a range of activities that need have no single feature in common."[81] As another study puts it, "at times [sacrifice] is considered to be nothing but a fossilized remnant of past dependence on cruel and demanding deities no longer worthy of human worship, while at others it is considered to be a necessary cathartic symbol of the human need for humility and service to another in order to

74 PERSUASIONS OF GOD

limit the devastating effects of one's natural preoccupation with the egotistical self."[82] Because of this range, many scholars have denied that "sacrifice" is a useful term for scholarly analysis. In "The Rhetoric of Sacrifice," for example, James Watts distills the negative critiques about the usefulness of the term into a terse judgment: "*sacrifice* is an evaluative term rather than a descriptive one."[83] Marcel Detienne adds, "the notion of sacrifice is indeed a category of the thought of yesterday, conceived of as arbitrarily as totemism . . . both because it gathers into one artificial type elements taken from here and there . . . and because it reveals the surprising power of annexation that Christianity still subtly exercises on the thought of these historians and sociologists who were convinced they were inventing a new science."[84] (Detienne names Girard as a prime example.)[85] Within the religious traditions that have apparently annexed Girard's mind, there is also no unitary theory of sacrifice available. David Janzen argues that no single explanation can cover the diverse purposes of sacrifice in the Hebrew Bible, let alone across cultures and traditions. Such universal theories "impose a theory on all sacrifices enacted in all societies with no regard to their cultural or historical contexts."[86] Even among Christian scholars sympathetic to Girard, his notion of sacrifice has received pushback. Girard's early resistance to the word itself seems to contradict the sacrificial vocabulary not only in the Christian scriptures (especially the Letter to the Hebrews) but also in the Roman Catholic liturgy. Moreover, it also seems clear that Jesus does not set out to abrogate all forms of sacrifice but rather recognizes that the ethics precedes it: "if you bring your gift to the altar, and there recall that your brother has anything against you, leave your gift there at the altar, go first and be reconciled with your brother, and then come and offer your gift" (Matt. 5:23–24).[87] Though the ethical relations of contrition and reconciliation take precedent, a sacrificial practice is maintained.

Yet Girard has made statements that seem to deny this more nuanced understanding of sacrifice. In *Things Hidden*, for example, he insists that the Gospel message indicates "*the complete elimination of the sacrificial for the first time—the end of divine violence and the explicit revelation of all that has gone before. It calls for a complete change of emphasis and a spiritual metamorphosis without precedent in the whole history of mankind.*"[88] The claim of an intervention "without precedent" deserves careful attention, not only in light of the rhetorical approach of the present study but also because of the claim's supersessionist implications, a matter that must be addressed.

Supersessionism, also sometimes called "replacement theology," is the pernicious but persistent idea that Christianity has "superseded" Judaism and therefore obviated it. Girard's particular claims for Christianity have raised the question of whether he is a supersessionist. Girard insists that he is not; when asked, he explicitly rejects the "heresy that consists in eliminating the Old Testament."[89] Girard also credits the Hebrew scriptures as offering the foundational insight into the relationship between violence and the sacred. Girard has also said that Christian misunderstanding of the Bible "is most often rooted in the inability of Christians themselves to see that the two Testaments are one."[90] For Jews, this claim of unity may threaten erasure; for Christians, however, it is an important reminder that Christian theology and ethics remain dependent on the Judaism from which they grew.

In fact, for these reasons, Sandor Goodhart argues that the divine rejection of violence is already revealed in the Hebrew scriptures. Goodhart reads Isaiah 52–53 (also known as the Song of the Suffering Servant and often taken by Christians as a prediction of Jesus) and asks, "What element of René Girard's theory of sacrifice is missing from this description? The sacrificial expulsion, the violent removal of the victim who has done no violence, who is removed by (and for) what his persecutors did and by whose removal they are healed—all of it is there."[91] Goodhart also denies that Girardianism is coequal with Christianity. "Perhaps because Girard himself remains a committed Christian, or perhaps for other reasons, his thinking has often been confused with Christianity."[92] For Goodhart, however, the *anthropological* insight is already articulated in the Hebrew scriptures; the *theological* import is an entirely different matter, one that mimetic theory is not obliged to address. Yet Girard also makes claims that seem to contradict Goodhart's read. In *Battling to the End*, his last major work, Girard argues that mimetic theory is "essentially Christian": "I would even go so far as to say that it tries to take Christianity to its ultimate meeting, to complete it in a way, because it takes violence seriously."[93] What is to be done with this rather maximalist claim that Christianity possesses a unique insight into the origins and problems of human culture? And how does that claim position Girard vis-à-vis the question of supersessionism?

As we have seen, when Girard is asked about supersessionism, he disavows it and recognizes that it is a heresy. In addition, Girard's reading of the Christian scriptures implies a serious critique of Christianity, which has failed to understand its own message about violence. But as true as those observations may be, they cannot fully assuage concerns about supersessionism. Nor will claims that

Christianity offers something "for the first time" or "without precedent in the whole history of mankind" or as "the climactic achievement" of the move away from the violent sacred.[94] Such arguments risk severing the Gospels from their Jewish roots.[95] Jesus certainly introduces innovations (e.g., "love your enemies"), but even these are intensifications of his own religious tradition. Reading Girard, one will be prompted to ask, Is Girard a supersessionist? Even as he explicitly rejects the position, his own statements can raise the question. For the study of religious rhetoric, the more pointed question is this: Can mimetic theory, despite some of Girard's claims for Christian exclusivity, be put to critical and inventive use unmarred by supersessionism? Here, we might consider Jonathan Sacks's *Not in God's Name*, which uses Girard's work to explain the stubborn persistence of antisemitism in Christian cultures. Sacks writes, "*wherever you find obsessive, irrational, murderous antisemitism, there you will find a culture so internally split and fractured that if its members stopped killing Jews they would start killing one another.*"[96] Sacks's Girardian argument makes plain that the current rise of antisemitism in the United States should be no surprise: riven by resentment and contempt, the citizens of a putatively Christian nation will turn their attention on the most familiar scapegoat rather than on each other; the tenacity of antisemitic attitudes quickly focuses their ire.[97] More importantly, Sacks's argument confirms Goodhart's claim that mimetic theory is not inherently or exclusively Christian. In addition, more and more scholars are using mimetic theory to study other religious traditions and discovering that the insight into the sacrificial origins of culture is not limited to Judaism and Christianity.[98] These studies suggest that a number of different traditions also recognize that the authentically religious does not require violent sacrifice.

That insight leads Girard, at least initially, to reject the word "sacrifice" as a means of understanding Jesus's death. "Sacrifice" is too redolent of the idea of a sulking deity requiring propitiation. That lingering framework distorts the Gospel message, creating a malformed "sacrificial Christianity" still articulated through a sacred imaginary.[99] (We will turn to specific theological examples of this problem in chapter 3.) This allergy to sacrifice leads Girard to suggest that the Letter to the Hebrews, which presents the apostolic writings' most elaborate picture of sacrifice, should be eliminated from the Christian scriptural corpus. But the most essential problem with Girard's suspicion of sacrifice is that it seems to eliminate altogether the idea that Jesus's death had any moral character or decisive effect. Without the former possibility, there can be no meaning, religious or otherwise, to the statement, "Greater love has no one than this, that a person will lay down his life for his friends" (John 15:13). Without the latter possibility, there is no Christian theological possibility of understanding Jesus's death as revealing something essential about the violent sacred.

As we have seen in other keywords, Girard's understanding is challenged and refined by his interpreters, in this case the Swiss Jesuit Raymund Schwager, who in a long correspondence convinces Girard that he has eliminated the idea of sacrifice too hastily.[100] "If we abandon the word sacrifice, the danger would be to not sufficiently underline the *solidarity* of Christ with *us*, who are still terribly embedded in a sacrificial world."[101] Ultimately, Girard acknowledges the force of this critique, admitting that he was mistaken to miss the paradoxical relation by which God "reuses the scapegoat mechanism, at his own expense, in order to subvert it."[102] This constitutes another implicit acknowledgment of the need for complicit invention, particularly as a post-Christian project of recycling "our stock of old labels."[103] Otherwise, to jettison sacrifice would be to jettison kenosis, the idea that constitutes the Gospel expression of rhetorical capacity, of emptying oneself as a means of making oneself available. Understood in this way, self-sacrifice is not mere self-diminishment but rather a profound, nearly reckless form of generosity. To enter into such solidarity is an act of sacrifice in the most fundamental sense of making holy (*sacer*, holy + *facere*, to make).

From a Christian theorhetorical standpoint, God empties Godself to sustain an exposure to humanity, including the human cult of the kill. Through this exposure, God practices a kind of complicit invention in which God becomes "a scapegoat in order to desacralize those who came before him and to prevent those who come after him from being sacralized."[104] Girard articulates the end of a certain kind of sacrifice by borrowing from Levinas, who borrows from the Talmud: "If everyone is in agreement to condemn someone accused, release him immediately for he must be innocent."[105] For the Christian, God attempts to persuade humanity of this idea by standing in the accused's place, not simply to replace the accused but *as* the accused. As a result of this intervention, a new intensity of the persuasion of God is made available through an act of sacrifice, which can no longer operate as an automatic mechanism of deity propitiation. Instead, sacrifice can operate only as appeal, an appeal expressed primarily through solidarity.

For Girardians, the idea of God as a rhetorician who makes appeals may seem counter to the general orientation of Girard's project. As the title of his magnum opus suggests, Girard sought to uncover "things hidden from the foundation of the world." The idea is to expose essential truths lurking under

78   PERSUASIONS OF GOD

misapprehension. We have already seen that when Girard mentions rhetoric, it is always as something to be gotten past or beyond. In addition, the kind of communal activity in which rhetoric trades is in Girard's writing almost always equated with the scapegoating mob. To say that Girard's project is in any way "rhetorical," therefore, is to cut against the grain of his thinking. Nevertheless, my argument is that Girard's work has implications that can only be construed as rhetorical. Girard's self-implicating understanding of Christianity challenges conventional understandings of ideas of the sacred and sacrifice, thus occasioning a demand for inventing persuasions of God in an "alienated" or post-Christian key.[106]

Girard's Theorhetorical Demand

Girard's theorhetorical demand begins to emerge in his critical questions about the concepts of the sacred and sacrifice. Regarding the word "sacred," Girard insists that the word cannot apply to the central events of the life of Jesus as Christians understand them: "For the power of the Resurrection, it would be better to use a word other than 'sacred,' if we reserve this word, as I do, for the religions of the hidden scapegoat."[107] The sacred designates the disguised violence of scapegoating, and the effects of the Crucifixion will therefore require some other description, not least because the word covers such a wide range of practices and beliefs. Similarly, Girard argues that the notion that Jesus's death is a "sacrifice" is perhaps misleading. The term "surpasses our understanding and our powers of expression."[108] Likewise, he writes, "We must beware of calling [Jesus's] action sacrificial, even if we then have no words or categories to convey its meaning. The very lack of appropriate language suggests that we are dealing with a type of conduct for which there is no precedent in the realm of mythology or philosophy."[109] Here, Girard expresses a rhetorical demand quite radical in its request for language for which there is no precedent, even though this implied ex nihilo position contradicts the foundations of his own religious critique. Only through a form of complicit invention is Jesus's "sacrifice" persuasive. But Girard's antipathy to what he sees as the linguistic excesses of the postmodern turn prevents him from imagining interventions appropriate to his own anthropology. Meanwhile, his implicit project of religious and rhetorical intervention is stymied by his own intellectual and cultural instincts. Girard recognizes what he describes as "a new felt need for religion, in some form."[110] Though he would probably never put the matter in terms of the post-Christian, the suggestion of a "new felt need," along with the vagueness of "some form," indicates the recognition of a decisive shift.

Despite his antirhetorical instincts, Girard also seems to recognize the complicity of all repurposed form. Older forms of religious expression, he argues, "form part of a great drama, a spectacle, and perhaps it ought to be staged some other way. But if we were to get rid of all the sanctions and all these, so to speak, 'theatrical' and dramatic aspects, we would be eliminating an extremely important part of our lives."[111] To speak of drama in this context is to observe the implicit theorhetorical implications of Girard's work, implications that go beyond the simple presentation of a new understanding of Jesus's life, death, and resurrection. It is the drama of Jesus's life, death, and resurrection that is important, not simply the declarative conclusions one might draw from that drama. "We are beings both aesthetic and ethical at the same time."[112] The intersection of the aesthetic and the ethical is where rhetoric lives. For a thinker who so often seemed to frame his conclusions as ideas to be understood rather than appeals to be experienced, this observation is notable for its implicit rhetorical need. Girard admits, as if in response to critiques that we will examine in a moment, that his conclusions cannot ultimately be grasped primarily as concepts.

From other examples of Girard's theological considerations, we can continue to divine a theorhetoric. Because of the enduring relationship between violence and the sacred, he argues, God will have to perform the basic rhetorical task of suiting the message to the audience. "Behaving in a truly divine manner, on an earth still in the clutches of violence, means not dominating humans, not overwhelming them with supernatural power; it means not terrifying and astonishing them."[113] The mystics might beg to differ on whether God astonishes. But the more important point is that Girard acknowledges that God has a style, a persuasion. Elsewhere, Girard links theological and rhetorical considerations in his insistence that God must play a role: "The word *persona* is a Greek word that means 'actor.' We mustn't bemoan the fact that the word has a literary and theatrical origin, because it's a concept that is absent from philosophy and that had to be borrowed from literature, which is always stronger than philosophy where existential relationships are concerned."[114] We encounter in this statement an incipient theopoetics, a recognition that drama (narrative, story, and spectacle) may be the most ethical and reliable means of divine encounter. Paradoxically enough, God is available only insofar as God plays a role and wears a mask.

An implied rhetorical demand appears in some of the most significant critiques of Girard's work. In an oft-cited challenge, the theologian John Milbank argues that Girard conceives of the Gospels as delivering a piece of information rather than a new vision for human relations. This "extrinsicist" argument, as Milbank describes it, risks rendering Jesus's message incomprehensible: "if Jesus suffered perfectly, or if he alone really refused a dominating violence, then how do we *know* this, how does it 'come through to us'?"[115] This question seems to point to Girard's claim that Jesus's "sacrifice" has "no precedent." Without any precedent, Milbank suggests, there is no way for us even to grasp that something new has happened. Girard's reading of the Gospel texts appears to require an intervention so singular as to be unhearable. In the terms of the present argument, Girard's conclusions appear to imply an entirely noncomplicit form of invention in which there are no available means for the "uptake" of Girard's insight.

Nor is there any means for making that insight "workable," something with some practical effect. We need, Milbank writes, to know the "idiom of peaceable behaviour if we are to be able to distinguish it from the coercive."[116] If we cannot make this distinction, then even the imitation of a "good" model remains fundamentally, ontologically rivalrous. Even as Girard accepts Adams's argument for a positive, loving mimesis, he also sometimes reverts to language that suggests that the only salutary response to the world's brokenness is to withdraw. In *Battling to the End*, Girard's last book, he argues, "The aspect of Christ that needs to be imitated is his withdrawal."[117] To offer the most generous reading of Girard's meaning here, one might see a form of appropriate withdrawal in John 8, where Jesus defends the woman caught in adultery. In a sense, Jesus "withdraws" from the anger of the crowd by refusing to mirror it. This is a rhetoric of meekness par excellence, an "apathetic" rhetoric in which there is a withdrawal from mirroring and rivalry—but not from the situation or, most importantly, from the victim. If anything, Jesus's "meekness" paradoxically allows him to take over the scene and redirect the rage of the crowd. Yet "withdrawal" cannot serve as a primary heuristic for responding to confrontation, even applied to Jesus. As a fully human person, Jesus is ontologically unable to withdraw from mimetic desire. His human subjectivity, which must be a product of relationality and prior rhetoricity as surely as any other human subjectivity, is what allows him to be moved by the woman's plight in the first place. Jesus had human models: Mary and Joseph, his cousin John, the prophets. There must have been those with whom he could be complicit in order to articulate an idiom of peaceable behavior.

In a similar way, Milbank argues that Girard's understanding of mimetic desire seems to trap humanity in an inescapable cycle of violence: "given Girard's identification of culture with a mimetic desire, and apparent denial of the possibility of an objective desire or a benign *eros*, it is difficult to see what 'the Kingdom' could really amount to, other than the negative gesture of refusal of desire."[118] This "negative gesture" would deny Girard's most fundamental premise, which is that all desire is mimetic. The "kingdom," therefore, cannot be built solely on a refusal of rivalrous desire, a refusal that is by Girard's own understanding impossible.[119]

The theologian David Bentley Hart faults Girard in terms similar to Milbank's. The problem with Girard's understanding of salvation, argues Hart, is that it "makes out the salvific motion of Christ's life to be almost purely negative, a motion of alienation, running dialectically against history." The intervention of Jesus may seem purely negative, an anti-idolatry so stringent as to erase the Incarnation (which may be the most divine gesture of theorhetorical complicit invention). Though Hart acknowledges that Girard does not mean to reduce the Incarnation to a kind of gnostic revelation, he argues that that is where Girard's conclusions inexorably lead. "Christ looks suspiciously like a figure who saves simply by pointing beyond every economy—and every world."[120] Hart notes that Girard acknowledges this context; his understanding of the Gospels can make sense only in relation to the previous scriptures on which they draw. But Girard's articulation of Jesus's intervention sometimes seems to express a hermeneutic of rupture so complete that there is no context left in which to interpret Jesus's message. "Does Christ then offer a new order of exchange and sacrifice, or is he simply the abnegation of human solidarity, a revolutionary outcry that forever interrupts the story of the world but tells no story of its own?"[121] Again, what is the peaceable idiom that Jesus's intervention might suggest?

To be fair, Girard does admit that knowledge alone is not enough to redirect mimetic desire away from its tendency toward rivalry and resentment. "In reality, no purely intellectual process and no experience of a purely philosophical nature can secure the individual the slightest victory over mimetic desire and its victimage delusions." An authentic recognition of our implication in mimesis requires a change "on the most intimate level of experience," a change that will

82   PERSUASIONS OF GOD

end up "shaking to their very foundations, all the things that are based on our interdividual oppositions."[122] Girard makes this statement in *Things Hidden Since the Foundation of the World*, considered his magnum opus, which appeared in 1983. Thus, relatively early in his work, he makes clear that recognizing the full depth of desire requires something like a conversion experience (though at that point Girard is talking mostly about novelists who reveal the mechanics of desire in their work). When Rebecca Adams outlines the contours of a loving mimesis—one that calls us into affirmative selfhood and loving relationship—she is furthering a possibility that Girard himself recognized. The "gnostic charge" against Girard is therefore not entirely fair, though refuting it fully does require some extension of Girard's work.

Whatever the theological strengths and weaknesses of the "gnostic critique," which itself has been repeatedly challenged, Milbank and Hart essentially fault Girard for a lack of rhetorical awareness.[123] Milbank puts the rhetorical critique explicitly: "Christianity does not claim that the Good and the True are self-evident to merely objective reason, or dialectical argument. On the contrary, [Christianity] from the first qualified philosophy by rhetoric in contending that the Good and the True are those things of which we 'have a persuasion,' *pistis*, or 'faith.'"[124] Within the Girardian context, Milbank's argument pushes back against any notion that some purportedly objective revelation of truth is readily tantamount to the idiom of peace. Put in rhetorical terms, the idiom still needs to be invented.

Conclusion

Following the anthropologist Lucien Scubla, my purpose in this chapter has not been "to cast discredit on the whole of [Girard's] output; it is on the contrary to return to the original core of the theory and to continue building on the solid foundations our author himself set."[125] That original core points to a vigorous, clarifying, kairotic, and—most importantly—*religious* critique of the violent sacred. Most crucially, that import is one of self-criticism. The methodological choice I have made in this book is to see Girard as a religious critic rather than an anthropological one. That choice maintains attention on Alberg's observation that mimetic theory is "self-implicating."[126] For the Christian reader, then, the first and most important conclusion one might draw from Girard's theory is a critique of Christianity, which often "covers the texts with a veil of sacrifice. Or, to change the metaphor, it immolates them in the (albeit splendid) tomb of Western culture."[127] Christianity violates its own Gospel by founding a sacred order that inevitably requires victims. It is for this reason that Girard's work becomes so important for articulating a post-Christian theorhetoric, a rhetoric of meek witness to the Gospel without the rivalry that leads to violence. This is what Girard means when he imagines a Christianity without sacrificial (i.e., violent sacred) crutches.

To be sure, it is unlikely that Girard would have seen things this way. Regarding the formulation "post-Christian," Girard insists that "the more evocative word is the second one."[128] Yet Girard's ideas imply a need for rhetorical invention, a claim not entirely novel or foreign to Girardian thought. In *René Girard, Unlikely Apologist*, the theologian Grant Kaplan describes mimetic theory as a "heuristic," by which he means "a model that allows theological narratives and positions to become more intelligible."[129] This does not mean, Kaplan cautions, that Girard wanted his ideas to serve only theological ends; he still aspires to push his conclusions into the realm of social science. Yet the notion of mimetic theory as heuristic confirms the rhetorical trajectory that this chapter has tried to follow. Even Girard's idea that mimetic theory "completes" the Christian message, far from being an exclusivist claim, is one that implies complicit invention—an adherence and commitment to tradition deep enough to reinvent it, a translation that is willing to betray, though piously. This pious betrayal is the work of chapters 3 and 4.

3

Overcoming Christianity

There is no choice but to keep shuttling back and forth between alpha and omega. This
constant movement, back and forth, imposes a form of composition resembling a snail,
or a volute, or a spiral.

—René Girard, *The One by Whom Scandal Comes*

Chapter 2 presented a rhetorically oriented, critical appraisal of René Girard's
religious critique. In addition to reviewing Girard's work for an audience who
might be unfamiliar with it, the chapter also outlined the ways in which Girard's
project makes a theorhetorical demand. Though Girard himself would probably be skeptical of such a project, he also acknowledged that his work indicated
possibilities that he himself had not anticipated. "I am not necessarily hostile to
all the things which I do not mention in my writing. The people who complain
about not finding this or that in my books are the same, as a rule, who ridicule
the excessive ambition of *le systeme-Girard*."[1] My purpose was not to complain
about not finding a fully developed rhetorical theory within Girard's writings,
nor was my purpose to ridicule the ambition of the Girardian system.[2] Yet there
can be little doubt of that ambition. Girard claims to have discovered the
authentic message of Christianity, a message that Christians have misunderstood for the greater part of the last two millennia: "In a remarkable paradox,
but one that accords well with the sacrificial course of mankind, the sacrificial
reading . . . refashions the mechanism that has been revealed and thus of necessity annihilated—if the revelation were genuinely accepted—into a kind of sacrificial cultural foundation. This is the foundation that both 'Christianity' and
the modern world have rested upon, right up to our own time."[3] In other words,
Christianity has allowed its antisacrificial message to be subsumed into the very
sort of sacrificial structures that the Gospels reject. Though Girard often feels
compelled to defend Christianity against its fashionable despisers, his religious

critique begins with the admission that Christian theology and practice have often gotten things backward.

Sorting through some of the specific theorhetorical implications of this reversal is the project of the present chapter. Since the introduction, we have been building toward an idea of an alienated theorhetoric, a post-Christian theorhetoric that critically engages the Truth/truths of Christianity. That project began by theorizing a rhetoric of meekness and continued in chapter 2's study of Girard through a practice of rhetorical criticism that observed both Girard's implicit rhetorical demand and the paradoxical understanding required to see Girard as a post-Christian theorhetor. In Girard, we find a thinker both orthodox and alienated, an avowed Christian who has raised the question of whether, as David Dawson writes, "the story of Jesus is inimical *to religion as such* and *the narrative codifications of theology in particular*."[4] Can what Burke might call the Gospel imaginative be bureaucratized without distortion? Girard acknowledges the difficulty when he laments that "the Christian text is able to found something that in principle it ought never to have founded: a culture."[5] Insofar as cultures are founded on victimage, a "Christian culture" should be a contradiction in terms. To observe this, however, is also to suggest that the Christian message cannot help but be apocalyptic in both senses of the term: revelatory and destructive.

My hope in this chapter—and I think it is best characterized as a hope—is to point to how a rhetoric of meekness might do more than buy time against destruction. Pursuing this possibility will require an intensification of the practices of complicit rhetorical invention pursued so far in this book. In what follows here, complicit invention will be expressed through an overcoming that is not rivalrous. I borrow this idea from Gianni Vattimo's take on Martin Heidegger's notion of *Überwindung* (overcoming), which for Heidegger designates a complex relationship to the history of Being. In this history, Heidegger suggests, metaphysics does not simply disappear but rather "returns transformed, and remains in dominance as the continuing difference of Being and beings."[6] Metaphysics, Heidegger insists, "cannot be abolished like an opinion."[7] That is to say, tradition and history cannot be simply jettisoned, a response that (as a meek rhetoric would observe) simply mirrors the move it attempts to reject. For Vattimo, this means that the best way to relate to the history of Being is rather through *Verwindung*, a word related to but distinct from *Überwindung*. Vattimo understands *Verwindung* to refer to overcoming, but with a twist. If *Überwindung*

86   PERSUASIONS OF GOD

indicates a decisive break, *Verwindung* constitutes "a resigned acceptance that continues the metaphysical tradition in a distorted form."[8] This is why Vattimo interprets *Verwindung* as a form of a kind of "twisting." A relation to history and tradition endures, but the relation is altered; there is a sense of recovery and recovery *from*—recovery in the sense of convalescence. This kind of twisting offers a protocol for complicit invention of a post-Christian rhetoric.

What follows in this chapter, then, are three movements of complicit invention, each created through different encounters occasioned by Girard's thought. The first of these movements has been stalking this book since the beginning—namely, the influence of Kenneth Burke. Rhetoricians will have long since recognized the ways in which Girard echoes Burke's thought. Burke argued not only that religion is unequal to the task of forestalling global homicide-suicide but also that religion is shaped by the same structures that draw us toward that apocalyptic fate. By contrast, Girard finds in the Jewish and Christian scriptures a critique of those structures, but a critique that implicates Christianity as a means of making that critique persuasive in a post-Christian context.

This engagement between Girard and Burke will lead us to a second and related movement of complicit invention, a movement that takes up Christian theologies of atonement, or the reconciliation between God and humanity brought about by Jesus's life and death. Atonement theology plays a central role in Burke's thinking in *The Rhetoric of Religion*, where Burke reproduces a form of "penal substitution," in which the son endures a punishment that properly belongs to sinful humanity. This idea structures Burke's logology and his political-theological conclusions. Yet penal substitution, and the "satisfaction" theory from which it derives, is only one way to understand the hotly contested Christian idea of atonement. Other possibilities, including those suggested by Girard, indicate a rhetoric of religion based in persuasion rather than an inescapable dialectical structure. A different rhetoric of religion might be imagined by a different theology.

Our third and final movement of complicit invention will move between and through a dialogue between Girard and Vattimo, who is most famous for his idea of *il pensiero debole*, or "weak thought." Weak thought follows from the announcement that "the strong frameworks of metaphysics—*archai, Gründe*, primary evidences and ultimate destinies—are only forms of self-assurance."[9] These kinds of arguments will be very familiar to rhetoricians; indeed, Vattimo is singular among postmodern philosophers of religion for his acknowledgment that rhetoric is what follows in the wake of collapsing self-assurance. But what makes Vattimo's thought pertinent for the present discussion is his connection between his own project and Girard's. For Vattimo, Girard's thought provides the basis for a Christianity commensurate with Vattimo's mistrust of ultimate destinies. Vattimo thus finds in Girard a religious confirmation of his philosophic trajectory. For Girard, however, Vattimo's self-described "optimistic nihilism" misconstrues the effects and demands of dismantling the violent sacred. The religious demand of the Gospel is more arduous than Vattimo suggests. If Vattimo endorses the gentleness of the dove, Girard thinks that gentleness must be supplemented by the wisdom of the serpent (Matt. 10:16).

A Nonovercoming Overcoming

The basic idea of *Verwindung*, as Vattimo understands it from Heidegger, is that metaphysics cannot simply be "overcome" by being escaped, defeated, or left behind. In "Overcoming Metaphysics," Heidegger argues that "we may not presume to stand outside of metaphysics because we surmise the ending of metaphysics."[10] This presumption is still shaped by metaphysics, which does not simply disappear. "It returns transformed, and remains in dominance as the continuing difference of Being and beings."[11] Elsewhere, Heidegger writes, "To overcome does not mean to dispose of, but to have at one's disposition in a new way."[12] Whatever is overcome remains within the new dispensation, though it does so precisely as something that has been overcome. Heidegger analogizes his idea of "overcoming" to Christian conversion. Though the change of conversion may be decisive, the convert's prior disposition is preserved in the new disposition, which is itself defined in relation to the old: "One's pre-Christian existence is indeed existentially, ontically, overcome in faith. But this existentiell overcoming of one's pre-Christian existence (which belongs to faith as rebirth) means precisely that one's overcome pre-Christian Dasein is existentially, ontologically included within faithful existence."[13] To describe oneself as a convert who has "overcome" a prior existence is to define oneself precisely by a relation to this overcoming. The notion resonates deeply with complicit invention and singular rhythms, both of which refuse the gesture of overcoming in an ordinary sense of defeat. Similarly, Vattimo understands *Verwindung* to express the paradoxical relation between a decisive difference marked by an ongoing relation to the same. If overcoming aspires to "a capacity for leaping out of the tradition into which our very existence is 'thrown,'" *Verwindung* constitutes instead a "resigned

88   PERSUASIONS OF GOD

acceptance" that "continues the metaphysical tradition in a distorted form."[14] This idea underwrites Vattimo's "optimistic nihilism": nihilism because of the weakening of Being, but optimistic insofar as that weakening might free us from anxious assertion or panicked domination. "Is it not possible," Vattimo asks, "that many of the dramatic problems of our civilization depend for their drama on a neurotic effort to reaffirm a strong sense of reality in a context where emancipation resides rather in the weakening of that sense?"[15] For Vattimo, an optimistic nihilism promises the possibility of letting go of such neuroses.

Vattimo admits that his own take on *Verwindung* represents its own "distortion," which he describes as a "left-wing" reading of Heidegger insofar as it emphasizes the forgetfulness of Being as an event, an event that "gives itself fully, not provisionally or pedagogically, in its suspension, in its weakening and dissolution." This reading, he argues, avoids the "negative theology" of the rightwing reading, which assumes that Being is "given" in a transcendent realm. The left-wing reading "takes more seriously the basic purpose of Heidegger's critique of metaphysics, namely the purpose of overcoming the identification of being with beings."[16] The "overcoming of the overcoming" constitutes a kind of surrender to tradition, but a surrender characterized by convalescence, distortion, and twisting.

Throughout the remaining three sections of this chapter, we will rely on this idea of twisting as an available means of practicing a meek rhetoric that refuses rivalry. My purpose, then, is not to adjudicate between Girard and Burke, Girard and theologians of atonement, or Girard and Vattimo. Rather, my purpose is to read these encounters for the unexpected possibilities of post-Christian theorhetorical invention they might produce.

The Religion-(Mis)using Animal

Burke's 1961 *Rhetoric of Religion* remains a standard work on its titular subject; it is also a book that suggests the extent of Burke's influence on Girard, whose interests and obsessions track closely with Burke's.[17] If Girard is the hedgehog who knows the one big thing of scapegoating, Burke is the fox who knows many things. Burke's interest in rhetoric indicates the central difference in their anthropologies: Burke takes language far more seriously than Girard does—the human is "the symbol-using (symbol-making, symbol-misusing) animal."[18] By contrast, Girard would call the human the mimetically desiring animal, the animal whose desire and whose participation in victimage precedes all symbolicity. "Burke," Girard observes, "sees victimage as a product of language rather than language as a product of victimage (indirectly at least, through the mediation of ritual and prohibitions)."[19] If Burke thinks our language inclines us toward victimage, Girard argues that victimage occasions language. If, as Burke insists, the very structure of language inclines us toward victimage, Girard insists it is because language, like all culture, is ultimately a product of victimage.

Both agree that humans are the sacrifice-using and -misusing animal, the animal that builds its cultures through sacred violence. But if Burke sees Christian theology as symptomatic of the ultimately violent structure of language, Girard sees in Christian theology, particularly the study of the scriptures, the discourse par excellence for revealing the mimetic source of violence. If Burke launches his critique from outside of religion, Girard launches his critique from within religion. This difference has important consequences for any study of the rhetoric of religion. Can we imagine a post-Christian theorhetoric as a distortion/convalescence of Christian tradition, or must a post-Christian theorhetoric proceed on a decisive break from its past?

Prompting this inquiry is a question Burke himself poses: "With a culture formed about the idea of redemption by the sacrifice of a Crucified Christ, just what happens in an era of post-Christian science, when the ways of socialization have been secularized?"[20] This question reminds us that *The Rhetoric of Religion* is not simply a work that draws on theology but a work that forwards a political theology, as Steven Mailloux defines the term: "any implicit or explicit theory relating worldly action within power relations to speculative thinking about a world beyond."[21] Political theology presumes that the political is always infused with the theological, for better or worse. This mutually constitutive relationship has obvious implications for rhetorical practice, which draws on the means made available by a given culture at any given moment (the commonplaces of justice and injustice, crime and punishment, unity and disunity). Because these matters are inherently theological, their study requires an engagement with theology, which John Freccero describes as "the ideology of religion," adding that "religion is a system of action—specifically, of governance. God's self-identity in the creative act is at the same time a defense of the idea of order."[22] Within modern rhetorical theory, Burke's *Rhetoric of Religion* is perhaps the most thoroughgoing examination of the ideology, articulated through a pervasive atonement theology, that structures equally pervasive political beliefs, symbols, and images.

To "get at" this ideology requires a trip through the theology that underwrites it, as the theologians Peter Scott and William Cavanaugh explain. "All politics has theology embedded in it. The task [of political theology] then might become one of exposing false theologies underlying supposedly 'secular' politics and promoting the true politics implicit in a true theology."[23] This is a project occasioned by *The Rhetoric of Religion*, despite Burke's nearly obsessive insistence that logology is an entirely secular subject that makes no actual theological statement.[24] Logology, he argues, studies theology *"not directly as knowledge but as anecdotes that help reveal for us the quandaries of human governance."*[25] But political theology suggests that this division cannot be so easily maintained. William Rueckert suggests as much when he characterizes Burke's intellectual project as a "secular variant of Christianity." "The whole dramatistic system," writes Rueckert, "is laid out with a moral-ethical, Christian-Catholic bias, and is presented in such a way as to make perfectly clear Burke's belief that he has developed a new 'scientific' religion which twentieth-century man can 'believe' in, but which, unlike the old one it replaces, is designed to save man in this world."[26]

Whether this claim accurately characterizes Burke's aspirations, the theology of *The Rhetoric of Religion* suggests that there is no saving man in this world after all. This discouraging possibility had stalked Burke's thought since the 1930s, when he observed the parallels between the violence of the Jim Crow South and the incipient violence of Nazi Germany. Both these expressions of violence were formed by a religious structure: "the use of a sacrificial receptacle for the ritual unburdening of people's sins."[27] Lynching becomes an implicitly religious act insofar as it mimics the formal religious act of transferring a people's sins onto the back of a victim. Before Girard, Burke observed that such scapegoating was "quite efficacious" and "met the pragmatic tests of success" insofar as it seems to occasion "the feeling of relief."[28] This exchange of blood for peace seems a persistent feature of human culture, as Burke explains in his seminal "The Rhetoric of Hitler's 'Battle'": "people, in their human frailty, require an enemy as well as a goal."[29]

The question that has long troubled scholars of Burke is whether we can find any way out of the sacrificial structure that assuages guilt through violence. *The Rhetoric of Religion* seems to conclude that we are doomed with forestalling a future structured by the sacrificial principle with resources that are themselves structured by the sacrificial principle. The poison is the cure, and the cure, the poison (which is also Girard's explanation for why violence so often works). "For it seems that," Burke writes, "even if one believes in the idea of a perfect, supernatural, superpersonal victim, by identification with whose voluntary sacrifice one can be eternally saved, there is still the goad to look for victims here on earth as well."[30] Burke believes that the goad endures because there is something in the structure of language itself that makes us prone to victimize. Synecdoche becomes the "'basic' figure of speech" because it reveals our fundamental orientation toward substitution, and the "'scapegoat' becomes another kind of 'representative,' in serving as the symbolic vessel of certain burdens, which are ritualistically dedicated to it."[31] Logology extends this focus on representation into a study of words about words so formalistic that it "must suspend at least provisionally the referential function of language and treat the various linguistic realms as semiological fields whose force is defined not in terms of their content but, rather, in terms of their form."[32] Yet this focus risks disabling the logologer from considering the contents of the scriptures and traditions that produce theology.

Throughout his thinking on these matters, Burke wrestles with the question of whether the addiction to malevolent synecdoche is fundamentally religious. Cary Nelson offers this provocative framing of the issue, describing Burke's later work (i.e., *The Rhetoric of Religion* [1961], *Language as Symbolic Action* [1966] and beyond) as "the result of placing 'the rhetoric of Hitler's battle' over 'the rhetoric of religion' and asking what their homologies reveal about 'the form underlying all language.'"[33] If the same structure animates both Hitlerian and Christian rhetoric, then perhaps no rhetoric of religion is equal to the task of disrupting vicious representational thinking. Burke had tried to resist coming to this dark conclusion. In "Hitler's 'Battle,'" he had insisted that Hitler's rhetoric presented an "astounding caricature of religious thought" and "a bastardization of fundamentally religious patterns of thought."[34] By the time of *The Rhetoric of Religion*, however, Burke no longer seems certain that the violent sacrificial patterns of religion represent a misuse.[35] This is not to impute a cynicism to Burke but rather to suggest that his methodological choice disposes him to look for certain forms of theological expression, forms that reveal a rotten perfectionism. The perfection of Christianity, Burke suggests, lies in the way it follows the sacrificial principle to its ultimate conclusion. Jesus is the "perfect" victim not simply in a theological sense but also in a logological sense. Anticipating Girard, Burke observes a pattern of violent sacrifice across cultures. "Thus the idea of a personally fit victim could lead to many different notions, such as: (1) the ideal of a perfect victim (Christ); (2) the Greeks' 'enlightened' use of criminals who had been condemned to death, but were kept on reserve for state occasions when some ritual sacrifice was deemed necessary; (3) Hitler's 'idealizing' of the Jew as 'perfect' enemy."[36] By this logic, it becomes even less clear whether there is a decisive difference between "the rhetoric of Hitler's battle" and "the rhetoric of religion."

This growing sense of futility emerges in the first pages of *The Rhetoric of Religion*, where Burke presents the argument in a brief lyric poem: "Here are the steps / In the Iron Law of History / That welds Order and Sacrifice."[37] Nevertheless, Burke attempts to dilute the gloom of the "trilogy of solemn tragedies" (chapters on logology, Augustine's *Confessions*, and Genesis) with the closing "satyr-play" between "the Lord" as patient tutor and "Satan" as an overeager pupil. Incorrigibly moral, Satan is repeatedly scandalized by the Lord's patient explanation of how the symbol-using animal will manage to resolve their guilt theologically.

> **The Lord.** On the contrary! And here enters the principle of perfection. The Earth-People will consider themselves so guilt-laden, that only a perfect sacrifice would be great enough to pay off the debt.
> **Satan.** The morbid devils! Then they will think of themselves as permanently lost?
> **TL.** No, they will conceive of a sacrifice so perfect that it could cancel off all their guilt, however mighty that guilt might be.
> **S.** But only a god would be perfect enough for that!
> **TL.** Quite right.
> **S.** I tremble! You mean . . .
> **TL.** Yes. And finally a cult will arise which holds that I, in my infinite mercy, will send my only begotten Son as the perfect sacrifice for the Earth-People's redemption.[38]

Burke here echoes theologies of satisfaction and substitution, which we will turn to more directly in the next section. For now, however, it is enough to note the sacrificial equipment for living structured by the myth of redemptive violence. The Lord sees that Christian typology has simply grafted the Greek *pharmakos* onto Hebrew sacrifice. "For sheerly logological perfection," the Lord goes on to explain, "few religions will be able to rival the religion (with its close variants) that names itself after my son. . . . Its merger of monotheism with the circumambient rites of pagan polytheism will be a major dialectical triumph."[39] Once merged, this perfected theology will be disabled from mounting any sort of critique of the myth of redemptive violence. Christianity becomes the most persuasive version of that self-perpetuating myth, claiming explicitly that sacrifice is abrogated for all time while all the while animating repeat performances of the same violence.

Fortunately, Burke can be challenged on both theological and, even more importantly, rhetorical grounds. Theologically speaking, for example, we might question Burke's methodological choice to employ "order" rather than "covenant" as his foundational term. Though Burke is interested in the idea of "covenant," he admits that it is not "wholly convenient for our purposes."[40] "Counter-covenant" may imply either a rejection of order per se or an alternate order (as in "to reign in hell"). Barbara Biesecker notes that this methodological choice is perfectly consistent with Burke's program, but it is a choice and, like all choices, excludes other possibilities. Even according to his own sources, there is more than one available understanding of covenant. Such other understandings include a covenant of relationship or, as the scripture scholar N. T. Wright describes it, "a covenant of vocation," in which Israel is called to sanctify creation by defending the defenseless and welcoming the alien.[41] "You too must befriend the stranger, for you were strangers in the land of Egypt" (Deut. 10:15–19). There is a command here, but it is not a moralization by the negative. What kind of political theology might *The Rhetoric of Religion* have produced if Burke had begun with Deuteronomy: "It is not because you are the most numerous of peoples on earth that the Lord set His heart on you and chose you—indeed you are the smallest of peoples; but it was because the Lord favored you and kept the oath He made to your fathers" (Deut. 7:7–8). Here, the Lord sets his heart rather than the rules. If a works contract is about maintaining a moral code, the covenant of vocation is about being God's image-bearers "with genuinely human tasks to perform as part of the Creator's purpose for his [sic] world."[42] An alternative understanding of covenant produces a theology based first and foremost not on order but on ethics.

If Burke ends up in a cul-de-sac that curtails human agency, it is because he is simply reflecting a theological framework that reduces human agency to a desperate form of bargaining, in which there are no persuasive means available. That framework is a particular view of "the atonement," the term that refers to attempts at understanding the reconciliation between God and humanity effected by Jesus's life, death, and resurrection. As we will see in the next section, the idea of atonement is often reduced to an exchange in which a debt of guilt is paid off by Jesus's suffering. In a powerful critique of Burke's *Rhetoric of Religion*, Kristy Maddux notes that the "the ideology of the atonement cycle is

94 PERSUASIONS OF GOD

particularly troubling" in that it "creates a world order potentially so powerfully constraining that the individual rhetor cannot assert agency in his or her social situation."[43] To imagine something different, we must begin with a more thorough examination of the theology on which Burke is drawing, along with the possibilities of a different theology, possibilities indicated by Girard's religious critique. In addition, Burke's *Rhetoric of Religion* might be challenged on rhetorical grounds, including the basic question of whether the book is actually about rhetoric. Timothy Crusius distinguishes Burke's understanding of dialectic, which is "the disinterested pursuit of a vocabulary's implications," from rhetoric, which seeks "*the overcoming of estrangement.*"[44] By this definition, *The Rhetoric of Religion* is more dialectic than rhetoric, more interested in the implications of a supernatural vocabulary than in whether such a vocabulary is persuasive to the supernatural (a question that Burke forecloses). If we insist on theological discourse as epistemology or dialectic (a claim that many theologians would dispute), we are left with a study of the closed fist rather than the open hand, a gesture not generally considered one of reconciliation.

Ostensibly a book about rhetoric, *The Rhetoric of Religion* seems to preclude persuasion. The iron law of history leaves no room for appeal, rhetorically or juridically. For this reason, many scholars have critiqued *The Rhetoric of Religion* on the grounds that it erases any form of agency and by extension rhetoric. "The deepest tension in *RR* [*Rhetoric of Religion*]," writes Robert Wess, "is between its methodological commitment to the most 'thorough' example and its logological project: the method directs attention to history, but the project produces a psychology that puts history into eclipse."[45] That psychology, (de)formed by a sense of persistent guilt at our failure to maintain order, cannot help but cast about for victims, and even the "perfect victim" of Christ is not enough to break the habit.[46] History repeats itself so regularly that there is no history.

Biesecker, however, suggests that *The Rhetoric of Religion* ends up being a rhetoric despite itself. "To what extent," she asks, "can the human being intervene in a structure that always and already antedates it?"[47] The "iron law" appears to exclude the situated, context-bound expressions of the temporal. Yet the only thing that makes such a structure possible is the negative, a purely human invention without natural analogue. For Burke, Adam's sin is a logological necessity; the formal properties he is trying to observe demand a beginning that implies its own end. If Adam had not sinned, the "Pauline logic" that links the "Fall" to "Redemption" through a "tragic sacrifice" would not work.[48] But, as Biesecker observes, Adam's logological act first must be a temporal act.[49] The introduction of the negative as a concept requires the introduction of the negative as an act. Put another way, the narrative or temporal must precede the logical or essential, which puts us back onto the plane of history, event, and persuasion. "Thus," writes Biesecker, "it becomes possible for us to say that what Adam's sin performs within the creation story is not a logological but, rather, a *rhetorical* necessity."[50] Some role for human agency in what has already happened and what still may happen is preserved.

This also means that narrative (and, by extension, theological content) matter. To recall Crusius's terms, the story of Genesis is one of an estrangement that needs to be overcome (rather than a dialectic that needs to be diagrammed). God's first question is, "Where are you?" (Gen. 3:9). God's creatures seem lost, and God appears anxious about finding them. Crusius's language of "overcoming" estrangement also recalls this chapter's central methodological keyword. How is estrangement overcome? How can reconciliation be occasioned? Burke incisively exposes the limitations of a certain approach to reconciliation, an approach that frames "overcoming" as an act of propitiatory violence. Such an act of overcoming is the precise sense that the idea of *Verwindung* would reject—that is, overcoming as an act of strength, assertion, finality. This framework also excludes the persuasion of God since no appeal is possible or necessary.

The complicit invention of estrangement-overcoming rejects this framework, along with the valorization of the negative as the primary means of historical subjectivity. Nevertheless, even a complicit style of invention must recognize the force of Burke's critique, a critique that sets the agenda for any project of post-Christian theorhetoric. But rather than simply "overcoming" Burke's critique with alternative theologies (of which there are many), my intention is to allow Burke to set the terms of the challenge for a post-Christian theorhetoric. How can rhetorical theory accommodate some notion of reconciliation without repeating a gesture of overcoming that would buy reconciliation at the price of the kill? That is the central question of atonement, which I take up in the next section.

The Reconciliation-(Mis)using Animal

The Rhetoric of Religion introduces atonement theology into rhetorical criticism. When the Lord observes "sheerly logological perfection," in the religion that blends "monotheism with the circumambient rites of pagan polytheism," when

96   PERSUASIONS OF GOD

he describes Christianity as a "cult . . . which holds that I [the Lord], in my infinite mercy, will send my only begotten Son as the perfect sacrifice for the Earth-People's redemption," he repeats the claim that Christianity is simply the most globally influential expression of the violent sacred.[51]

Though Burke's view is reductive, his observations cannot be dismissed. The version of Christian theology on which he draws—a theology that holds that reconciliation requires the "sacrifice" of an innocent who takes on himself the punishment that is properly owed to sinful humanity—has been enormously influential, at least in the West. This idea, along with a great many other related ideas, has gone under the name of "atonement," the term that designates "man's [sic] reconciliation with God through the sacrificial death of Christ."[52] This is the idea by which Burke's Lord is bemused and his Satan scandalized. Yet whatever this idea may mean theologically, rhetorically it is a dead end. "Increasing numbers of people," writes the theologian Mark Heim, "find this language empty, literally unintelligible, or actively offensive."[53] Heim perfectly articulates the context and need for a post-Christian theorhetoric. Maddux echoes Heim's critique, writing that the idea of atonement is "objectionable because it condones violence and encourages Christians to accept their suffering."[54] Girard also recognizes the fundamental rhetorical problem: "Not only does God require a new victim, but he requires the victim who is most precious and dear to him, his very son. No doubt this line of reasoning has done more than anything else to discredit Christianity in the eyes of people of goodwill."[55] It is difficult to imagine that such a story would be persuasive in a post-Christian context, where the premises that underwrite this story no longer hold.

The question for a post-Christian rhetoric is whether atonement might be understood as appeal rather than appeasement. Fortunately, other theologies are available. But even these must come to some understanding of the cross, without which no atonement theology makes sense. "Any atonement theology," writes John Stoner, "dealing with the cross as it does, must be able to make a credible interpretation of Jesus' words in Mark 8:34."[56] "If any want to become my followers, let them deny themselves, and take up their cross, and follow me." When St. Paul says that the cross is "foolishness," particularly to the "debater of this age" (1 Cor. 1:18, 20), he is recognizing a scandalous theorhetorical challenge. That challenge persists into the present post-Christian context, where the cross can seem to fetishize suffering.

Yet the matter cannot be settled by manufacturing some new theory of atonement, which the literature repeatedly suggests is a fool's errand. The theologian

Lisa Sowle Cahill puts the issue clearly: "The key plank of Christian faith, salvation in Jesus Christ, has never been explained definitively by any creed or council. *That* we are saved is clear; *how* we are saved is not."[57] Though Burke's logology, with its dialectic of ultimate terms, may lead one to think otherwise, there is no unified or consistent theory. Many theologians also point out that there is no scriptural warrant for forwarding such a theory. Though Paul's writings are usually cited as the ultimate source, those writings offer "a rich yet hardly coherent matrix of interpretive metaphors."[58] Even Gustaf Aulén, whose 1931 *Christus Victor* more or less set the parameters of contemporary thought on this issue, argues that within the Christian scriptures "there is not to be found . . . a developed theological doctrine of the Atonement, but rather an idea or motif expressed with many variations of outward form."[59] As persistent as that motif may be, it does not appear to add up to a "logically articulated theory of salvation," as Elizabeth Johnson describes it. "There are no theories, syllogisms, or tightly reasoned arguments," which creates a problem for those thinkers who would formulate a rationally coherent and complete explanation of "the" atonement.[60]

The issue is theorhetorical. In a study of atonement, Stephen Finlan examines Paul's use of metaphors, which have led to much of the modern controversy. Part of the problem, argues Finlan, is that Paul was thinking rhetorically. "In the interests of making the Gospel marketable, Paul poured new wine into old conceptual forms, spiced with a dose of spiritualizing, and enlivened by the real spiritual experience that he and his fellows were having. But this means that some incompatible religious ideas were yoked together."[61] Paul's primary motivation, put in Augustinian/Ciceronian terms, was to move, not to teach. This rhetorical motivation defies any attempt to make Paul's use of metaphors function as a single rational account. Finlan writes, "Whatever could 'preach' could stay; but this has caused confusion to later Christians. This is the danger of atonement metaphors, however rhetorically effective they may be: they carry their baggage with them, and leave these little bags like time bombs . . . prepared to explode into manifestations of fear, suspicion, and scapegoating."[62] Though Finlan's remarks seem to betray the usual suspicions about rhetoric, they also suggest the way in which persuasive discourses can be misread as systematic theological accounts. Rhetorical discourse designed to move is easily distorted into a dialectical discourse designed to instruct. Finlan's theorhetorical observations suggest that we will do better to understand atonement as an expression of God's persuasion.

The theorhetorical nature of Paul's metaphors, however, has not stopped theologians from trying to work them into a rational explanation of atonement.

98   PERSUASIONS OF GOD

There is not room enough here to review the entire tradition, but a brief sketch can orient the reader. In the West, at least, the contemporary popular notions of atonement begin with Anselm of Canterbury (1033–1109), who put his stamp on the idea with his *Cur Deus Homo* (*Why the God-Man?*). Anselm's treatise is an attempt to clarify why God had to become human in order to effect a reconciliation with God's creation. James Alison summarizes the basic argument:

> God would have been perfectly within his rights to have destroyed the whole of humanity. But God was merciful as well as being just, so he pondered what to do to sort out the mess. Could he simply have let the matter lie in his infinite mercy? Well, maybe he would have liked to, but he was beholden to his infinite justice as well. Only an infinite payment would do; something that humans couldn't come up with; but God could. And yet the payment had to be from the human side, or else it wouldn't be a real payment for the outrage to be appeased.[63]

Because Jesus is human, he answers the human debt; because Jesus is divine, he is in a sense "big enough" to cancel the debt. Jesus's death thus satisfies God's honor through an ultimate act of divine/human self-giving. The *Westminster Dictionary of Christian Theology* sums up the work this way: "At the centre of [Anselm's] argument he asserted that it was impossible for God to leave his world in a state of *disorder*. Yet man had disobeyed and dishonoured his creator, and it was impossible for him to make adequate amends. Only God could achieve what man was incapable of doing."[64] Human sin had offended the honor of God so deeply and publicly that no human act could repair the damage. Yet God's honor must be satisfied if reconciliation between God and humanity is to happen. So, the son becomes a human (*Deus* becomes *homo*), and his dual nature allows him to satisfy the father's honor.

As the problem of "disorder" may suggest, Anselm is writing in a feudal context in which honor is crucial to a secure social order. Anselm extends this idea to God, whose honor secures the order of creation.[65] To allow "insults" to God's honor would be to suggest that God's honor could be violated without consequence, with the result that the entire plan of creation is thrown into doubt. God's honor, therefore, has to be "satisfied," and thus the notion of satisfaction enters into atonement theology. Despite Anselm's laudable attempt to preserve an idea of God's justice and to link it to God's mercy (in that God is willing, in the person of the son, to take on the punishment properly owed to humanity), it also seems inescapable that Anselm's God demands suffering. That surmise contributes to the impression that God seems willing not only that an innocent should suffer but that the innocent must be his own son. This is the idea that Burke's Satan finds so revolting and that has had such a wide influence on Western Christian thinking. Johnson writes, "I sometimes think that Anselm may well be the most successful theologian of all time, for what other theory has dominated theology, preaching, and liturgical practice for a thousand years?"[66]

From a theorhetorical standpoint, Anselmian atonement presents what Johnson calls a *"disastrous image of God,"* a god who demands the blood of his own son as satisfaction.[67] This idea, Johnson notes, contradicts what many people construe as Jesus's central image of God, the father from the parable of the Prodigal Son (Luke 15:11–32), who races out to meet his lost son and embraces him without precondition. Johnson goes on to catalog other problems with satisfaction theory, including its neglect of the life and resurrection of Jesus along with the self-destructive spirituality and attitudes that it can encourage. Atonement theologies can lead one to believe that "suffering, more than joy, is the best avenue to God."[68] In the terms we have been developing throughout this book, however, the most damning critique she offers is that satisfaction sacralized violence and thereby authorizes the Christian use of it. Satisfaction theology and its derivatives are thus a key source of the myth of redemptive violence, which have been casuistically stretched to include a myth of redemptive suffering.[69]

These myths have come under many critiques, which I outline briefly here. In *God of the Oppressed*, James Cone, widely considered the founder of North American Black liberation theology, insists that any theology that fails to account for the political and social effects of the Gospel is no theology at all. For people living under oppression, Cone argues, the biblical message of liberation is not theoretical; it is a living reality with both theological and political consequences. The "principalities and powers" over which Jesus would claim victory include those systems that "oppress the poor, humiliate the weak, and make heroes out of rich capitalists."[70] As long as such unequal systems persist, "then we know that Satan is not dead."[71] That means that there is still work to be done. God may liberate, but God also demands that the liberated must live as though they were liberated and that the oppressors stop oppression, which means "joining God in the fight against injustice and oppression."[72]

In addition, feminist theologians have argued that the myth of redemptive suffering is especially damning for women. In a searing indictment of this theology, Joanne Carlson Brown and Rebecca Parker refer to it as "divine child abuse."[73] As Rita Nakashima Brock and Parker put it, commonplace Christian ideas of "sacrifice" are especially dangerous for women, who under its influence may come to understand violence "as divine intent, pain for their own good. And the Christian tradition reinforced this impulse by upholding Jesus as a son who was willing to undergo horrible violence out of love for the father, in obedience to his father's will."[74] The grammar of this kind of "sacrifice" conforms to this understanding of Jesus's sacrifice, distorting the moral imaginations of those who believe it. Mary Daly sums up the matter succinctly: "The qualities that Christianity idealizes, especially for women, are also those of a victim: sacrificial love, passive acceptance of suffering, humility, meekness, etc. Since these are the qualities idealized in Jesus 'who died for our sins,' his functioning as a model reinforces the scapegoat syndrome for women."[75] Despite our efforts to capture a more robust and rhetorical notion of meekness in chapter 1, Daly's comments offer a salutary caution about an overeager embrace of a self-distorting humility.

Challenging and extending both the Black liberation and feminist critique is the womanist critique, which, Delores Williams writes, "especially concerns itself with the faith, survival and freedom-struggle of African American women. Thus womanist theology identifies and critiques black male oppression of black females while it also critiques white racism that oppresses all African Americans, female and male."[76] Womanist theology thus represents a kind of *Verwindung* of Black liberation and feminist critique insofar as it draws on but also challenges and intensifies those earlier arguments. It identifies the notion of Jesus's "surrogacy" as particularly problematic for African American women, whose surrogacy has been exploitative and violent. "It is therefore fitting and proper for black women to ask whether the image of a surrogate-God has salvific power."[77] Williams argues that the new understanding of the "salvific value" of Jesus's life and death made possible through the reflection and experience of African American women "frees redemption from the cross and frees the cross from the 'sacred aura' put around it by existing patriarchal responses to the question of what Jesus's death represents."[78] In key ways, this critique of surrogacy resonates with the Girardian understanding of the cross. Counter to Girard, however, Williams argues that the Bible and biblical criticism have not attended victims nearly enough.[79]

With this admittedly brief critical overview in mind, we must finally turn to a challenging question posed by Brown and Parker: "If we throw out the atonement is Christianity left?"[80] Many theologians argue that the doctrine is not central and that there is no way of coming to a decisive and final understanding of it. Yet that does not necessarily mean we can "overcome" atonement by throwing it out. Thelma Megill-Cobbler writes in her own feminist response that Christians "cannot do away with the idea of the atonement and the terrible cross that remains at the center of the gospel and continue to call [themselves] Christians." Yet she also cautions that Christians cannot "simply repeat the formulas of previous generations."[81] How, then, do Christians speak of the cross in a post-Christian context in a way that does not simply double down on distorting rhetorical appeals?

For Girard, the revelation of the violent sacred upends the entire atonement question. As discussed in chapter 2, Girard argues that the central insight revealed decisively by the Jewish and Christian scriptures is that God does not demand propitiation by blood in order to overcome estrangement. The need for victims is a human need, not a divine one. Girard thus rejects any idea of overcoming in any sense that someone else has paid off a debt once for all. That does not mean that Girard denies that something decisive has happened, but what is decisive is the revelation of human violence. "Henceforth," he writes, "we can no longer pretend not to know that the social order is built upon the blood of innocent victims. Christianity deprives us of the mechanism that formed the basis of the archaic social and religious order."[82] If the Crucifixion is decisive, it is not because it soothes God's wrath but because it exposes human wrath. For this reason, Girard's view of atonement is sometimes understood as a form of "exemplarity," which tends toward self-implication insofar as it reveals how mistaken religion and the religious can be.[83] This idea particularly applies to the apostles, who, Girard notes, "do not understand much while they are listening to Jesus. They misunderstand everything."[84] At the moment Jesus calls Peter "Satan" for misunderstanding why the Messiah must go to Jerusalem (Matt. 16:23), the text confirms the self-implicating nature of the Gospel vision.

At other times, however, Girard seems to endorse the idea of a triumphant messiah, though in the paradoxical sense suggested by Paul: "He [Jesus] thus disarmed the principalities and powers and made a public spectacle of them, drawing them along in his triumph" (Col. 2:14–15). This idea echoes "Christus Victor" theory of atonement, the idea that Jesus somehow defeats Satan through the cross. Girard writes, "the idea of Satan overcome by the Cross is an essential one that unfortunately, in Western Christianity, has been suspected of being magical, irrational, and is dismissed as a result."[85] For Girard, the victory is one revelation: Jesus defeats the principalities and powers—that is, the rivalrous desire that results in scapegoating, the foundation of culture—by exposing their

102   PERSUASIONS OF GOD

workings. "Through Jesus' rejection and crucifixion this satanic undertaking is exposed. . . . The satanic human will is thus overcome on the cross."[86] The "victory" of the cross is a victory of exposure. We might thus understand Girard's theory of atonement—if he can be said to have one—as a combination of moral exemplar and Christus Victor.

But Girard's theological conclusions lead to problematic theorhetorical conclusions. When Girard speaks of "overcoming," he seems to mean something final, irrevocable, something along the lines of the "once and for all" victory suggested by the Hebrews (10:10). This sense of a theological overcoming, however, leads Girard to articulate a theorhetorical overcoming formed by the very sort of rivalry and competition that his religious critique would expose, a position particularly problematic for a post-Christian context:

> Of all the Christian ideas, none nowadays arouses more sarcasm than the one that our text expresses so openly, the idea of a *triumph of the Cross*. To progressive Christians, proud of their humility, it seems as arrogant as it is absurd. To characterize the attitude that they condemn, they have brought the term "triumphalism" into fashion. If there exists somewhere a charter of triumphalism, it must be the text I am discussing here [Col. 2:14–15]. It may seem to be expressly written to arouse the indignation of the modernists, who are always very concerned to summon the Church to its obligation of humility.[87]

Theologically, Girard's view may be persuasive. Theorhetorically, however, Girard's idea of victory is less so. It seems rhetorical insofar as it recognizes that the paradoxical victory of the cross is a public event meant to effect a radical change in attitude and a complete renunciation of violence. Yet Girard's notions of triumph and overcoming also end up browbeating both Christianity's modern critics and modern adherents. In Girard's view, both of these groups conspire to obscure the full impact of the Gospels, the first by humiliating Christian ideas and the second by making the humility of Christian ideas a trained incapacity. Lest he be misunderstood on this point, Girard elsewhere insists that the "idea of silencing Christianity in the name of Christian humility is a Christian idea gone mad."[88] The suggestion is that some Christians (i.e., "progressives") so wish to avoid rivalry with other faiths or worldviews that they end up silencing their own belief. Girard himself has no such compunction. When asked if he favors converting non-Christians, Girard answers, "Jesus said, 'I am the way, the truth, and the life,' and he told his disciples to go into the world and make converts. If we give that up, are we still Christian?"[89] Here, a theological notion of triumph appears to devolve into a notion of triumphalism, and the paradoxical sense of victory suggested by Paul is replaced with a rivalrous sense of victory.

How, then, might this team-sport sense of overcoming be reconciled with the Vattimanian sense of overcoming? The challenge is to express the triumph of the cross as a theological matter without lapsing into rivalrous theorhetorical triumphalism. The seeds of an answer must be found in an understanding of atonement that also rejects any notion of satisfaction or substitution. Timothy Gorringe articulates such an understanding by construing atonement as an expression of God's *solidarity* with those who suffer. Gorringe finds the roots of solidarity in the idea of kenosis, the Christian scriptures' expression of rhetorical capacity. Again, the relevant passage is, "Rather, [Jesus] emptied himself, taking the form of a slave, coming in human likeness; and found human in appearance, he humbled himself, becoming obedient to death, even death on a cross" (Phil. 2:7–8). Gorringe suggests that the theological radicalness of this idea would have been perfectly clear when it was first expressed. "Paradoxically," however, "this way of reading the cross plays no part whatever in the history of Western atonement theology until the twentieth century."[90] But in the wake of Auschwitz, this way of reading the cross resurfaces Christian theology. To take one example, Jürgen Moltmann's *Crucified God* argues that God will be found in solidarity with victims of violence, not with the seemingly triumphant perpetrators of violence. This solidarity is witnessed to on the cross, which is not the canceling of a debt, or the undergoing of a punishment, but rather a sign of Jesus's obedience to what Dolores Williams calls his own "ministerial vision."[91] Similarly, Moltmann argues that Jesus's suffering is the result first and foremost of "his actions, from his preaching of the imminence of the kingdom as a kingdom of unconditional grace, from his freedom towards the law, and from his table-fellowship with 'sinners and tax collectors.'"[92] Jesus's suffering is not, therefore, some obligation-satisfaction mechanism that could have propitiated God, without his public life. Rather, Jesus's suffering is precisely a result of that public life.

In a remark that resonates with a rhetoric of meekness, Moltmann continues, "Jesus did not suffer passively from the world in which he lived, but incited it against himself by his message and the life he lived."[93] Moltmann's point is not to blame the victim but rather to suggest that suffering is the foreseeable result of solidarity with the powerless. The solidarity expressed here, argues Gorringe, "implies a quite different understanding of power, a move from the passive—the victims, who are acted upon—to the active, where unity is strength."[94] Moltmann's and Gorringe's remarks recall Daniel Gross's notion of rhetorical listening, which hovers somewhere between the active and passive. Gorringe's idea of power also resonates with a reconstructed notion of sacrifice, one that decisively reconfigures the word's meaning away from scapegoating and toward commitment to the scapegoats themselves.[95] The sacrifice of Christ is not the sacrifice of debt payment or punishment substitution but the sacrifice of the sort described by Terry Eagleton: "A god who loves his creatures so dearly that he is prepared to be done to death by them"—in other words, God loves God's creatures so dearly that God empties Godself in order to stand in the place of the victim so that there may be no more victims.[96]

This sort of kenotic, capacious sacrifice has existential implications for Christian religion, implications that Brown and Parker recognize when they wonder whether Christianity can survive the rejection of traditional theories of atonement.[97] Moltmann senses the same possibility: "The 'religion of the cross'" he writes, "is a contradiction in itself, for the crucified God is a contradiction in this religion."[98] In Girardian terms, the cross's rejection of the violent sacred is by extension the rejection of religion as the management of the chronic problem of violence through controlled bursts or symbolic reenactments of violence. Insofar as the cross finally rejects this avenue of overcoming estrangement, we are left with both a theological problem and a theorhetorical problem. Moltmann writes, "The Christian faith which once 'conquered the world' must also learn to conquer its own forms when they have become worldly. It can do so only when it breaks down the idols of the Christian West."[99] This conquering of form implies the need for a radical, even scandalous, reimagining of the cross in which the cross becomes an icon of iconoclasm.

As examples, I would turn our attention to two iconic-iconoclastic renderings of the cross and its meaning, one ancient and one modern. The ancient commentary comes in the form of a Roman graffito, scratched into a wall sometime between the first and third centuries of the common era. The image in question features two figures: a man raising his arms, possibly in prayer, and a donkey-headed figure on a cross. The text accompanying the image reads, "Alexamenos worships his god." Some scholars believe that this may be the earliest depiction of the Christian cross. The graffito indicates that "early cultured despisers of Christianity had no trouble mocking the very idea of worshiping a crucified man."[100] The idea of a crucified god would have seemed utterly perverse to Jesus's contemporaries, whose primary association with the crucified was probably the six thousand who were hanged along the Appian Way after the slave revolt of 73–71 BCE.[101] To suggest that a god might have suffered a punishment reserved for the lowest of the low would have seemed ridiculous; only an ass could represent such a god. Like all true insults, however, the graffito captures something essential about the scandal of the cross, a scandal of iconoclasm that has been lost with the symbol's ubiquity.

The modern commentary comes from the film *Lenny*, the 1974 Lenny Bruce biopic starring Dustin Hoffman. In the film, Bruce confronts Christianity's oldest libel: "And a lot of people say to me, 'Why did you kill Christ?' 'I dunno . . . it was one of those parties, got out of hand, you know.' We killed him because he didn't want to become a doctor, that's why we killed him."[102] This lampooning of the charge of deicide is accompanied by an unforgettable commentary on the cross: "There's a good thing that we nailed him when we did, because if we had done it within the 50 last years, we'd have to contend with generations of parochial schoolkids running around with little electric chairs hanging around their necks."[103] In these remarks, Bruce articulates a powerful post-Christian theorhetoric. The disturbing image of an electric chair—a horror to contemporary people as surely as the cross would have been to Jesus's contemporaries—suggests that Bruce senses its meaning far more deeply than many Christians do. In addition, Bruce's attack on Christian antisemitism reminds Christians of their faith's original sin, a sin whose scapegoating structure should have been apparent from the cross itself. Bruce's radical defamiliarization offers a modern version of the Alexamenos graffito's defamiliarization; both perceive the full perversity of a crucified god.

Both also recognize both the power and the risk of complicit invention. The power is the opportunity to subvert a structure from within it; the risk is that the subversion is very easy to miss. Girard writes, "God Himself reuses the scapegoat mechanism, at his own expense, in order to subvert it. This tragedy is not devoid of irony. Indeed, its connotations are so rich that most of them escape us. The irony has to do in part with the structural similarity between the two kinds of sacrifice."[104] Theologically speaking, God enters into this ritualized violence in order to reveal its origins from the inside. But God enters so fully inside this structure that it can be easy to think that the violence is the point. That mistake leads to the myths of redemptive suffering and violence. The

106   PERSUASIONS OF GOD

mistake has been made so frequently that one might ask whether kenosis was the most effective rhetorical strategy. But without the risk of kenosis, the full revelation of the violent sacred may not be possible.

Heim suggests a reading of the Gospels commensurate with the idea of complicit invention: "The Gospel accounts are written in stereo, we might say. On one side is the underlying pattern with all its mythic components in place. On the other side is a constant counterpoint of elements that reveal the hidden realities, the true structure of scapegoating."[105] Only through the interplay of these complementary elements can we see the myth being undone. Through this complicit invention, a God can be detected attempting to persuade an audience, through the means of self-emptying, that redemption requires no violence. Rather, it requires a solidarity with the victims of violence, a solidarity so perverse that often the critics of Christianity recognize it more readily than Christianity's own adherents do.

The Nihilism-(Mis)using Animal

A third movement of complicit invention emerges from an encounter between Gianni Vattimo and Girard, whom Vattimo credits with influencing his own reconversion to Christian faith. Vattimo is an unlikely revert. A philosopher in the tradition of Nietzsche and Heidegger, Vattimo's project would seem to put him directly at odds with conventional metaphysical grounds of faith. Yet in Girard, Vattimo finds a religious confirmation for his philosophical trajectory. Vattimo also finds himself a stranger to his own roots. Girard brings him back to those roots, but only through the twisting path of *Verwindung*. That trajectory includes a role for rhetoric, which Vattimo recognizes as a way forward in the absence of secure grounds.

Like Girard, Vattimo also expresses a theorhetorical demand: "I want to interpret the word of the Gospel as Jesus taught us, by translating the often violent letter of precepts and prophecies into a language more concordant with the supreme commandment of charity."[106] Vattimo's idea of charitable communication is thoroughly, even radically, post-Christian: "I am merely defending the right to hear the word of the gospel again, without being obliged to share in the outright superstitions that obscure the official doctrine of the Church in philosophical and moral matters."[107] For Vattimo, charity, or love, is the central characteristic of Gospel rhetoric; the church's official doctrine and dogma are stumbling blocks. Girard, however, insists on the centrality of doctrine and dogma, which include the truth of the victim, the central revelation of the religion-canceling religion of the crucified God. The public dialogues between Girard and Vattimo—recorded in the volume *Christianity, Truth, and Weakening Faith*—have become a landmark event for scholars of Girard. Nevertheless, I present this encounter not to adjudicate it but rather to practice a complicit invention of post-Christian rhetoric of meekness.

Vattimo is most famous for his notion of "weak thought" (*il pensiero debole*), a project of postmetaphysical philosophy that has been described as "the most striking current of thought in Italian philosophy in the post-WWII period."[108] Weak thought emerges from the erosion of "*archai, Gründe*, primary evidences and ultimate destinies."[109] This "enfeeblement" characterizes Vattimo's take on Heidegger, whom he credits with the decisive announcement that Being can no longer be construed or experienced as a source of certainty and security. However, his particular understanding of Heidegger is shaped by his hesitation to overcome Being: "even the discovery of the superfluousness of metaphysics ... risks resolving itself into a new metaphysics—humanistic, naturalistic, or vitalistic—if it goes no further than substituting 'true' being in place of the one that been revealed as false."[110] Vattimo recognizes this as the response of dialectical thinking, the desire to assert a "strong" response as a way to manage insecurity.[111]

By contrast, Vattimo speaks of Being having a "nihilistic vocation," which recognizes that "diminishment, withdrawal and weakening are the traits that Being assigns to itself in the epoch of the end of metaphysics."[112] The "end" of metaphysics does not therefore imply either erasure or replacement, impulses that still operate out of a sense of insecurity. Weak thought is paradoxically strong enough to face what Vattimo calls the "enfeeblement of being," the sense that the grounds of Being have given way, which should be understood to mean both the crumbling or erosion of foundations and the unveiling of new paths. For this reason, Vattimo's nihilism is optimistic, hopeful about the possibility of freeing us from the need for domination or control. Nihilism presents "an opportunity to be grasped," an opportunity to free ourselves from the neuroses of "nostalgia for strong reality, for clear authority, for a unique and apodictic system of values."[113] It is this philosophical orientation that predisposes Vattimo toward Girard's project. "It was he [Girard] who re-Christianized me (albeit in my own way), it was with him that I began to think that it might be possible to bind weakening, secularization, and Christianity closely together."[114] This connection leads Vattimo to imagine a nihilistic approach to Christian faith.[115] Weakening and secularization, understood in connection to Girard's project, become the paradoxical bases for Vattimo's religious turn. The history of Being is characterized by weakening and nihilism in which the kenosis of Christ Jesus serves to abolish the violent sacred. The weakening of Being becomes "nothing but the transcription of the Christian doctrine of the incarnation of the Son of God."[116] Vattimo also connects this to kenosis, which he sees as the nonviolent God embracing a weakening. Weak thought becomes weak faith.

Weak faith might also describe the role of rhetoric in both Vattimo's philosophy and implicit theology. For Vattimo, "truth does not have a metaphysical or logical nature but a rhetorical one."[117] It "is not the object of a noetic prehension of evidence but rather the result of a process of verification that produces such truth."[118] Those processes of verification require a particular community to deliberate at a particular time and in particular circumstances. This process of verification does not unmoor us from history or tradition, however. If anything, it binds us to tradition more closely. Because "we no longer believe in the (by now presumptuous) value of making tabula rasa of all that we inherited in order to seek some 'new' foundation or beginning, then our condition is that of dealing with a mass of existing interpretations which we can summon or even invent to make sense of the world."[119] This idea of truth suggests both the "strong" and "vulnerable" varieties discussed in chapter 1: strong insofar as truth is the product of construction, vulnerable insofar as rhetorical fashioning is always constrained by the traditions to which we are anchored. For all Vattimo's talk about weakening and nihilism, his dependence on tradition is profound.

In fact, for a thinker so closely associated with radical hermeneutics, Vattimo's vocabulary is strikingly conservative. He describes the ideal of tradition as one of *pietas*, which he links to *Verwindung* as another appropriate expression for "the weak thought of post-metaphysics."[120] For Vattimo, *pietas* acknowledges "mortality, finitude, and passing away" but also "devoted affection, respect."[121] *Pietas* for Vattimo suggests something similar to the attitude that a young person might have toward her older relatives. She admires them, respects them, loves them, even if she does not share all their political or cultural ideas. Preserving the relationship is more important than adjudicating every disagreement. "You may have a special respect for their experience and the language they have inherited. In this sense, interpersonal relationships are much more about charity than truth."[122] Here, we see that Vattimo's embrace of *caritas* does not proceed from some lack of respect for truth but from a deeper devotion to relationship.[123] It would be more accurate to say that Vattimo sees truth as both rhetorical and religious, the product of pious interpretation, affectionate commitment. Truth does not simply assert but binds (*re-ligare*: to bind over or again); "no one ever starts from scratch but always from a faith, a belonging-to or a bond."[124] Weak thought becomes weak—or meek—rhetoric, a rhetoric whose primary orientation is one of dependence, relation, belonging.

For Vattimo, weak faith is a matter of secularization. Like many contemporary scholars and critics of religion, Vattimo recognizes that secularization is not simply the absence or withdrawal of religion but is instead a function and result of religious influence: "a secularized culture is not a culture that has simply left behind the religious contents of its tradition; it is one that continues to live them as traces, as models that are hidden and disfigured but nonetheless profoundly present."[125] Vattimo goes so far as to say that secularization is not the "abandonment of religion" but rather "the paradoxical realization of Being's religious vocation."[126] Secularization thus represents the fulfillment of religion's promise. Vattimo articulates this fulfillment in terms he learns from Girard: secularization represents "the effective realization of Christianity as a nonsacrificial religion."[127] The incarnation ultimately undoes the idea of divine sovereignty, just as the Crucifixion presents an icon of iconoclasm. In Vattimo's notion of secularization, we see not only a connection between Girard and *Verwindung* but also the theorhetorical implications of this connection: "I emphasize this matter of 'recovery,' because it concerns one of the themes of the argument I shall develop . . . , which seeks to characterize 'secularization' as the constitutive trait of an authentic religious experience. Now, secularization means precisely a relation of provenance from a sacred core from which one has moved away, but which nevertheless remains active even in its 'fallen,' distorted version, reduced to pure worldly terms."[128] Within this context, the dual influence of Heidegger and Girard comes into sharper focus. Recovery of the sacred core is not the reestablishment of it but rather a convalescence from it within an enduring relation. For Vattimo, the revelation of the violent sacred undermines notions of Christianity that have depended on a sacred culture. To expose to the sacred core is to enfeeble it, along with "the often violent letter of precepts and prophecies." This is why secularization is Being's religious vocation and why the weakening of "superstition" is a good sign. This weakening, moreover, will now have to be articulated in "pure worldly terms," or a translation of the Gospel into a language of *caritas* ostensibly free from traditional Christian commonplaces. Like Girard, then, Vattimo recognizes a theorhetorical demand; unlike Girard, however, Vattimo imagines that this theorhetoric will play a constitutive role.

Whatever its theoretical underpinnings, Vattimo's *Verwindung* sometimes appears to erase tradition rather than recover (from) it.[129] This is seen most fully in Vattimo's reference to "pure worldly terms," which suggests that Vattimo's post-Christian vocabulary will be stripped of all Christian reference. Yet Vattimo's vocabulary—piety, devotion, respect, history—hardly seems like the lexicon of someone ready to overthrow the past. In his dialogues with Girard, Vattimo insists, "I have no wish to behave like a bull in a china shop, wrecking the whole place."[130] When asked if he can still pray "Our Father," even though it is "culturally conditioned," he affirms that he can: "When I pray, I know precisely that the words I am using are not intended to convey some literal truth. I pray these words more for the love of a tradition than I do for the love of some mythic reality."[131] This idea suggests, at least at first hearing, a style of Christian discourse that is as Christian as it is post.

The question is whether Vattimo's piety and *caritas* are enough to sustain a Christian witness against Christendom. In the dialogues recorded in *Christianity, Truth, and Weakening Faith*, Girard and Vattimo shorthand the central issue of their debate as *caritas* versus *veritas*.[132] For Vattimo, *caritas*, love, represents the Gospels' first and central commandment, which is why Christianity opens "the way to an existence not strictly religious, if we take 'religious' to mean binding restraints, imposition, authority."[133] Augustine's injunction to "love God and do what you will" captures the spirit of Vattimo's conclusions (with the emendation to love the neighbor and do what you will). Ethics, writes Vattimo, consists of "charity plus traffic regulations."[134] The traffic regulations are there to make it possible for people to live together; charity makes it possible to allow maximum freedom. Beyond these, the traditional habits of religious identity are no longer necessary or appropriate.[135] This is what Vattimo seems to mean by a secularized "provenance from a sacred core," "reduced to pure worldly terms."[136] In a post-Christian culture, the completion of Christianity's vocation is that there is no longer any need for its traditional trappings. "Team-sport" religion withers away in inverse correlation to the ethics of love and traffic rules. A post-Christian theorhetoric is articulated under the sign of "post-" rather than "Christian."

In some ways, Girard is sympathetic to Vattimo's project. Though he acknowledges that some might refer to Vattimo as a "cafeteria Catholic," he also argues that "this characterization fails to capture the spirit of Vattimo's writing, which is entirely positive and conveys a real love for the Church." He also complements

Vattimo "for his peculiar talent for thinking vigorously without losing his serenity."[137] Most importantly, he recognizes a truth in Vattimo's claim that weakening and nihilism might make the Gospel hearable again. Despite his own antipathy to postmodernism, Girard acknowledges Vattimo's argument that, having lost confidence in the scientistic idea of objectivity, faith once again becomes both possible and necessary.[138]

Yet Girard also has serious reservations about Vattimo's *caritas* risks. First, Girard worries about what he sees as the unshackling of all restraint. Vattimo's "hedonistic Christianity," as Girard puts it, cannot account for the enduring risk of mimetic desire, a risk recognized in the Decalogue, which in many ways is designed to forestall the risks of competition.[139] Without such restraint, Girard argues, human beings will neither recognize nor resist the excesses of mimetic desire. Second, and just as importantly, Girard insists on the centrality of *veritas*, not in opposition to *caritas* but as something that is central to it. *Veritas* remains decisive for Girard because there are real victims buried at the foundation of culture, and through his own passion, Jesus indicates that all such victims are in fact innocent.[140] Girard is careful to say that this claim does not preclude *caritas*, but the commandment to love proceeds from what Girard takes to be the anthropological truth of the victim. "I think we ought to take very seriously this concept: the concept of love, which in Christianity is the rehabilitation of the unjustly accused victim, which is truth itself, which is the anthropological truth and the Christian truth."[141] Without the truth of the passion, Girard argues, we are left without a critical perspective on our scapegoat-structured human culture. For Girard, the cross is the central articulation, both event and symbol, of this critique. The triumph of the cross over the mythology that requires victims (i.e., over the iron law of history) cannot finally be reduced to pure worldly terms. Even in a post-Christian context, there needs to be some recognizable Christian content. The content to which Christians are bound, and which they must recover, is the Cross. Yet Vattimo is not wrong that Christians must also recover *from* it. Only by this strange twisting, this paradoxical overcoming, this complicit invention, can the contemporary Christian encounter the God who both triumphs and suffers. Only through this convalescence can one recognize with Moltmann that the "'religion of the cross' is a contradiction in itself."[142] The "religion of the cross" is, or at least ought to be, antireligion as much as it is religious, a critique of creed as much as it is a creed. A post-Christian rhetoric must claim the cross even as it recognizes the way in which the cross displaces its own commonplaces.

One last argument over the cross will indicate the complex challenge of post-Christian theorhetorical invention. In 2018, officials in the German and heavily Catholic state of Bavaria ordered that crosses be hung in all public buildings. Though crosses are far more common in German public spaces and schools than might be expected in a place like the United States, many nevertheless objected to the order. Some critics insisted that the move violated Germany's principle of religious neutrality. Others charged that the order was meant to manipulate anxieties over Muslim immigration. (The claim was that the ruling Christian Social Union was attempting to woo voters from the ultraconservative and anti-immigrant Alternative for Germany.) When challenged on the grounds of religious neutrality, Markus Söder, the minister president of Bavaria, responded by saying that the cross "is not a sign of religion." Rather, he insisted, it is merely a sign of culture and heritage. "The cross is a fundamental symbol of our Bavarian identity and way of life."[143]

One might expect religious leaders to be pleased by this public endorsement, but several raised objections. Munich's Lutheran leader argued that this sort of political use of the cross degraded its meaning. The cross, he stated, should be about "loving your enemy, helping the weak, a commandment of love for all, instead of using the cross to ward off others."[144] The Catholic archbishop of Munich argued in similar terms. "If the cross is seen only as a cultural symbol, then it's been misunderstood."[145] Yet other Christian leaders wondered how anyone could have objected. The papal nuncio of Austria rebuked his colleagues, saying, "I am deeply saddened and ashamed that when crosses are erected in a neighboring country, bishops and priests of all people protested."[146] He similarly complained about "religious correctness," which he suggested as a sort of analogue to political correctness.[147]

We have here, then, a strange case study of a kind of post-Christian rhetoric: a secular official makes a public endorsement of a religious symbol on the grounds that the symbol is not religious. At the same time, religious figures argue against the religious public display on the grounds that the symbol is too religious to be publicly endorsed. To put the matter in the terms developed in this chapter, the Bavarian minister appears to argue that the cross has been entirely secularized, but he does so in a way that certainly does not seem "more concordant with the supreme commandment of charity," as Vattimo puts it. Surely, Vattimo would object to this kind of public use, but in doing so, he would surely have to say that Söder's use of the cross is *insufficiently religious*, an argument that seems counter to his endorsement of secularization. We may yet need some traditional religious appeals.

At the same time, one could imagine Girard endorsing the papal nuncio's complaints about "religious correctness." Perhaps the Lutheran and Catholic bishops of Munich are practicing what Girard would dismiss as a Christian humility gone mad. That is not to suggest that Girard would approve of the cross being used to ward off the other, a use that is both sacred and sacrificial in the negative senses of those words—that is, a use meant to expel a perceived threat to order (i.e., "our identity and way of life"). But in contrast to the idea of an overpronounced Christian humility, I mean to suggest that Vattimo's sense of both recovery and recovery from are necessary for an appropriate Christian humility. One cannot deny that the cross has been used before in just the way Söder would use it now, and perhaps the most persuasive claim that the bishops could make is to remind Christians that the cross must not be allowed to be put to such use *again*. Söder, meanwhile, certainly seeks to recover something he thinks has been lost (i.e., "our identity and way of life"); the question to ask him is what he thinks he is recovering from.

In sum, my argument is that neither Vattimo's "love and the traffic rules" nor Girard's invocation of "I am the way, the truth, and the life" is alone sufficient for responding to this kind of post-Christian problem. Vattimo's secularization can leave the cross exposed to secular misuse; Girard's religiosity can leave the cross exposed to religious misuse. But, in keeping with the protocol of complicit invention, we can invent different kinds of appeals not by negating either argument but by traveling through and oscillating between them. The Girardian reading of the cross, along within the Girardian reading of atonement, insists on the cross's expression of solidarity with victims of scapegoating, including the Muslim immigrants whose presence is driving the order to hang the crosses in the first place. Such solidarity seems a more robust expression of the *caritas* that Vattimo endorses. But that invocation of the cross is not a triumphalist expression of the Gospel, at least not one that is in rivalry with other religious traditions. Indeed, the cross is at its most "religious" precisely when it expresses solidarity with those who adhere to another tradition. That is to say, the cross is most authentically Christian when it does not play the game of team-sport religion. And in refusing to play this game, it recovers the authentic meaning of Christianity by recovering from a distortion within Christianity itself, the lingering presence of a dangerous triumphalism born of the violent sacred.

This chapter has pursued this dual recovery project through its studies of Burke's religious rhetoric, of the theology of atonement that informed that rhetoric, and of an intellectual agon that might point to an appropriate theorhetoric, a theorhetoric that might escape that atonement theology. In these studies, my goal has been to avoid the principle of negation in which advocacy, critique, or synthesis are the only three options. Instead, I have tried to invent through the available positions, taking as my method the movement described by Girard in the chapter's epigraph: a shuttling back and forth, a constant movement that produces a form of composition resembling a spiral. My aim in doing this has been to invent a different rhetoric of religion, one shaped more directly by complicity with Christianity's theology and history. Drawing especially on the complicity of Vattimo and Girard, that theorhetoric has tried to recognize the terms "Christian" and "post-" as equally evocative. As proof of concept of a Christian theorhetoric that sees the "religion of the cross" as a contradiction, chapter 4 turns to a thoroughly Christian document that presents a post-Christian reinvention of a term as problematic as meekness, sacrifice, and atonement: holiness.

4

Uneasy Holiness

Holiness . . . is not about swooning in mystic rapture.
—Pope Francis, *Gaudete et Exsultate*

In *The Subversion of Christianity*, the French philosopher Jacques Ellul makes what would seem to be the most radically post-Christian theorhetorical argument, advocating for the abolishment of the word "Christianity" itself. According to Ellul, "Christianity" (*christianisme* in the original French)[1] has become a perversion of its original radical ideas in the same way that communism and existentialism are perversions of Marx and Kierkegaard. Anticipating Girard, Ellul argues that as a culture becomes Christian, Christianity devolves into a pale shadow of the Gospel. "People cannot see or understand that Christianity has been abolished by its propagation."[2] One cannot therefore blame some spectral "secularism" for Christianity's devolution into a hollow religiosity.

Some might prefer a hollow religiosity, which at least might be harmless. As I write, Pope Francis has just completed a weeklong "penitential journey" to Canada to apologize for the Catholic Church's participation in state-run boarding schools that served as mechanisms of cultural genocide—along with horrific cruelty and neglect. As of 2015, when Canada's Truth and Reconciliation Commission concluded its work, courts had received nearly 40,000 claims of physical and sexual abuse from the 80,000 survivors who were still alive. At least 150,000 Indigenous children were forced to attend these schools, many of which were run by Roman Catholic religious orders and organizations. The Canadian government describes this system as one "imposed on Indigenous peoples as part of a broad set of assimilation efforts to destroy their rich cultures and identities and to suppress their histories."[3] The cultural violence of this project was mirrored by other forms of violence against Indigenous children, "who were forcibly removed from their homes and, at school, were often subjected to harsh discipline, malnutrition and starvation, poor healthcare, physical, emotional, and sexual abuse, neglect."[4] Because of the Catholic Church's complicity in these events, Pope Francis went to Canada to apologize.[5] While Catholic media have largely praised Francis's effort, Indigenous media and activists have been less impressed. Francis was widely criticized, particularly for his failure to repudiate the Doctrine of Discovery, a fifteenth-century legal idea, promulgated by a series of papal bulls, that authorized European nations to colonize Indigenous lands because their inhabitants were not Christian.[6] From the perspective of these victims, the perversions of Christianity observed by Ellul may seem like a feature rather than a bug. Lest anyone accuse someone like Gianni Vattimo of exaggerating the dangers of metaphysical certainty, one need only read the Canadian Truth and Reconciliation Commission report.

Confronted by such history, Ellul can be forgiven for thinking that the word "Christianity" is utterly compromised. The problem is what might be used in its place. Ellul suggests three essential ideas that could replace the term: the revelation of God in Jesus, the community of the body of Christ, and the authentic witness of Christian lives. "Since we cannot keep repeating this triple formula," he continues, "we shall now use X to denote these three aspects. We need to keep the word *Christianity* only for the ideological and sociological movement which is its perversion."[7] Only by authentic Christian subversions (of the last being first, of table fellowship with outcasts, of touching lepers, of turning the other cheek) can the perversions of Christianity themselves be subverted. Ellul's stance is one to which we have returned throughout this volume: a stance of alienated theology, of a distorted convalescence, of a twisted double subversion. As Vattimo would insist, the needed restructuring is not just a recovery but always a recovery from. Ellul even offers a kind of mantra for this position: "One can be a Christian only in opposition."[8]

To be a Christian in opposition seems the most appropriate stance for a post-Christian theorhetoric. This is what it means to invent a theorhetoric of a Christian religion "infinitely more demanding because it's deprived of its sacrificial crutches."[9] This infinitely more demanding religion is one that refuses to maintain itself through the scapegoating activity of the violent sacred. For these reasons, Girard repeats a theological commonplace that *the holy* should replace *the sacred* as the most essential religious quality. "The real sacred—or let us say the holy, let's not use the same word—is love, divine love."[10] God's "pedagogical strategy," as Girard describes it, is "the gradual transformation of the *sacred* into the *holy*. The God of the Bible is at first the God of the sacred, and then more and more the God of the holy, foreign to all violence."[11] In other words, holiness, or the real sacred, is the religious phenomenon or experience that rejects violence. Unfortunately, Girard invokes holiness without ever fully developing what he means by it. His entire project can be seen as a kind of *via negativa* of holiness: the holy is that which is not sacred (i.e., occasioned by violence). Yet while this may tell us what holiness is not, it fails to tell us what holiness may be. Girard's project of disarticulation—and of rhetorical invention—therefore remains half finished.[12]

Recent rhetorical scholarship has also begun to grapple with the concepts of the sacred and holy. In *Responding to the Sacred* (2021), for example, editors Michael Bernard-Donals and Kyle Jensen argue that the sacred is both "a call that compels a response" and also "that which exceeds human capacity."[13] The idea of "sacred communication" forces rhetorical studies to reckon with the paradox that we encounter the severest limits of rhetoric within our deepest need for rhetoric. Like Girard, Bernard-Donals and Jensen sense that the sacred portends both possibility and danger. Meanwhile, Christian Lundberg imagines extrahuman communication as an expression of "the holy," which he argues is a more appropriate alternative for characterizing divine encounters. Lundberg fashions his argument on a distinction that has become familiar in both rhetoric and religion. Many theologians would likewise endorse Lundberg's claim that "the sacred represents a means of drawing lines or separating from the other as a means of fending off what it understands as the profane, while the holy is a mode of openness toward the 'otherness' of the other."[14] In Lundberg's understanding, the holy indicates a rhetorical ethics, an ethics of encounter, responsibility, and hospitality. In religious thought, the holy is often forwarded as a more ethical alternative to the sacred. Emmanuel Levinas, for example, described himself as a thinker of the holy: "You know, one often speaks of ethics to describe what I do, but what really interests me in the end is not ethics, not ethics alone, but the holy, the holiness of the holy."[15] Yet encounter with the divine is not always a happy occasion; it can portend what Bernard-Donals describes as displacement, deterritorialization, and even a kind of violence.[16] Extrahuman communication does not always offer assurance but sometimes something more destabilizing and disturbing.

This chapter attempts to finish Girard's implicit theorhetorical project of inventing holiness in ways that will advance the emerging conversation in rhetoric on these matters. If Lundberg is right that the holy is defined by the "possibility of affecting and being affected in turn," then holiness at least becomes an ineluctably rhetorical phenomenon, one that implies the possibility of profound influence. Yet the profundity of that influence, the vulnerability to it, is precisely what Girard fears is a prelude to the contagious violence of the violent sacred. The question therefore is whether holiness actually represents a decisive difference. The answer to this question is crucial to the post-Christian theorhetoric pursued in the previous chapters. To exemplify this rhetoric, I finally turn to Pope Francis's 2018 apostolic exhortation *Gaudete et Exsultate* (Rejoice and be glad), which is a persuasive call toward holiness, expressed in what I argue is a post-Christian style of complicit invention.

Ambiguous Rhetoric

"Rhetoric," Bernard-Donals and Jensen write, "has always had a vexed relationship with the sacred."[17] The same can be said for any attempt to account for extrahuman communication. As Steven Mailloux has argued, rhetoric still must invent a persuasion of God outside of a "humanist ontotheology," which "consists of speaking to and about God as a being, the Supreme Being, and then thinking being itself on the basis of this superior or perfect divinity."[18] This model, familiar though it may be, is both bad theology and bad rhetoric. It is bad theology insofar as it reduces God to a version of ourselves. It is bad rhetoric insofar as it constrains rhetoric to representation. Outside of such terms, however, rhetoric may be as strange and surprising as the divine itself.

As rhetoricians take up these matters, they will encounter a century-old interdisciplinary inquiry involving anthropology, sociology, psychology, political science, religious studies, and theology. Key to this inquiry is whether either the sacred or the holy possesses an autonomous existence—that is, whether there is something called "the" sacred/holy that somehow stands apart from human response or intervention. Another key issue is what is sometimes called the "ambiguity" or "ambivalence" of the sacred, the sense that the sacred portends allure and danger, promise and peril. Scholars including William James, Émile Durkheim, Rudolf Otto, Mircea Eliade, James Frazer, and William Robertson-Smith (along with Nietzsche and Freud and many others) have tried to explain why the sacred seems to occasion such opposed effects. This conversation was more or less halted by the shift to structuralism and poststructuralism.[19] Yet its key ideas and terms have endured, both in and outside the academy. When rhetoricians speak of "the" sacred or "the" holy, they are echoing this tradition.

The same is true for Girard, whose entire project could be described as the final action in what Camille Tarot calls "'the war over the sacred' in French sociological thought, perhaps even a Hundred Years' War, because it still has not ended."[20] For some, Girard is the last combatant of this war, a lone holdout who has not yet heard of the armistice. But while Girard does impute an ambiguity to the sacred, it is not because the sacred possesses an entirely autonomous existence; it is because he is tracing how the sacred becomes both an occasion and an obfuscation of the all-too-human propensity for violence. This is why Girard originally understood religion to be "that obscurity that surrounds man's efforts to defend himself by curative or preventive means against his own violence."[21] Later in his work, Girard distinguishes between types of religion: those that rely on the violent sacred and those that expose it. This is the lever by which Girard hopes to separate the sacred from the holy. But it is not clear that one can so easily escape the ambivalence of the sacred for a holy unicity.

The same sorts of controversy attend Rudolf Otto's attempt to isolate and observe the holy through a vocabulary of the "numinous," the Wholly Other (*ganz andere*), and the *mysterium tremendum et fascinans*—the mystery that is both tremendous (L. *tremendus*, to be trembled at, fearful, dreadful; related to *tremĕre*, to tremble) and fascinating (L. *fascināre*, to cast a spell on, bewitch). (Bernard-Donals and Jensen note Jeffrey Kripal's memorable translation: the mystery that is both "utterly fascinating" and "fucking scary.")[22] Otto coins these terms in his landmark *The Idea of the Holy* (1917), which tries to capture (in another neologism) the *numinous* (L. *numen*, divine, divine majesty, deity). The notion of the Wholly Other presents a fundamental rhetorical challenge: "either God is the 'wholly other' in an absolute sense, in which case we can experience and say nothing about him, even that he is the wholly other, or we experience something of God, in which case God's essence should not be designated 'numinous.'"[23] Like rhetoricians, scholars in religious studies recognize the conundrum of the ineffable (L. *in*, not + *effābilis* < *ef—fāri*, to utter < *ex*, out + *fāri*, to speak), a term that contains its own negative theology. Once again, we confront the dissatisfying choice between the "hyper-ascendant deity of mystical or negative theology" and "the consigning of the sacred to the domain of abyssal abjection."[24] The recent turn in rhetorical scholarship to the sacred and the holy represents an attempt to navigate around this choice.

Yet these kinds of ideas and the inquiry that produced them have both come under sharp critique. In *Theories of Primitive Religion* (1965), for example, the

British anthropologist E. E. Evans-Pritchard observed fundamental problems in the scholarship that helped cement the idea of autonomous sacred phenomena. Evans-Pritchard's criticisms are numerous, but perhaps the most damning concerns the way in which European scholars exoticized the peoples they studied. Scholars, he argues, gave "undue attention to what they regarded as curious superstitions, the occult and mysterious," thus emphasizing "the mystical" at the expense of "the empirical, the ordinary, the common-sense," with the result that "the natives were made to look childish and in obvious need of fatherly administration and missionary zeal, especially if there was a welcome bit of obscenity in their rites."[25] Giorgio Agamben makes a related point when he describes the entire inquiry into the numinous as a product of a late-Victorian unease with modernity, an unease that eventually infects French sociology. Worried over a decline in religious sentiment, Agamben argues, scholars looked to "primitive" religion to recover a sensibility that their own societies had lost. In Agamben's estimation, Otto's work is the apotheosis of this misguided inquiry: "a theology that had lost all experience of the revealed word celebrated its union with a philosophy that had abandoned all sobriety in the face of feeling. That the religious belongs entirely to the sphere of psychological emotion, that it essentially has to do with shivers and goosebumps—this is the triviality that the neologism 'numinous' had to dress up as science."[26]

While I would not claim that Evans-Prichard and Agamben are the final word on these matters, their critiques should caution rhetoricians about how we take up this language. Ironically enough, rhetoricians may find an appropriate opportunity to repair such language within the criticism that such language is rhetorical rather than analytical. Lynn Poland, for example, argues that Otto's attempt to define the holy fails precisely insofar as it becomes rhetorical. Otto's attempt to isolate the numinous becomes "a rhetorical problem as well as a theoretical one." She continues, "Otto's analytic, it seems to me, dissolves willy-nilly into rhetorical strategy."[27] Similarly, Carsten Colpe has argued that the distinction between the sacred and the holy "has a certain heuristic value, though admittedly only that and nothing more."[28] While these may be fighting words for anthropologists or sociologists, for rhetoricians there is no embarrassment in rhetorical strategy or heuristic value; the best way to use these terms may be precisely to shift them from concepts to topoi, which Wayne Booth has defined as "the almost-empty places-of-agreement where those who think they disagree can stand as they hammer out their disagreements."[29] Though there is something deeper than deliberation when it comes to sacred and holy matters, Booth's formulation reminds us that topoi are defined by their capacity: the emptiness that makes a space available for encounter. At the same time, the adverb "almost" suggests that these sacred and holy "places" come formed by their history, particularly the "war" through which these terms first became thinkable as concepts, as nouns available for analysis.[30]

That history is too long to recount here. But even a brief sketch of three central contributions—from Émile Durkheim, Mircea Eliade, and Rudolf Otto—indicates the difficulties of maintaining the sacred and holy as consistently applicable analytical concepts. So vexed is the problem that it is impossible to map the conversation in a way that both respects chronology and manages the slippage between sacred and holy. As Wolfgang Palaver remarks, with admirable understatement, the common terms—sacred, holy, numinous, *mysterium*, sanctity, saintliness—have been deployed "incoherently up until the present day in the Western languages that have shaped scholarly debates about religion."[31] Their meanings shift between different studies and within single studies; sometimes they are synonymous, sometimes antonymous. In the English translation of Otto's *Idea of the Holy*, for example, "sacred" and "holy" are used interchangeably to describe the same phenomenon. In French, Otto's book was translated as *Le sacré*, a translation that probably influenced Mircea Eliade's title for *The Sacred and the Profane* (1957). This kind of shift can impede efforts to discern a conceptual difference between the sacred and the holy.[32] With these challenges in mind, I have elected to follow chronology, even at the risk of eliding the difference.

"The" Sacred

Even when we can focus on a single term like "sacred," difficulties persist. While it is commonly deployed as a term of approbation (sacred duties, sacred honor, sacred pledge), the word also carries the opposite meaning—of being accursed, criminal, infamous. Raymund Schwager notes that the Latin *sacer* (Gr. *krateros*) can denote something that "is at the same time cursed and blessed, repulsive and attractive, ugly and radiant" (in other words, in ambiguous ways).[33] To be *sacer* is to be set apart in some way from the ordinary run of people and things, in ways both honorific and dangerous. A king or a bishop may be "consecrated," just as plants or animals or lands may be protected "against violation, infringement, or encroachment." The sacred person or thing enjoys "a religiously secured immunity from violence or attachment; sacrosanct, inviolable." But to be *sacer* is also, paradoxically, to be exposed to danger. "Consecration to a god is perceived by humans as a blessing, whereas being possessed by a god is perceived as a misfortune."[34] The sacred thus entails an ambiguity, an ambiguity that occasioned the sociological war over religion.

Within that ongoing struggle, Émile Durkheim is known for two central contributions to understanding the sacred: first, for observing the ambiguity of the sacred and, second, for defining religion in terms of the social. Durkheim first defines the sacred by distinguishing it from the profane (L. *pro*, outside of + *fanus*, shrine, sanctuary, temple). Durkheim was not the first to observe this division, but his work became the foundation and often the target of the conversation that followed.[35] Durkheim thought the sacred-profane distinction even more fundamental than the relationship between good and evil. The relation is one of total negation: "The sacred thing is, par excellence, that which the profane must not and cannot touch with impunity."[36] Though an item or a person may be transformed from profane to sacred, the transformation is *"absolute*. In the history of human thought, there is no other example of two categories of things as profoundly differentiated or as radically opposed to one another."[37] Yet Durkheim also notes that the sacred carries a certain ambiguity; it may be associated with both benevolent and malevolent spirits, just as it may be associated with the "negative cult" (that which you should not do) and the "positive cult" (that which you should). The sacred thus occasions an ambivalent response: "The fear inspired by malignant powers is not without a certain reverential quality. Indeed, the shades of difference between these two attitudes are sometimes so elusive that it is not always easy to say in just which state of mind the faithful are."[38] This is the source of the ambiguity.

Second, Durkheim understood religion to be primarily social; its central function is to cement community. "In history," Durkheim writes, "we do not find religion without Church," which is to say a community or group.[39] This fundamental social element underwrites Durkheim's definition of religion as *"a unified system of beliefs and practices relative to sacred things, that is to say, things set apart and forbidden—beliefs and practices which unite into one single moral community called a Church, all those who adhere to them."*[40] This idea came under sharp critique, both during the "war" and after. But Camille Tarot notes that Durkheim was not trying to understand religion as "a subjective phenomenon, an individual state of mind or an intellectual or mystical fact."[41] Put another way, Durkheim was trying to avoid both religious and antireligious reaction. The social could provide an explanation of religion that would avoid the most extreme positions.

Though it is not clear that Otto ever read Durkheim, his *Idea of the Holy* has sometimes been read as a response. Unlike Durkheim, Otto is attempting to isolate and observe "the holy" as a thing unto itself, irreducible to the social. He tries to observe the holy as a "*sui generis* reality."[42] This is what leads to Otto's neologisms, which have endured despite the book's waning influence.[43] Yet, however contemporary scholars regard Otto, his book succeeded in setting the terms of "the" holy, along with the numinous, the Wholly Other (*ganz andere*), and the *mysterium tremendum et fascinans*. Otto strives to drill down to the holy itself, below the moral accretions that have obscured its fundamental nature (moral accretions that presumably indicate the influence of the social). "The fact is we have come to use the words 'holy,' 'sacred' (*heilig*) in an entirely derivative sense," a sense shaped by cultural norms and practices.[44] This distillation project, however, encounters difficult rhetorical challenges, challenges that have invited the rhetorical criticisms mentioned earlier. "We are bound to try," Otto writes, "by means of *the most precise and unambiguous symbolic and figurative terms* that we can find, to discriminate the different elements of the experience [of the holy] so far as we can in a way that can claim general validity."[45] The paradox of "precise and unambiguous symbolic and figurative terms" indicates that, as much as he would like to find independent or objective grounds for the holy, he has to conclude that holiness "cannot be rationally conceived, but only evoked."[46] Evocation, however, is a matter of persuasion more than pure analysis.[47]

Whatever the holy may be, it is invented through a relation between both "nonrational" elements and "rational" expression. This is what Otto describes as the "warp and woof" that together work to produce the holy, an echo of what Otto earlier describes as the "harmony of contrasts" that produces the *mysterium*.[48] The "content" of the numinous is articulated through the "form" of the mystery.[49] Ultimately, then, Otto defines the holy as the "numinous completely permeated and statured with elements signifying rationality, purpose, personality, morality."[50] This means that Otto finally cannot isolate the numinous, which can be observed only through its relations to the ethical, relations that make up "the holy."

From an analytic standpoint, this notion may represent a failure. From a theorhetorical standpoint, however, we can see a possibility for complicit invention, an emerging topos that works through movement between the numinous

124   PERSUASIONS OF GOD

and the ethical, which can only be understood in relation to each other. (I am jumping ahead slightly in the argument, moving for a moment from a descriptive accounting of the sociological war to a prescriptive harvesting of resources for a theorhetoric.) A Christian theologian, Otto anticipates Girard in drawing on the Hebrew and Christian scriptures, where "the numinous is throughout rationalized and moralized, i.e., charged with ethical import, until it becomes the 'holy' in the fullest sense of the word."[51] There is a relation between the Wholly Otherness and the ethical.[52] For Otto, then, the holy cannot be understood as merely that which is left over after the numinous has been drained away. It is rather produced by the relation between the sense of the "irrational" (i.e., the numinous, the *mysterium*) and the "rational" (the ethical).[53]

In *The Sacred and the Profane* (1957), Mircea Eliade both takes up Otto's project and critiques its limitations. Like Otto, Eliade is inclined to grant the "sacred" an autonomous significance. Yet Eliade proposes "to present the phenomenon of the sacred in all its complexity, and not only in so far as it is *irrational* [i.e., non-rational]. What will concern us is not the relation between the rational and the non-rational elements of religion, but *the sacred in its entirety*."[54] By this description, Eliade announces that he is less interested in the warp and woof of holiness, as Otto understands it, and more interested in the full range of the effects of the sacred, which "ontologically founds the world."[55] He wants to maintain his attention on the so-called irrational sacred. This focus leads to his own coining of "hierophany," which is his name for moments in which the sacred is manifested—and manifests itself—in the profane world, so that something that was once ordinary (a stone, a tree, bread and wine) becomes extraordinary, sacred, "saturated with *being*."[56] A hierophany (Gk. *hiero*, sacred or holy + *phanein*, to bring to light, cause to appear, show) is a moment of "the manifestation of something of a wholly different order, a reality that does not belong to our world."[57] All religions, Eliade insists, are characterized by such manifestations, which ultimately seem beyond human power to manufacture or demand. The hierophany seems to show itself, independent of social or human control. Thus, while Eliade would preserve Durkheim's division between the sacred and the profane, he is much more interested in the sacred's own power.[58]

That power is certainly related to the social, as Durkheim insists. Of hierophanies, Eliade writes, "*Something* that does not belong to this world has manifested itself apodictically and in so doing has indicated an orientation or determined a course of conduct."[59] According to Eliade, that other quality founds a sacred order to which human beings orient themselves (i.e., the ontological foundation of the world). This is also true within "the wholly desacralized cosmos," which, he adds, "is a recent discovery in the history of the human spirit."[60] Even modern or "profane" (i.e., nonreligious) people cannot fully shake their orientation to *some* sacred order, even if it is not a sacred order as typically understood within religion. But Eliade's main point is that hierophanies have an objective, independent existence. Bernard-Donals and Jensen import this idea into rhetorical studies, describing a hierophany as a moment in which "the divine *shows itself* by punctuating the ordinary, whereby what had been previously considered profane—mundane, purely natural, ready-to-hand and readily assimilable to our previous experience—is endowed with another quality."[61] Rhetoric therefore possesses the capacity to account for such experiences and perhaps to occasion them.

Durkheim, Otto, and Eliade are certainly not the only three figures we could cite in this context, but they are major contributors to the conversation to which Girard is responding. Like Durkheim, Girard recognizes the social effects of religion, though he resists the conclusion that religion can be reduced to the social. Like all three, Girard recognizes a certain ambiguity or ambivalence in the sacred, though he resists the idea that the sacred has some independent or autonomous existence. "The ambivalence of the sacred," explains Frederiek Depoortere, "becomes intelligible when we understand that the sacred comes into being through externalizing violence, by dehumanizing it and turning it into a transcendent power."[62] Because the sacred hides human complicity in violence, it appears to be autonomous, but it is all too human. The revelation of the violent source of the sacred's false autonomy is the central act of nonsacred religion. That revelation is the basis for what Girard describes as "the gradual transformation of the *sacred* into the *holy*."[63] Yet because Girard only makes clear what holiness is not, we are left with the project of inventing what the holy may be. To begin that project of invention, we might start by discerning the shape of a topos of holiness.

"The" Holy

The English "holy" is of German origin and comes though Old English *hálig* (as in Otto's *Das Heilige*). *Hálig* suggests a sense of being consecrated or dedicated, but it also related to the Old English *hál*, meaning "free from injury, whole, hale," which is itself derived from the noun *hailoz-*, meaning "health, happiness, good luck." The pre-Christian meaning of *halio-* is not entirely certain, though the editors of the *OED* suggest that the word means "inviolate, inviolable, that must be preserved *whole* or intact, that cannot be injured with impunity." Even prior to its contact with Christianity, then, "holy" suggested a sense of being set aside and protected (which may explain how it came to be used to render both *sacer* and *sanctus*).[64] Most importantly, the sense of being "set aside" does not appear to imply any sense of exposure to violence. This lack of obvious connection to violence (other than the attempt to heal it) may suggest why "the holy" does not seem connected to a sense of community order. We speak of sacred duties, sacred honor, sacred rites, but holy is reserved for that which precedes human control (holy ground) or exceeds it (holy fools).

Beyond efforts at etymology and definition, scholars have once again tried to define "holy" by opposition. Jack Miles writes that holiness "can only be defined dialectically. Holy is what is *other than* unholy or profane."[65] Even everyday usage, writes the theologian Paul S. Minear, "recognizes these as the options: a thing is either holy or profane, sacred or secular."[66] Willard G. Oxtoby notes another contrast, this one between sacred and holy: describing something as "holy" puts the speaker squarely inside the tradition in question.[67] To describe something as "sacred," however, often places one on the outside, as when we describe something as a "sacred cow."[68] Outside of confessional contexts, "holy" seems to have atrophied into an epithet ("holy roller" or "holier than thou"). "Sacred" thus seems more appropriate for analytical claims, whereas "holy" cannot help but claim the one who speaks the word.

This may be why scholars tend to suggest that holiness has an implicit rhetorical character. "Holiness," writes the theologian John Rogerson, "is a word in the English language whose meaning depends on the contexts in which it is used and the interests of those who use it."[69] This implicit but unmistakable rhetorical understanding of holiness may weaken its use as an analytical tool, but it opens the possibility of seeing the word as a place of invention. The theologian David Blumenthal makes an even more overt case for understanding holiness rhetorically; in Jewish tradition, holiness occasions what rhetoricians would recognize as copiousness: "As one integrates the holy into life, *one needs other words*. One reaches outward: King, Lord, Name, justice, beauty, purity, Shabbat, Israel, You. One probes inward: awe, wonder, radical amazement, sublime, love, joy, bliss, bless, worship. One gropes for forms: holy day, temple, mitsva [*sic*], liturgy, charity, study, Torah, acts of kindness, martyrdom. *The failure of language is transformed into a rich vocabulary of response, always haunted by its own muteness*."[70] In Blumenthal's remark, we can observe similarities to the way rhetoricians have described the sacred as a phenomenon that motivates a rhetorical response even as it seems to undermine it. In the face of the holy, language wilts but then bursts forth to compensate for its own failure. Some sense of the frightening-fascinating endures, but it does so within an ethical relation. It is a form of complicit invention. As Rogerson puts it, holiness is the sense "that people can feel themselves to be grasped by an unseen reality that becomes something to be after for its own sake and which in this way liberates seekers from self-interest."[71] The numinous-ethical connection is revealed in the idea of an unseen reality that liberates seekers from self.

At this point, then, we have some sense of the shape of the available topoi of "sacred" and "holy," along with some sense of how these terms have developed over time. That development, in Western usage at least, cannot be separated from the influence of Judaism and Christianity. While that influence may limit the applicability of these ideas to any general idea of the "religious," it is not a limit for developing a post-Christian theorhetoric of the holy. In Jewish and Christian tradition, holiness is the means by which one comes to know God. The scripture scholar Walter Brueggemann writes, "Holiness is not an autonomous theme, but it is a way of discerning who this God is."[72] Holiness therefore returns us to the basic theorhetorical project of talking about talking to, for, and about God. We might then inquire about the available rhetorical resources, a question that returns our attention to the "vexed" relationship between rhetoric and the sacred.

Ambivalent Rhetoric

If the relation between rhetoric and the sacred is vexed, it is in large part because, as we have seen, our understanding of the sacred is itself quite vexed. But more than that, rhetoric has sometimes suffered from a bad conscience about approaching questions of the sacred. Though rhetorical studies has tended to understand itself as a secular discipline working in a secular academy, the collapse of such commonplaces as the "secularization thesis" and the "disenchantment of the world" have revealed that religion will not be so easily ignored or compartmentalized.[73] The world still has the capacity to surprise in ways that inspire responses that have gone under the name "religious." Whether to construe these responses as sacred or holy—or whether the distinction matters at all—therefore becomes a matter of some import.

As rhetoricians reimagine persuasion as primordial and ontological, they perhaps become more open to the possibility that there are more things in heaven and earth than are dreamt of in our philosophy. Perhaps the locus classicus of this possibility is Christian Lundberg and Joshua's Gunn's 2005 essay "Ouija Board, Are There Any Communications?," an essay that explicitly challenges rhetoric's investment in "ontotheological humanism."[74] In contrast to "covertly theistic discourse of the subject," they suggest "a negative theology of the subject," a theology that would be less certain of the powers of intention and control in any communicative encounter.[75] The Ouija board, for example, seems to distribute agency among the human, the technological, and the *we-know-not-what*. Even if messages from the Ouija board do not rise to the level of hierophany, they remind us of the limits of human control.

The emerging study of the sacred and the holy represents an attempt, not unlike that of the sociological war, to get at some notion of the sacred and the holy as phenomena that exceed human control even as they seem to demand human response. As the notion of a Ouija board suggests, the tension around the sacred lies at least in part within the tension between its status as autonomous phenomenon and human achievement. The sacred is "received" but is also occasioned—fostered but not effected, "effect" being the verb of grace alone. Though the sacred exceeds human intention, we cannot help but search for ways that, in Jody Nicotra's memorable formulation, we might "hack the sacred"—to tune into and even bolster its signal.[76] Eliade similarly notes that *homo religiosus* has always developed "techniques of *orientation* which, properly speaking, are techniques for the *construction* of sacred space. But we must not suppose that *human* work is in question here, that it is through his own efforts that man can consecrate a space. In reality, the ritual by which he constructs a sacred space is efficacious in the measure in which *it reproduces the work of the gods*."[77] In this idea, we may detect not only the ambiguity of the sacred but the ambivalence of rhetoric, which operates somewhere between effects we occasion and effects beyond our control.

The tension I am trying to observe here can be stated with reference to ideas that we have already invoked. Diane Davis understands rhetoric to designate a "fundamental structure of exposure," which is to say that prior to any conventionally persuasive activity, there must be a prior openness to persuasion, or indeed a persuasion that is itself an openness.[78] So fundamental is the exposure that it can never be fully closed off. This "primordial rhetoric," as Allen Scult calls it, is necessary for any rhetorical activity.[79] Even the answer "no" attests to a response-ability that we cannot ultimately reject. "You might whip out your Blackberry or plug in your iPod or feign sleep or complete absorption in your magazine, iPad, or Nintendo DS, but the active refusal to be responsive is a response and so no longer complete indifference."[80] Because of prior rhetoricity, indifference is not possible. In the parable of the Good Samaritan, for example, the three who pass by the wounded man are not practicing indifference. They *cannot* practice total indifference; they can only bind his wounds or let him bleed.

But some intentional rhetorical activity, even if such activity can never be reduced to intention, is also an irreducible part of sacred communication. Recall John Caputo's claim that theopoetics constitutes an attempt to "sustain an exposure to the inbreaking of something."[81] Sustaining the exposure implies something beyond prior rhetoricity. It implies a human desire, an attempt to "hack the sacred." After primordial rhetoric comes some response that sustains the exposure (or not). The exposure may endure, whatever our response to it. But the response matters nonetheless. Bernard-Donals and Jensen, for instance, draw on Girard to note that "ritual or liturgic expressions as responses to the sacred do not involve the identification of an already sacred object, but rather the production of sacred objects through ritual acts."[82] The things of the sacred are made, up to and including the gods themselves. But Girard also observes the grave danger in that kind of theopoiesis: "The peoples of the world," Girard insists, "do not invent their gods. They deify their victims."[83] The question, then, is what role rhetoric might play in sustaining the exposure while not creating any victims along the way?

In asking that question, I am not trying to force a false choice between an ontological and intentional rhetoric. In juxtaposing the sustaining of exposure against the fact of exposure, my intention is not to reassert representational or epistemic terms. Nor is my argument that sustaining the exposure is primarily a representational or epistemic matter, a stance that Caputo and his fellow theopoets also reject. It is simply to note that, insofar as we hope to attune ourselves to the sacred, we maintain some relation, however cautious, to ideas of intention, aim, and cooperation. We must proceed carefully, particularly in light of the victim-deifying tendency noted by Girard. Yet we proceed; the sacred prompts us to proceed.

These risks can be observed in an emerging argument about whether the sacred is even amenable to rhetoric. "The sacred," argues Scult, "may even be defined hermeneutically by the impossibility of human discourse to fully comprehend it, or, more specifically, by the incapacity of human discourse to explain the rhetorical function of the sacred, its way of making itself known."[84] Drawing on Levinas, Bernard-Donals describes divine encounter as one of displacement, deterritorialization, and even violence. The divine "presents us with the paradigmatic case in which the subject is compelled or called by that which exceeds our capacity to understand it—to name the relation—and in which meeting the demand to answer that call is in fact impossible."[85] The sacred thus "serves as a limit to rhetoric: as that which compels a response, albeit an unsettled one, and as the response itself, which does not do justice to or contain adequately the compulsion to respond."[86] Encountering the divine, the human may retreat to a rhetoric that is not fully responsive.

The limits of rhetoric can be observed in Moses's encounter with the Lord in Exodus 3. Moses comes upon what Eliade would describe as a hierophany: a bush that is aflame but unconsumed. "Do not come closer. Remove the sandals from your feet, for the place on which you stand is holy ground" (Exod. 3:5). (In this passage, the English "holy" is a translation of the Hebrew *qadosh*, which was translated as *hagios* in the Septuagint and *sanctus* in the Vulgate.) Bernard-Donals writes that the sacred undermines "the subject's certainty about the ground on which she stands and the name that she provides for herself as a resident of that community or territory."[87] In this case, the ground is holy but shifting under Moses's feet. If Moses had thought he could remain in Midian and forget his past, he is now ordered to go home again, where he must face his double alienation from both the Israelites and the Egyptians, unsure whether he can finally reside anywhere. In Girardian terms, Moses has all the familiar trappings of the scapegoat: like Oedipus, he is both foreign and native, stranger and kin. He is marked by a disability (tradition holds that Moses had a speech impediment), and most importantly, he is out in front and set apart. Kings are as likely as beggars to be blamed for the community's woes. Encounter with the sacred radically displaces both the subject and the subject's response. In the sacred encounter, "the speaker essentially herself empties of names, regularities, and knowledge at the moment of encounter, a literal turning inside out."[88] One might call it a kind of violence insofar as it ejects the subject from the familiar and conventional, but it not a violence that excludes the other in order to protect the familiar. If there is an exclusion, it is of the self. "But this coring out of the self is the only way in which individuals as subjects can catch a glimpse of what resides beyond the regularities of reason that restrict human action and that foreclose the possibility of real contact between and among individuals."[89] Only through this coring out, through this creation of capacity—through this empty-ing of what we thought we knew about ourselves, the other, and God—can we be made available for the ethical call.

Yet this same encounter between the Lord and Moses also displays the characteristics of more familiar rhetorical exchange. Fearing that he lacks the necessary oratorical skill to move Pharaoh, Moses begs to be let off. "Please, O Lord, I have never been a man of words, either in times past or now that You have spoken to your servant. I am slow of speech and slow tongue" (Exod. 4:10). As Moses presses his case, the Lord starts to lose patience: "Who gives man speech? Who makes him dumb or deaf, seeing or blind? Is it not I the Lord?" (Exod. 4:11). But then he suddenly relents. "There is your brother Aaron the Levite. He, I know, speaks readily. . . . You shall speak to him and put the words in his mouth—I will be with you and with him as you speak, and tell both of you what to do—and he shall speak for you to the people" (Exod. 4:14–16). Sophistically, Moses's weaker position becomes the stronger argument to which the Lord must yield. Even more strikingly, the Lord of wonders has no miracle cure for fear of public speaking. In fact, both parties win by losing: God concedes Moses's point and sends rhetorical backup; Moses concedes God's point and agrees to go. The Lord, in a sense, has also been displaced. In Bernard-Donals's terms, they have both "cored themselves out" in order for the project to be carried forward.

This aspect of Moses and God's exchange raises the possibility that divine encounter is a matter not only of displacement, deterritorialization, and vio-lence but also of appeal, argument, and deliberation. In a friendly challenge to Bernard-Donals, David Frank argues that within the sacred, we can also detect a God who is more traditionally rhetorical, one to whom humans can relate by means of "reason, speech, language, conversation, argument, and debate."[90] While Frank does not deny the displacement and violence that Bernard-Donals observes, he nevertheless insists that the Hebrew scriptures reveal a God open to persuasion. Through a reading of Genesis, Exodus, and Job, along with the Hebrew scriptures beyond the Bible, Frank observes an ongoing conversation in which God is moved by human appeal to a deeper sense of mercy and justice.[91] The Hebrew of Genesis, for example, suggests that God does not order the earth and sky into existence but rather persuades them to cooperate in the process of creation in Genesis 1.[92] Despite committing the first murder, Cain persuades God toward mercy, and God spares him from further punishment (Gen. 4:13–15). In contrast to Agamben's notion of *homo sacer*, the Lord makes absolutely certain that Cain will not be exposed to violence. "'I promise, if any-one kills Cain, sevenfold vengeance shall be taken on him.' And the Lord put a mark on Cain, lest anyone who met him should kill him" (Gen. 4:14–15). As Girard would probably note, the Lord's action stops the cycle of revenge (though Cain also becomes the founder of a city [Gen. 4:14], suggesting the link between violence and order). Abraham likewise persuades the Lord toward mercy before he destroys Sodom and Gomorrah (Gen. 18:23–32). Abraham asks, "Will You sweep away the innocent along with the guilty? What if there should be fifty innocent within the city; will You then wipe out the place and not forgive it for the sake of the innocent who are in it?" (Gen. 18:23–24). When the Lord agrees to spare Sodom if there are fifty good people, Abraham presses ahead. What about forty-five? What about forty? By the time Abraham is finished, he has persuaded the Lord down to ten.

Frank's God is rhetorical not only because God persuades but also because God is persuadable. "Genuine argument with the divine is possible because God can yield to the stronger argument. . . . The divine becomes, through argument, capable of disagreeing with the human via argument and is thereby willing to cede power to reason."[93] That is not to say that rhetorical engagement with God carries no risk. Frank acknowledges the force of Bernard-Donals's argument that communication requires vulnerability, and vulnerability exposes us to risk; the God of the scriptures can appear to be both good and bad, abusing and lov-ing. Yet, the Jewish scriptures and traditions on which Frank draws also depict a God who "develops the capacities for mercy and justice as a function of engage-ments with and confrontations by humans."[94]

In keeping with the rhetorical protocols of this book, my intention here is not to adjudicate this argument but to note that sacred encounter can be con-strued as both ontologically and conventionally rhetorical. Encounters with the divine can be deeply unsettling, driving us from our familiar haunts and regular ruts. But they can also be occasions for argument and deliberation, in which conventional rhetorical appeal can persuade and even change God. The divine is at once "Wholly Other" and willing to submit to mediation (in all senses of the term).

This brings us to Girard's claim that God's "pedagogical strategy" is to trans-form "the *sacred* into the *holy*. The God of the Bible goes from the violent sacred to holiness." In many ways, the framing of this statement is incorrect. As we have seen, God eschews violence in the earliest pages of the Jewish Bible. And taken out of the larger context of Girard's work, the statement seems to repeat the false and pernicious Old Testament versus New Testament trope (though Girard explicitly rejects the "Marcionite attitude" in the same breath). Most importantly, his point is that the general tendency of the scriptures is to move away from the "violent sacred," whose central purpose is to maintain order and identity. When, therefore, Bernard-Donals observes that the sacred "puts into crisis the subject's capacity to establish a community," he is making an observation that resonates with Girard's thought.[95] The divine call interrupts the tendency to build identity and community on the backs of the excluded. To be emptied of names, regularities, and knowledge, to be turned inside out, is to be incapacitated from any security occasioned by means of exclusion or expulsion. The mirror image of this capacity is witnessed in Abraham's pleas to the Lord to spare Sodom. There, it is not that an innocent must suffer for the security of the community; it is that an innocent is enough to redeem an otherwise inhospitable city. But this ethical conclusion comes about only through the most traditional rhetorical means of reason, speech, language, conversation, argument, and debate. Theorhetoric, which includes speaking to God, is what moves God to be who God says God is.

It may not matter very much in the end whether we describe Abraham's persuasively redemptive arithmetic as "sacred" or "holy." One might describe life as sacred in order to spare it; one might describe a place as sacred in order to defend it. The only question is whether the numinous calls for the expulsion of the other or the expulsion of ourselves from safety and security. As Bernard-Donals and Frank have shown, the "sacred" can occasion both events. The point is not, therefore, to set up some linguistic regulation that favors the "holy" over the "sacred." The point is to have the means of discerning what sort of sacredness or holiness is being invented. Indeed, perhaps the advantage of a topos of the sacred would be that it recalls the stakes of any numinous encounter, any hierophantic event. If, therefore, a topos of the holy is to be preferred, it is because it offers a space more hospitable to the other, a space that is never formed by the exclusion of the other. For Girard, that is the main point: the sacred cannot be built by means of exclusion or expulsion. Within the framework of a rhetoric of meekness, a topos of holiness cannot be built on mirroring or rivalry, even in relation to the sacred.

Within rhetorical studies, the clearest call for a rhetoric of holiness has come from Lundberg, who describes holiness as that which "holds open a caveat that the context within which the human subject lives among others, as a gift, is fragile, contingent, and often outstrips our representational faculties."[96] Holiness recognizes the interdependence and vulnerability of the human subject, for whom holy ground may be a place of displacement. The sacred, by contrast, "implies an affirmation of context not as gift but as given (or natural), and of the human faculties of representation and signification as unproblematically, effortlessly, and transparently referencing this naturalized reality and the social and political orders that underwrite them."[97] This notion of the sacred recognizes the relationship between the sacred and order in the ways Girard, Eliade, and others would recognize. "Hierarchy," after all, means sacred (*hiero*, sacred or holy) order (*arche*). The danger of such order is indeed that it is naturalized (though in Girard's estimation, that which appears to be transparent is actually an obscuring of the constitutive role of violence). Lundberg's idea of holiness, however, implies an orientation of vulnerability rather than violence.

In many ways, Lundberg's distinction between the sacred and the holy articulates the distinction that Girard is trying to draw. Lundberg reads this distinction through a "rhetorical/affective motif: sacred commitments serve as a means of organizing affective investments against the other, while a holy commitment draws succor from relationship to the other."[98] Within Lundberg's understanding, the sacred is produced by organizing *against*, a claim that resonates with Girard's (and Levinas's) understanding of the sacred. The holy, by contrast, does not create identity through separation but rather is an exposure to the other. In James Crosswhite's terms, the holy becomes "a way we open ourselves to the influence of what is beyond ourselves and become receptive, a way we participate in a larger world and become open to the lives of others, a way we learn and change."[99] The holy strips our human pretensions to construe the other in advance of—or even in spite of—encounter. This vision of the holy thus resonates with an ontological construal of rhetoric as a kind of constitutive vulnerability. This understanding can include some of the features of the sacred described by Bernard-Donals. Numinous encounter or experience can be radically precarious and destabilizing, but it is only through this exposure that we can be open to new possibilities.

Lundberg pursues this project through a particular theological framework, in this case an "unapologetically and intentionally theological register rooted in the Christian traditions."[100] Lundberg's point is not that Christianity has cornered the market on holiness. But a specific religious content offers a "means of understanding what we might borrow from theological traditions to better understand rhetoric's ambivalence regarding its rational/calculative impulses around meaning and the elements of rhetorical force that are not reducible to ideation, meaning, or intention."[101] In many ways, then, Lundberg's project parallels Girard's: rather than reading Christianity through another discipline, Lundberg reads rhetoric through Christianity. How might theological concepts of holiness inform rhetoric's own reflection on the tension between rhetoric as prior, ontological, and constitutive and rhetoric as artful, technical, and purposive?

My question is somewhat different: How might Christian theological ideas of holiness inform a post-Christian theorhetoric? How might we invent a rhetoric of holiness appropriate for a moment when, as Ellul suggests, "X" might be a more persuasive title than "Christianity" (*christianisme*)? In the following section, I proceed by means of what we might call a "perspective by congruity," that is, a perspective that might be gained by seeking a post-Christian theorhetoric in what may seem to be the most traditional and non-post place possible: Pope Francis's apostolic exhortation *Gaudete et Exsultate*, or "Rejoice and Be Glad."

Rejoice and Be Glad

Promulgated on March 19, 2018, *Gaudete et Exsultate* (GE) would hardly seem to fit the bill for a post-Christian theorhetoric.[102] GE is an entirely intra-Christian discourse, written by a Christian leader for Christian readers.[103] Yet GE is a perfect text for the present purpose. First, it is a thoroughly rhetorical document: an "apostolic exhortation," written precisely to persuade readers toward some new action or renewed commitment. In the traditional offices of the Christian rhetor as imagined by Augustine, an apostolic exhortation is meant to move. Francis can be understood as an anonymous rhetorician, a rhetorician most concerned with the canon with which rhetoric is most commonly equated: style.[104] In his intellectual biography of Francis, Massimo Borghesi writes that the pope does not consider style "merely an intellectual paradigm, a 'technique' with which to settle conflicts; it is something more profound." Style, for Francis, is "a mode of being."[105] Luis Orlando Jiménez Rodríguez echoes that position, arguing that style is ultimately a theological theme for Francis; it is the word that Francis employs when he links the attitudes and values that emanate from the Gospel and the actions and concrete relationships that should follow.[106] In GE, Jiménez Rodríguez notes, the word "style" appears seven times, with the related word "mode" appearing several more times.[107] In all of these uses, Francis is going for something more profound than everyday conceptions of "mere" style might suggest.

Throughout *GE*, Francis is articulating holiness as a style particularly appropriate for a post-Christian context. Though his is clearly a Christian call, it is not one that construes the church as what Massimo Faggioli describes as "an island of grace for the conspicuously holy surrounded by a sea of sinfulness."[108] The church is instead what Francis famously dubbed "a field hospital after battle."[109] The call of holiness therefore means resisting the temptation "to flee to a safe haven." Those havens, Francis writes, "can have many names: individualism, spiritualism, living in a little world, addiction, intransigence, the rejection of new ideas and approaches, dogmatism, nostalgia, pessimism, hiding behind rules and regulations."[110] As many of the items on this list indicated, Francis is more concerned with the stylistic failings of the conventionally religious than he is with those of the irreligious. These failings focus on shoring up imaginative dams against the flood of the outside world. By contrast, *GE*'s "hospitable style," as Jiménez Rodríguez calls it, "does not enter into violent relations either with postmodern pluralism nor with the coexistence of diverse ways of living in the world."[111] The style of *GE* thus reflects a rhetoric of meekness that refuses to see the other (or other ideas or modes of life) as rivals to be defeated through traditional argument.

Most importantly for the present argument, the central purpose of *GE* is to move its readers toward holiness. It thus takes up Lundberg's central theme in the unapologetic and intentional theological register of Christian tradition: "At its core," Francis writes, "holiness is experiencing, in union with Christ, the mysteries of his life" (20). It may be hard to see how such claims could be construed as post-Christian. My claim, however, is that *GE* construes holiness within the framework of complicit invention that we have observed throughout this book. Throughout *GE*, Francis articulates holiness through a tension between the ordinary and the extraordinary. This is the enabling *agon* through which Francis produces a holiness that is for ordinary people but that makes extraordinary demands. Francis insists, "He [the Lord] wants us to be saints and not to settle for a bland and mediocre existence" (1). But he also makes clear that holiness is not reserved for saints. Francis is talking to what he calls "the middle class of holiness" (7), those who make up of "the humblest members" of the people of God (8). It is this seeming contradiction—an extraordinary demand on ordinary people—that articulates the tension through which Francis moves, inventing while resisting any temptation toward resolution or synthesis. Francis implicitly construes holiness as a kind of topos whose frontiers (topoi are almost-empty places) are set by the gravitational tension between the ordinary and the extraordinary.

Outside the church, holiness has come to be "regarded as a special sort of hybrid hobby for the piously impractical at best, and escapist sissy stuff for the weak at worst."[112] Things are no better inside the church, where another theologian asserts that holiness "remains one of those 'I know it when I see it,' vague and impressionistic theological concepts that escape the grip of any attempt at explicit definition."[113] Facing this problem, Francis does not pursue the kind of *"a transformation through a translation that maintains the meaning intact"* urged by Latour.[114] Rather, he is pursuing something closer to Girard, who insists that we have to "recycle our stock of old labels."[115] This recycling is what Francis attempts in *GE*, and his approach resonates with the protocol of convalescent distortion and impious piety described in chapter 3. Though Francis would be no more likely than Girard to endorse Vattimo's expression of this protocol, Francis's idea of holiness reflects the same complex relation to tradition, which Francis defines with recourse to the American religious scholar Jaroslav Pelikan: "Tradition is the living faith of the dead, traditionalism is the dead faith of the living."[116] Those who cling to the latter to the exclusion of the former Francis describes not as traditionalists but as "backwardists."[117]

Written to laypeople, *GE* is not an academic study of holiness, nor is it an analytic attempt to isolate holiness as a phenomenon. Rather, it is an attempt to move readers toward holiness: "What follows is not meant to be a treatise on holiness, containing definitions and distinctions helpful for understanding this important subject, or a discussion of the various means of sanctification. My modest goal is to repropose the call to holiness in a practical way for our own time, with all its risks, challenges and opportunities" (2). Such a project cannot help but imply some redefinition, but redefinition is not his primary aim, at least not in the kind of analytical sense we observe in the sociological war over the sacred. Francis makes absolutely clear that he is not after analysis. "There can be any number of theories about what constitutes holiness, with various explanations and distinctions. Such reflection may be useful, but nothing is more enlightening than turning to Jesus' words and seeing his way of teaching the truth" (63). Narrative and example—what Girard would call positive mimesis—is the most persuasive available means of holiness.

One can see this tension between Francis's construal of holiness as a mission and his insistence that it is a mission for all. First, the idea of mission: in keeping with the themes around the sacred that we have observed in this chapter, Francis understands holiness to be a call, "a powerful summons to all of us. You too need to see the entirety of your life as a mission" (23). In the opening chapter, "The Call to Holiness," Francis repeatedly uses the word "mission" to characterize the nature of the call, crystallizing this idea in a line he borrows from the theologian Hans Urs von Balthasar: "life does not have a mission, but is a mission" (27). To ignore this is to settle for the "bland or mediocre existence" against which Francis warns. For a Catholic audience especially, the radicalness of this exhortation is unmistakable, so unmistakable that Francis immediately has to reassure his readers. "Do not be afraid of holiness" (32). In offering this assurance, Francis seems to worry that his readers will think holiness will somehow sap one's "energy, vitality, or joy" (32). (Perhaps this equation of holiness and joylessness is a particularly Roman Catholic hang-up.) Whatever its source, however, Francis spends on entire section offering this reassurance: "Do not be afraid to set your sights higher, to allow yourself to be loved and liberated by God. Do not be afraid to let yourself be guided by the Holy Spirit. Holiness does not make you less human, since it is an encounter between your weakness and the power of God's grace. For in the words of León Bloy, when all is said and done, 'the only great tragedy in life, is not to become a saint'" (34). For Francis's audience, saints are likely to be perceived as so extraordinarily virtuous that they cannot be models in a Girardian sense. But Francis is pushing back against this perception. One does not need to fear that holiness will somehow separate one from what makes us human. Nor does it isolate us from ordinary life. "We are frequently tempted," he writes, "to think that holiness is only for those who can withdraw from ordinary affairs" (14). But the "middle class of holiness" cannot withdraw. They cannot be the typical saintly heroes enshrined in stained glass. Francis quotes St. Teresa Benedicta of the Cross: "Certainly the most decisive turning points in world history are substantially co-determined by souls whom no history book ever mentions. And we will only find out about those souls to whom we owe the decisive turning points in our personal lives on the day when all that is hidden is revealed" (8). Most holiness is hidden from public view.

Francis even challenges the notion that saints are extraordinarily virtuous. In his estimation, the saints are not a special class who possess special powers. "Their lives may not always have been perfect, yet even amid their faults and failings they kept moving forward and proved pleasing to the Lord" (3). Holiness is not a matter of a moral code, as some notions of atonement theology would have it. "Not everything a saint says," he adds, "is completely faithful to the Gospel; not everything he or she does is authentic or perfect" (22). Though he does acknowledge that saints may display heroic virtue and, of course, self-sacrifice, saintliness is not for heroes only. It is not a "heroic" virtue at all. It is not reserved only for "those already beatified and canonized. The Holy Spirit bestows holiness in abundance among God's holy and faithful people" (6). We might recall here Girard's suspicion of heroism, which he links to violent religion.[118] "We are never completely ourselves unless we belong to a people. That is why no one is saved alone, as an isolated individual" (6). Striking a Levinasian note, he closes the second chapter this way: "Jesus clears a way to seeing two faces, that of the Father and that of our brother. He does not give us two more formulas or two more commands. He gives us two faces, or better yet, one alone: the face of God reflected in so many other faces" (61). For Francis, holiness is not an individual project but one entirely dependent on sustaining the exposure to the other. We must belong to others if we have any hope of holiness.

At the same time, that belonging does not imply uniformity. In keeping with the Second Vatican Council, one's approach to holiness can be particular to that person. We are called "each in his or her own way" (10), as outlined by Vatican II.[119] Some people have in fact read *GE* as an extension of *Lumen Gentium* ("Light of Nations"), a document promulgated in 1964 as one of the central statements of Vatican II. *Lumen Gentium* is a "dogmatic constitution," a public document that in effect "legislates" church teaching on important matters. In the case of *Lumen Gentium*, the matter in question concerns the roles of members of the church's project of salvation, from the pope to the clergy to all believers. Key to this statement is its fifth chapter, "The Universal Call to Holiness in the Church," which makes clear that each and every member of the church is called to holiness: "Therefore, all the faithful of Christ are invited to strive for the holiness and perfection of their own proper state."[120] *GE* intensifies this general call. But rather than concentrating on the various "ranks" in the church (i.e., bishop, priest, catechists, etc.), Francis concentrates primarily on the laity: "To be holy does not require being a bishop, a priest or a religious" (14). Francis also reflects the rhetorical, accommodating practice of the Society of Jesus, of whom Francis is a member, writing that "all are called to be witnesses, but there are many actual ways of bearing witness." There are no "hard and fast rules for all" (11). Finally, Francis's understanding of holiness also reflects a Girardian theorhetoric: we need models, but models whom we follow by means of singular rhythms, produced by repetitions that also occasion change: "There are some testimonies that may prove helpful and inspiring, but *that we are not meant to copy*, for that could even lead us astray from the one specific path that the Lord has in mind for us" (11; emphasis added).

Though Francis has insisted that he is writing to and for an audience of ordinary Christians, he then takes a somewhat surprising turn by beginning a discussion of Gnosticism and Pelagianism, two early Christian heresies that he describes as "two subtle enemies of holiness," the title of the second chapter. The introduction of a pair of somewhat obscure and archaic terms seems to threaten Francis's project to speak to the middle class of holiness, and in this chapter, he does occasionally slip into the specialized language of a theology seminar, speaking of "anthropocentric immanentism disguised as Catholic truth" or a "narcissistic and authoritarian elitism" (35). He describes Gnosticism as "a purely subjective faith whose only interest is a certain experience or a set of ideas and bits of information which are meant to console and enlighten, but which ultimately keep one imprisoned in his or her own thoughts and feelings" (36). Perhaps this shift to more elevated language is meant to address those who have succumbed to the temptation of Gnosticism, those who "judge others based on their ability to understand the complexity of certain doctrines" (37). Gnostics essentially reduce faith to an intellectual project, one that serves to "'domesticate the mystery,' whether the mystery of God and his grace, or the mystery of others' lives" (40). "Mystery" is the keyword in Francis's discussion of Gnosticism; he continually pivots to the claim that there is a mystery at the heart of faith and doctrine that cannot be known or grasped.[121]

Gnosticism becomes a prelude to Pelagianism, which becomes its mirror and rival. If Gnosticism reduces holiness to knowledge, Pelagianism reduces holiness to will: as Francis quotes his own *Evangelii Gaudium*, Pelagians "ultimately trust only in their own powers and feel superior to others because they observe certain rules or remain intransigently faithful to a particular Catholic style" (94). Contemporary Pelagians refuse to acknowledge human limitation or finitude. "Unless we can acknowledge our concrete and limited situation, we will not be able to see the real and possible steps that the Lord demands of us at every moment" (50). Ironically enough, the "heroic" virtue of Pelagianism actually disables one from hearing the divine summons. The Pelagian cannot core out the self in a way that opens up the possibility of real contact. It is this second heresy that allows the church to "become a museum piece or the possession of a select few. This can occur when some groups of Christians give excessive importance to certain rules, customs or ways of acting" (58).

By the third section, Francis is fully recycling the old forms by reimagining the Beatitudes, the central teachings of the Sermon on the Mount (Matt. 5:3–12; Luke 6:20–23), known by their anaphoric structure: "Blessed are the poor, blessed are the peacemakers" or sometimes "Happy are the poor, happy are the peacemakers." Francis describes the Beatitudes as "a Christian's identity card," the best answer to the question of what Christianity is. "There can be any number of theories about what constitutes holiness, with various explanations and distinctions" (63). All well and good, Francis suggests, but the best explanation of holiness is expressed in the Beatitudes, where the word "'happy' or 'blessed' thus becomes a synonym for 'holy'" (64). Already, Francis is embarking on the kind of translation project imagined by Latour, a project that he continues throughout the third chapter. Though the Beatitudes are among the most iconic Christian scriptural texts, GE reimagines them as expressions of holiness. Each section addresses a different beatitude, and each closes with a refrain of religious translation. "Blessed are the meek" becomes "Reacting with meekness and humility: that is holiness."

Francis proposes meekness in a world beset by "conflict, disputes and enmity on all sides, where we constantly pigeonhole others on the basis of their ideas, their customs and even their way of speaking or dressing" (74). Against this, Francis proposes meekness, citing some of the key texts cited in the present book's chapter 1 (Matt. 11:29, 21:35; Zech. 9:9; Gal. 5:23, 6:1; 1 Pet. 3:16; 2 Tim. 2:25). "In the Church," he writes, "we have often erred by not embracing this demand of God's word" (73). Francis adds, "Meekness is yet another expression of the interior poverty of those who put their trust in God alone. Indeed, in the Bible the same word—anawim—usually refers to both the poor and the meek" (74). Francis is at pains to make sure that "poor" is understood to include the materially poor as well as the spiritually poor. "Poor in spirit" is not to be understood as only an "interior" state independent of actual material security or precarity (67–68, 70). It is a condition and a call that demands solidarity, as Francis makes clear in his discussion of "Blessed are those who mourn." Against a world saturated with "entertainment, pleasure, diversion and escape," in which the "worldly person ignores problems of sickness or sorrow" (75), holiness calls one to suffer with those who suffer. Those who mourn "sense that the other is flesh of our flesh, and are not afraid to draw near, even to touch their wounds" (76). In keeping with the understanding of meekness developed in chapter 1, Francis's notion of "blessed are the peacemakers" is not one that is conflict-averse. To be

142 PERSUASIONS OF GOD

"artisans of peace," as *GE* puts it, requires that one "face conflict head-on" (89). As with the injunction to mourn with those who mourn, the art of peace will be demanding and difficult.

GE is not without its critics, even among Francis's admirers. Despite the radicalness of this call, Francis occasionally slips into shopworn commonplaces, including and especially his persistent blind spot toward women and their alleged "feminine styles of holiness." In keeping with the orientation of *GE*, Francis's stated intention is to call attention to the "unknown or forgotten women" who "tended to be most ignored or overlooked" (12). But he does so in a way that betrays his persistent sexism. He imagines the "small gestures" of holiness through the example of a woman who is tempted to gossip but resists and who then goes home and listens to her children despite being tired (16). As Jamie Manson observes, "Perhaps Francis thought he was being cutting edge by using a female character in his paradigmatic example of the path to holiness, but the scenario reveals that his perception of women's lives continues to be painfully antiquated."[122] Later in the document, he argues that there is no humility without the risk of humiliation, without being willing occasionally to suffer in silence. While this may be true in the abstract, concretely it reads differently for women than men. Francis insists that he is not taking about masochism (120), but even with this caveat, he leaves open the kind of dangers we examined in chapter 3, in which the example of a suffering Christ is interpreted as an endorsement for putting up with abuse.

Nevertheless, Francis also construes holiness as a form of *parrhesía*: "it is boldness, an impulse to evangelize and to leave a mark in this world" (129). Francis thus invites the very sort of criticism articulated by Manson. As we might expect from Francis's comments on style, *parrhesía* is not only a matter of speaking boldly but also a means of living boldly. "Those who choose to remain neutral, who are satisfied with little, who renounce the ideal of giving themselves generously to the Lord, will never hold out" (163). This includes work for political change; holiness means that commitment cannot be reduced to private works of charity (99). But nor can it be the pursuit of political change without regard for the "luminous mysticism" characteristic of the saints (100).[123] Maintaining a relation between the two, especially in a relation of tension, seems necessary for inventing a topos of holiness that includes the irreducible ethical relation and the *mysterium tremendum* that outstrips our representational faculties.

Such tension is a characteristic notion not only of *GE* but of Francis's overall thinking. Borghesi describes the profound extent to which Francis's thought is articulated through the idea of *coincidentia oppositorum* or *complexio oppositorum*, which Jorge Mario Bergoglio (prior to be elected pope) described as "a unity that does not annul differences or reduce conflict."[124] There is a unity, Bergoglio insists, but not a unity that is meant to resolve conflict in a synthesis.[125] "The unity of the Christian is a dramatic, agonical [*sic*] unity, projected in the eschatological expectation of a fulfillment that only Christ can achieve."[126] Agonism is not resolved in the notion of unity in Francis's thought; it is preserved. This kind of preservation of difference and maintenance of conflict is key to the thinking of many of Francis's influences, including the theologians Romano Guardini (1895–1968) and Alberto Methol Ferré (1929–2009). Methol Ferré, for example, describes the danger of synthesis in this way: "Placing emphasis on a single pole ends to deviation and heresy; if a rectifying, corrective movement is not permitted, it becomes contradictory opposition. . . . The balance is always unstable, moving, being restored."[127] The instability is a requirement of maintaining a living tradition. Citing Guardini, Francis insists that "opposition opens a path, a way forward": "Speaking generally, I love oppositions."[128] He is not interested in "easy 'compromises' or cheap 'irenicism.'"[129]

The maintenance of this tension is required to practice a life of holiness. Otherwise, Francis writes in *GE*, the risk is "to sink into an obscure mediocrity" (90). The holy person must therefore strike out into a sea of oppositions, complexities, and tensions.[130] Perhaps not surprisingly, then, the pursuit of holiness requires a life of "constant and healthy unease" (99). This phrase is perhaps the most demanding aspect of the call to holiness, the central requirement of not sinking into an obscure mediocrity. To respond to social injustice and exclusion, to sit with conflict and disagreement, to relate religiously to the many who do not share the theology of the church and the many more who have been alienated by it—all of these require a kind of permanent discomfort or restlessness.

Conclusion

I began this chapter with Ellul's assertion that Christianity had been so compromised by its propagation that the word itself should be replaced by the letter "X." I end with an exhortation written by Pope Francis. From the most radical post-Christian theorhetoric imaginable, we turn to a theorhetoric so obviously and traditionally Christian that it would seem to undermine the goal of this entire project. The urge to reconcile these positions would contrast with Francis's own inclination to let oppositions stand.

In place of the label "Christian," Ellul suggested that only authentic Christian life, expressed within community, could convince anyone that the Gospel had something to say. This idea is captured in a line frequently but erroneously attributed to St. Francis of Assisi: "Preach the Gospel always. When absolutely necessary, use words." That St. Francis almost certainly did not say this is beside the point; the line nevertheless captures as essential idea about theorhetoric, which is that deeds are more persuasive than words. In *Evangelii Nuntiandi, The Proclamation of the Gospel*, Pope Paul VI emphasized the importance of witness: "Modern man listens more willingly to witnesses than to teachers, and if he does listen to teachers, it is because they are witnesses."[131] To be sure, Paul VI also argues that the Gospel must be explained in words and traditional preaching.[132] The "X" label will not suffice. But before the label "Christian" can have any meaning, there must be Christian life, "proclaimed by witness. Take a Christian or a handful of Christians who, in the midst of their own community, show their capacity for understanding and acceptance, their sharing of life and destiny with other people, their solidarity with the efforts of all for whatever is noble and good."[133] The way of living should set Christians apart, but the Christians themselves are not set apart. They stand in solidarity with others, sharing their destiny.

This locates the witness in the world, where the constant and healthy unease of holiness becomes the ethos of the infinitely more demanding form of religion imagined by Girard.[134] That Christianity can no longer lean on the sacrificial crutches of exclusion. It cannot steady itself through rivalry, with other traditions, with secularity, or even with different versions of itself. That does not mean that Girard would be in any way content with Ellul's argument (which is, after all, ultimately offered as a thought experiment). For Girard, the "idea of silencing Christianity in the name of Christian humility is a Christian idea gone mad."[135] But the trajectory of his thought points toward a Christian solidarity with and within the world, rather than a triumphalist Christianity set apart. For Girard as for Francis, the more evocative word in "post-Christian" is "Christian," but that word must be articulated through the "post" topos for a context in which its commonplaces have been subverted by Christianity itself. This, too, is part of the uneasiness demanded by Francis's call to holiness: any recovery of Christianity is also always a recovery from it; the latter is predicated on the former.

Acknowledging this recovery is essential to an authentically Christian theorhetoric and, judging by Francis's trip to Canada, remains an unfinished project. Such a theorhetoric would be meek in its loving apathy, sacrificial in its hospitable emptiness, atoning in its suffering solidarity, holy in its healthy unease. In this almost-empty place of exposure, one has the best chance of encountering the God-who-is-*probably*, the God who has no rivals, not because God has triumphed but because God has triumphed by refusing rivalry itself.

Postscript | Holy Envy

No philosophical thought will master the shift to charity.
—René Girard, *Battling to the End*

As I close this book, I think about further directions of theorhetorical inquiry, along with future engagements between mimetic theory and rhetorical theory. The future of theorhetorical inquiry raises many possibilities. What other theo-rhetorics might be invented with and within other religious traditions, in alienated relation to such traditions, or even outside of such traditions altogether? What else might be learned about religion, the sacred, the holy—along with rhetoric's role in all those experiences—from pursuing a rhetorical encounter with René Girard? What other complicit Christian rhetorics might be invented for a post-Christian era? What other complicit religious and spiritual rhetorics proceed from other traditions? The second possibility raises other questions. First and most basically, what might mimetic theory teach rhetoric, and rhetoric mimetic theory? How might the study and teaching of rhetoric be different if we assume the Girardian account of mimetic desire to be true? What might such a starting position reveal to us about rhetoric's role in argument, conflict, or reconciliation? Many of these potential projects would also claim the theological as a place for rhetorical invention and inquiry. (This would be the theological with a small *t*.) Such projects need not take the character of "big" rhetoric, in which other fields are revealed as secretly rhetorical, or for that matter of "little" rhetoric, in which rhetorical tropes and figures are observed within the symbolic exchange within other fields. Instead, recalling James Crosswhite, such projects might pursue a deep rhetoric, a rhetoric that observes the way in which various appeals and means of cooperation imply any community's ultimate questions and deepest aspirations.

My particular project has focused on Christianity, an area of religious inquiry that remains urgent, despite—or perhaps because of—premature reports of its demise. The reinvention of meekness, sacrifice, atonement, and holiness provides the barest beginnings of post-Christian theorhetoric. Even if rhetoricians confine their attention to lexicon alone, the scope of the work remains formidable. What, for example, might be the post-Christian understandings of salvation? Of judgment? Of forgiveness or faith? There is an endless need for new permutations of old language. And that is before rhetoricians turn to rhetorics of liturgy, ritual, contemplation, meditation, and prayer, all of which are arguably richer rhetorical contexts than the theological concepts I have studied here. These other domains require the sort of bodily, sensory, and material rhetorics that remind us that whatever "religion" may be, it is not merely verbal, cognitive, or even emotional. The Jesuit priest and antiwar activist Daniel Berrigan was once asked this question: "Is faith where your head is or where your heart is?" He is supposed to have replied, "Neither; faith is where your ass is." Liturgy, ritual, meditation, contemplation, prayer—these remind us that religion is not so much a matter of what a mind thinks as what a body does. Perhaps religious rhetoric cannot be reinvented until we truly apprehend this fact. If there is a critique to be made of the arguments I have presented here, it is that they are too conceptual, too much in the head. Still, if one recognizes the persuasions of God—that God enters situations, adopts styles, entertains and offers appeals—then there will always be a need for lexical reinvention. Religion is what a body does, but bodies often do what a language says.

Christianity is of course not the only tradition that might be reinvented by theorhetorical inquiry. Work is already under way in reading non-Christian and non-Western traditions in relation to mimetic theory. Scholars have produced work on the mimetic insights provided by the other major world religions of Buddhism, Islam, and Hinduism.[1] Girard's short work *Sacrifice* also contributes to this effort through a study of the Brahmanas of Vedic India. Despite Girard's exclusivist claims for Christianity, even he saw that non-Western religious traditions also detect the dynamics of mimetic theory. In his final major work, *Battling to the End*, Girard writes that Christ, by decisively separating the holy from the sacred, "*also* confirmed the divine that is within all religions."[2] And as we have already seen, the insights expressed in the Christian scriptures are founded on insights already in the Jewish scriptures. As a religious critique, then, not only is mimetic theory inherently interreligious; it also forces scholars and adherents of Christianity to recognize the Jewish roots of their faith.

As a starting place for a reader interested in the interreligious application of Girard's thought, I turn briefly to Rabbi Jonathan Sacks's *Not in God's Name*, an exploration of both interreligious conflict and the ways in which religion might resist such conflict.[3] Sacks uses mimetic theory to explain why antisemitism remains so intractable, particularly in Christian and Islamic cultures. There are many historical reasons, but following Girard, Sacks argues that the heart of the problem is mimetic desire. Why do the two younger children of Abraham so often vent their fears and anger upon the oldest? "Their relationship," writes Sacks, "is one of sibling rivalry, fraught with mimetic desire: the desire for the same thing, Abraham's promise."[4] Were these three cultures radically different, Sacks argues, they might each consider themselves specially chosen and simply ignore the others. But they all lay claim to the same covenant. It is the basic problem of the model-obstacle, in which subjects cannot face the fact that their desires are borrowed from their seeming rivals. Mimetic theory also helps explain the paradoxical nature of antisemitism, which combines two contradictory ideas. The first condition is that the scapegoat cannot fight back. "*If the scapegoat were actually powerful, it could no longer fulfil its essential function as the-victim-of-violence-without-risk-of-reprisal.*" The second condition, however, is that the scapegoat must be perceived as powerful enough to pose a threat: "*if the scapegoat were believed to be powerless, it could not plausibly be cast as the cause of our present troubles.*"[5] Thus, the other must be cast as conspiratorial, shadowy, sinister.

In just the past few years, the United States—to take the example of just one nation—has seen an alarming rise in antisemitic violence: Nazis chanting in Charlottesville in 2017, eleven Jews murdered at the Tree of Life synagogue in Pittsburgh in 2018, another murder at Chabad of Poway synagogue in California in 2019, a hostage incident at a Texas synagogue in 2022, along with innumerable smaller incidents of violence. Both the Anti-Defamation League (ADL) and the Center for the Study of Hate and Extremism at California State University, San Bernadino, report record levels of antisemitic hatred in 2021 and 2022. The ADL's 2023 *Audit of Antisemitic Incidents 2022* found a 36 percent increase in antisemitic incidents tabulated in 2021, the highest number since the ADL began monitoring such incidents in 1979.[6] From the perspective of mimetic theory, this violence raises alarming questions. Even an allegedly post-Christian culture has yet to cast out its original sin. Though we might expect that the collapse of institutional Christianity would be followed by the collapse of this type of scapegoating violence, the evidence suggests otherwise. This resurgence of antisemitism places a rhetorical demand on churches to confront this evil explicitly and openly. In addition, this ongoing threat suggests that violence is no longer working. The scapegoating of Jews cannot mend a fractured US society. "Because of Jewish and Christian influence," Girard writes, "scapegoat phenomena no longer occur in our time except in a shameful, furtive, and clandestine manner. We haven't given up having scapegoats, but our belief in them is 90 percent spoiled. The phenomenon appears so morally base to us, so reprehensible, that when we catch ourselves 'letting off steam' against someone innocent, we are ashamed of ourselves."[7] But the fact that victimage no longer works has not yet indicated that victimage will cease. If victimage is a *pharmakos*, it remains a highly addictive one, precisely because its effects are no longer as powerful as they once were.

The identification of the victim ruins the illusion that scapegoating would seek to maintain. But the undoing of that illusion means that order must find some other way of maintaining itself. For Girard, it was unclear whether we would find a way to save ourselves from ourselves, whether the revelation of scapegoating would be enough to free us from its lure. This question confirms the paradoxical sense in which Christianity is both religion and antireligion: "Christ took away humanity's sacrificial crutches and left us before a terrible choice: either believe in violence, or not; Christianity is non-belief."[8] Contrary to conventional wisdom, authentic religion demands that we stop believing—in rivalry, violence, scapegoating. But, freed of that false belief, we now face the challenge of relating to others without recourse to sacrificial habits. Being religious in a post-Christian sense is a matter of confronting the violence born within oneself and nurtured, as often as not, within religious communities. A complicit Christian rhetoric demands examination of Christian complicity. "Hope," Girard writes, "is possible only if we dare to think about the danger at hand."[9] Hope demands constant attention to the sources—and history—of violence as the mark of a post-Christian witness. Though Girard might resist this latter demand as a Christian humility gone mad, he also implies the need for it when he rejects the topos of an "essential" Christianity versus a "historical" Christianity. "On the contrary, we have to think of Christianity as essentially historical."[10] Without a historical consciousness, Christianity cannot address the heart of violence, including its own. Girard captures this difficult position—a position in which Christianity does and does not overcome itself—by borrowing a line from Friedrich Hölderlin: "But where danger threatens / That which saves from it also grows."[11] If the sacred is a means of putting away danger by pharmacologically concentrating it, the holy finds salvation by recognizing the ways in which the contagion was always already within.

The question is how this difficult posture might be maintained. One way would be to practice what the Lutheran theologian Krister Stendahl called "holy envy."[12] For Stendahl, holy envy is a foundational practice of interreligious study and dialogue that asks us to identify the value and beauty in traditions different from our own. That is to say, holy envy asks us to name our desires and to identify how those desires are occasioned and animated by other traditions. Certainly the idea that envy might be made holy may seem strange at this point in the book. For Girard, once described as "the prophet of envy," envy is the source of all our troubles: the spark of our resentments, the fuel of our conflicts.[13] Yet the inescapability of mimetic desire means that we have no choice but to make our envy holy. Paradoxically, holy envy becomes precisely the kind of practice and attitude that rhetoricians should cultivate, not only as an interreligious virtue but as a professional, social, and personal one.

As an interreligious virtue, the need for holy envy is made plain by Sacks's analysis of the roots of antisemitism. The sibling rivalry felt by the younger children of Abraham cannot be alleviated without their admission of mimetic desire. The first covenant belongs to the eldest, and contrary to common misunderstandings about some decisive break with the past, that covenant has never been abrogated. God has seen fit to express Godself in new ways without erasing or canceling any of the old ways. That means that we must welcome the other so that the most divine promise may be realized: "There is more than one way of being-in-the-world under the sovereignty of God."[14] Sacks demonstrates the ways in which this message is both essentially Jewish and utterly universal. The witness to God's covenant is paradoxically articulated through scriptures that relentlessly expose the foibles and failings of their own authors. "The Hebrew Bible is the supreme example of that rarest of phenomena, a national literature of self-criticism."[15] It is also a national literature of sibling rivalry, in which the older is so often displaced by the younger: Cain and Abel, Jacob and Esau, Joseph and his brothers. From these stories of sibling rivalry, Sacks concludes that "biblical ethics is a prolonged tutorial in role reversal."[16] Isaac, not Ishmael, is recognized as Abraham's legitimate heir. Joseph, not his older brothers, becomes the greatest. Jacob, not Esau, becomes Israel. Yet the scriptures also demand that the reader imagine what it is like to be the one left outside, to be Hagar, Ishmael, or Esau.

This reversal is encoded in the Lord's foundational command to his chosen people: "You shall not wrong a stranger or oppress him, for we were strangers once in the land of Egypt" (Exod. 22:20). This command is a warning against what Sacks calls "pathological dualism," which would divide people (and, we could add, nonhuman animals, other living creatures, and nonliving things) into camps— the inside and outside, the blessed and the cursed, the saved and the damned, even the animate and inanimate.[17] Perhaps we must begin to define the religion to which we might aspire as any set of beliefs, practices, scriptures, and liturgies that resist pathological dualisms. Meanwhile, Christians must practice a holy envy by recognizing their debt to Judaism and by imitating the capacity for self-criticism. We find the roots of such capacity in the Gospels, which relentlessly expose the failures of the apostles, particularly Peter, the rock on whom the church is built. For Christians, a holy envy would more readily admit what we want: an understanding of the incarnation as God's most radical antisacrificial act. Christians would thus acknowledge the central theological difference between Christianity and Judaism, a difference that cannot be elided or erased. But they would also acknowledge that their understanding of that difference is understandable only through a framework made available by Judaism in the first place.

As a professional rhetorician interested in religion, I have other envies I would make holy. I recognize my own desires in Sacks's implicitly rhetorical claim about religion: *"Religion is at its best when it relies on strength of argument and example. It is at its worst when it seeks to impose truth by force."*[18] Certainly, religious rhetorics will be embodied, emplaced, and enacted, but they must also be argued, a claim that not only requires traditional rhetorical activity but recognizes the inherent ethical norm of such activity. "To argue," writes Henry Johnstone, "is inherently to risk failure, just as to play a game is inherently to risk defeat. An argument we are guaranteed to win is no more a real argument than a game we are guaranteed to win is a real game."[19] In the game of rhetoric, argues Robert Wess, the only rule is that rules can be changed. Johnstone, however, reminds us of the one rule that cannot be changed: if you play the game, you might lose. Religion is at its best precisely when it risks failure, which is to say that it adopts persuasion as its way of proceeding. When persuasion fails—as it frequently will—we will know we are playing the game in a way that recognizes more than one way of being-in-the-world under the sovereignty of God.

This is a lesson that God teaches. In a study of God's interactions with Abraham, Moses, and Job, David Frank observes that the God of the Hebrew scriptures is persuasive—willing to persuade and willing to be persuaded. God gives way to appeals to ethics, compassion, and justice, as we see in Abraham's defense of Sodom and Gomorrah (Gen. 18:23–24). In the Hebrew Bible, human creatures have the capacity to persuade God to change, and God is willing to lose the game (even if God sulks sometimes). "God's arguments with Abraham, Moses, and Job make claims open to conscious scrutiny and criticism; freedom reigns."[20] That freedom also extends to the arguments themselves. In a Jewish style of rhetoric and argumentation, even "defeated" claims are preserved as the game continues. "Unlike the classical tradition," writes Frank, "this reversal of terms in Jewish thought does not mean the elimination of or lack of respect for the second term, as philosophical pairs nest opposites in the same system; philosophy and rhetoric can coexist, apodictic logic and argumentation can complement one another."[21] For "classical tradition," we might read Christian/ Hellenistic tradition, in which the game of argument is more likely to name a clear winner and loser.

God's persuasive capacity is perhaps most apparent in his arguments with Job, in which Job rightly accuses God of being unjust. "It is Job, not God, who emerges as the character seeking *Tsedek* [justice]."[22] God, moreover, never quite meets Job's arguments on their own terms; God's final speech simply overpowers Job, a fact that is obscured in Christian translations of the Bible, in which Job concedes that he is out of his depth: "I have dealt with things that I do not understand; things too wonderful for me, which I cannot know" (42:3). But this appears to be a bowdlerization of the original Hebrew, better captured in Jack Miles's translation: "You know you can do anything. Nothing can stop you. You ask, 'Who is this ignorant muddler?' Well, I said more than I knew, wonders quite beyond me.' You listen, and I'll talk,' you say.'" Miles's version gets closer to Job's sarcasm and frustration. We might even call it a form of the meek defense, insofar as Job's acquiescence to the Lord's overpowering diatribe is a challenge rather than compliance. In fact, writes Miles, "Job has won. The Lord has lost."[23] "With this defeat," writes Frank, "God falls silent; this is God's last argument in the Hebrew Bible." But even though God falls silent, God's argumentative persuasion has been definitively established, as has the human capacity and obligation to "remain true to justice in the face of power."[24]

As this turn to the book of Job suggests, my own envy, which I would seek to make holy, is drawn toward the argumentative God witnessed to in Jewish rhetorics. Frank's work is a representative example of this rich rhetorical tradition, which has been recovered and explicated by Michael Bernard-Donals, Patricia Bizzell, Davida Charney, Janice Fernheimer, Lauren Fitzgerald, Susan Handelman, and Deborah Holdstein, along with many others.[25] How, I am prompted to ask, might Christian tradition have developed differently if it had recognized God's argumentative capacity? What if Christianity had remained more attuned to the incarnational, a God so wrapped up in human creatures that God had to come to earth to argue with them? Recalling Kenneth Chase, what if we had understood that Christ is "embodied persuasion"? "That we ever came to believe anything other than this is, theologically speaking, heretical."[26] For the Christian religious rhetorician, to read of the Jewish capacity for argument with God is to feel an envy, an envy that must be made holy by seeing it as aspirational rather than rivalrous.

As both a social and personal virtue, finally, I want to suggest holy envy as the avenue to positive or loving mimesis, both in and outside of religious traditions. Recall Girard's claim that mimetic desire is not something from which we can simply withdraw. Because we always have models who animate and occasion our mimetic desire, the only question is whether we are in rivalry with these models. If we are, the question becomes whether we can adjust our relations to be more salutary or whether we need to find different models. The potential for envy is always there; how do we direct it so that it becomes holy? From the perspective of mimetic theory, the fundamental question of becoming rhetorical—of developing the capacity for rhetoric as an orientation, a stance, or a practice—is attending to the question of discerning models. Mimetic theory recalls rhetoric's most fundamental insight, which is that imitating the forms and styles of another is not a "mere" surface matter. Rather, it is to express the deep desire to inhabit another's being. To imitate therefore is to risk one's very being, to place a wager on a model as a means of becoming. For this reason, rhetorical pedagogies, religious or otherwise, must take account of the interdividual dynamics observed by Girard. It must even cultivate them. In so doing, it might equip students with the capacity to recognize not only their need for models but also the way in which they are always already bound up with models, the way in which their desires have been borrowed. In this way, rhetorical pedagogy might serve to make envy holy by acknowledging where it is complicit and where it is competitive. If antagonism is conflict degraded by mirroring—that is, reflexive, reactionary imitation—agonism might be defined as conflict elevated by deflecting imitation toward some pacific model outside the present confrontation. Only by this aspirational desire, this holy envy, can we unlock ourselves from reflexive, rivalrous conflict.

Cultivating such desire is the work not only of rhetorical education but also of self-persuasion, which is to say, practices that have been described by Michel Foucault as "technologies of self" and by Pierre Hadot as "spiritual exercises."[27] As rhetoricians continue to rethink notions of agency, subjectivity, intention, art, and *techne*, we would do well to consider this scholarship. Daniel Gross's *Being-Moved* leads us in this direction in his claim that rhetoric is "not a skill but rather a way of life, dependent upon what kind of life one lives."[28] To see rhetoric a way of life reframes arguments about whether rhetoric is primarily ontology, condition, technique, or capacity. All are encompassed in the idea that rhetoric is a way of being in the world. Gross further develops this idea in his attempts to name the kind of passive-active subjectivity that might emerge from deep rhetorical listening. Two of these attempts include forms of life that imply the need for practices of self-persuasion: (1) "directed inaction," which Gross links to Stoicism, and (2) *satyagraha*, the term that Mahatma Gandhi coined to name the style of nonviolent resistance practiced in the Indian independence movement. Each of these analogies imply not simply tactics or strategies for a deeper form of listening rhetoric but rather ways of life and attendant practices of self-persuasion.

To take *satyagraha* first, the word refers to the kind of nonviolent resistance used in the Indian independence movement and later in the US civil rights movement. It was a strategy of nonviolent noncooperation with British imperial forces with the aim of gaining self-governance. Gandhi coined the term from the Sanskrit words *satya*, meaning "truth," and *āgraha*, meaning "polite insistence." This etymology suggests that *satyagraha* is something like a rhetoric of meekness, which confronts the violence of oppression without mirroring the violence of the oppressor. Gandhi's vision for the *satyagrahi*—the practitioners of *satyagraha*—was extremely rigorous and explicitly religious. The *satyagrahi* was to keep vows, including vows to truth, universal love, chastity (even within marriage), sobriety, and a nonpossessive attitude toward all things. In addition, Gandhi insisted both on a living faith in God and on an equal respect for all religious faiths.[29] What this admittedly brief overview should suggest is that, for Gandhi at least, *satyagraha* should not be considered a tactic or even an overall strategy but rather a total way of life that demanded rigorous ascetical practices from all those who would pursue it. My point here is not to recommend these particular practices but rather to insist that invoking *satyagraha* as a model for an appropriate kind of rhetorical passivity or vulnerability also implies the need for similarly rigorous styles of self-discipline.

The same is true for Stoicism. In *Philosophy as a Way of Life*, Pierre Hadot argues that in the ancient world, philosophy "appears in its original aspect: not as a theoretical construct, but as a method for training people to live and to look at the world in a new way." For the Stoics, along with the Epicureans and the

Platonists, the "proof" of the philosophy is in the living, not the arguing.[30] Most importantly for a discussion of rhetorical practice, Hadot observes a central role for the language arts in a truly philosophical way of life, including "the rhetorical and dialectical techniques of persuasion, the attempts at mastering one's inner dialogue, and mental concentration."[31] These were part and parcel of philosophy's "spiritual exercises," a phrase made popular by Ignatius Loyola's *Spiritual Exercises* (1522–24), which itself is an inheritor of the philosophic tradition described by Hadot. Michel Foucault also confirms the centrality of spiritual exercises to philosophic discipline. These included "purification, ascetic exercises, renunciations, conversions of looking, modifications of existence, etc.," all of which were undertaken "not for knowledge but for the subject, for the subject's very being, the price to be paid for access to the truth."[32] The disciple took up spiritual exercise not to "learn philosophy" in the contemporary sense of that phrase but rather to become a different sort of person. "The philosophical act," writes Hadot, "is not situated merely on the cognitive level, but on that of the self and of being. It is a progress which causes us to *be* more fully. It is a conversion which turns our entire life upside down, changing the life of the person who goes through it."[33] My point here is not to trigger another round of philosophy versus rhetoric (nor is it to suggest Stoicism, a philosophy incommensurate with Christianity's attitude toward suffering, as a model for a post-Christian theorhetoric). Rather, my point is to suggest once again that, insofar as Stoicism may be a model for rhetorical passivity, its self-discipline and self-persuasion are likewise implied.

The stakes of such practices are high: they may turn a life upside down and cause the practitioner *to be* more fully. For a post-Christian theorhetorical subjectivity, Loyola's *Exercises* may prove particularly apt in that they have often been seen "as a paradigm of a spirituality of desire."[34] For Ignatius, desires could be "ordered," meaning oriented toward the love of God, or "disordered," meaning attached to distractions from that love. Even outside religious confession, we can distinguish between desire ordered toward our highest hopes and aspirations and the disordered desires that serve only to distract. Further rhetorical engagement with mimetic theory will animate questions of how desire both animates persuasion and interferes with it. These questions will lead rhetoric to consider those practices of self-persuasion that ask us to name what we want, the first step to making desires holy.

Burke also recognized that to practice rhetoric was to practice a way of life. In *The War of Words*, Burke insists that his aim in studying rhetorical devices is not to teach his readers to employ them more effectively. "Rather, we aim at an ethical approach to them, a method of meditation or contemplation that should be part of a 'way of life.'" The purpose of such a method is not, Burke clarifies, to "win" at the "Scramble." The devices are "useful . . . not for throwing an enemy, but for purposes of solace and placement, and for the cultivation of mental states that make one less likely to be hurt by enemies."[35] Burke's view seems halfway to the meek rhetoric that I described in chapter 1. It is clearly a refusal of rivalry, but one whose primary purpose is not to practice a generous vulnerability or productive confrontation but rather self-protection.

Burke explains his position by sketching a scenario: two old friends meet. One is rich, the other poor; one has succeeded in the game of life, the other struggled. The old friends strike up a conversation, and the poor man follows the rich man to the latter's office to continue the catch-up. The conversation proceeds, with the rich man "swinging competently in his swivel chair," until the poor man voices a contrary opinion. At that point, the rich man, affronted, rises to his feet. "With Quiet Dignity, he has indicated that The Interview is Over." The poor man slinks away, humiliated at the curt dismissal he has received. "Now," wonders Burke, "what are you [the poor man] going to do with that?" You might feel sorry for yourself, vow vengeance, get drunk, take out your frustrations by kicking a dog. "Or drop into a dismal church and pray?"[36] It is telling that Burke seems to think that all these acts are equally futile. In contrast, Burke suggests a different method of meditation and contemplation, in which the poor man "collects" the incident as a specimen of a rhetorical situation. Rather than brooding on the incident, you can study it, classify it, compare it. You become a critic of situations rather than a victim of them.

For the aspiring rhetorician, the benefits of this advice seem clear. Through dispassionate analysis, one observes the rhetorical motivations in a variety of such situations, collecting data as a means of cultivating the comic frame. This approach even elicits a kind of empathy, in that the poor man may come to recognize that the rich man "was but handing down to you what had, by a superior in the office that very day, been handed down to him." The critic Lee Siegel argues that Burke is after "vicarious introspection," a process of "imagining yourself into the other person's 'inwardness.'"[37] The poor man recognizes that the rich man is himself wrapped up with some other model-obstacle. But ultimately, Burke's critical practice is concerned primarily about the poor man's interests, not the rich man's. It is about protection from vulnerability, not the cultivation of it as a means of more ethical encounter with the other. This rhetorical way of life moves the practitioner "*Stoically* in the direction of order, solace, placement."[38] The Stoic connoisseur of situations practices a kind of self-protective detachment.

This kind of detachment cannot be squared with either a Girardian anthropology or a post-Christian theorhetoric. Burke himself makes the latter point very clearly. In collecting the situation, he writes, the poor man is at least being honest. "You haven't lied to yourself. You haven't turned the other cheek. You haven't tried to persuade yourself that you love the stinker all the more. You haven't made up fantasies of some great table-turning day in the future, when *you* can rise as a sign for *him* that the interview is over."[39] Here, Burke's usual care in separating religion's uses from its misuses deserts him, as he dismisses (and misunderstands) key Christian teachings about turning the other cheek, loving one's enemies, and reversing the first and the last.

The limitations of Burke's approach are also revealed by Girard's insight into mimetic desire. The two friends are rivals. The rich man is model-obstacle for the poor man; otherwise, there would be no need to manage his poisonous desire for revenge by drinking himself into a stupor or kicking the nearest dog. Such a transparent act of scapegoating might relieve some pressure from the abscess, but it will not heal it. The poor man is trapped, as are we all, in the dynamics of mimetic desire, dynamics that can distort our personalities or enrich them. Yet Burke's method of detachment does not seem to recognize the pull of desire. Even the dismissal of religious response is distorted by the misrecognition contrary to Burke's cynical characterization: the point of the poor inheriting the earth is not so that they may lord it over the rich. In Burke's hands, prayer becomes a way to anesthetize anger, and the meek defense becomes a delayed revenge.

If, as Girard suggests, philosophical thought cannot alone engender the compassion necessary to resist scapegoating, we will need practices that reach deeper even than rhetorical connoisseurship. We will need practices that order desire rather than denying it. This is especially true for theorhetorics, whose transcendent aspirations make it particularly vulnerable to rivalry's lure. A post-Christian theorhetoric will still find some of the needed resources even in dismal churches, and it will hold to the faith that loving one's perceived enemies might free both them and us from us-and-them.

Notes

Introduction

1. Other versions of this parable appear in Matt. 17:20 and Mark 4:30–32.

2. See also Ezek. 31:3–9.

3. Levertov, *Door in the Hive*, 83.

4. Mailloux, *Rhetoric's Pragmatism*, 86.

5. As Bruno Latour (riffing on William James) has argued, prepositions "mark a *position-taking* that comes *before* a proposition is stated, determining how the proposition is to be grasped and thus constituting its interpretive key." A preposition offers no specific domain of inquiry, but each "plays a decisive role in the understanding of what is to follow (*Inquiry into Modes of Existence*, 57).

6. Augustine, *On Christian Teaching*, IV.14, 103.

7. Meister Eckhart, *Complete Mystical Works*, 422 (emphasis added).

8. D. Davis, *Inessential Solidarity*, 2.

9. Rickert, *Ambient Rhetoric*, 33–34.

10. Hyde, "Introduction," xiii.

11. Bendavid, "Europe's Empty Churches."

12. As my invocation of "WEIRD" suggests, my interest is particularly within Western Christianity. This interest should not be taken to exclude global Christianities; rather, I mean to focus on the particular Christian inheritance that, for good or ill, has shaped and continues to shape the West. Catherine Keller would caution us about the Eurocentric nature of the entire death of God conversation: "frankly, the Euromodernism of the mere death of God and its posttheology still seem to evince dubious world-changing potential—*if* the world includes . . . the Americas, the populations of Latin America, Africa, and much of Asia" ("Theopoetics," 35).

13. See, for example, Berger, "Desecularization of the World."

14. Vahanian, *Death of God*, xxxiii. James Cone, considered the father of Black liberation theology, has critiqued death of God theology for its myopic focus on the problems of white Christianity: "If theology fails to re-evaluate its task in the light of Black Power, the emphasis on the death of God will not add the needed dimension. This will mean that the white church and white theology are dead, not God" (*Black Theology*, 89).

15. Vahanian, *Death of God*, xxxii.

16. Ibid., 5.

17. Ibid., 13.

18. Duve, "Come On, Humans," 665.

19. Gauchet, *Disenchantment of the World*, 4.

20. Vattimo, *Belief*, 21.

21. A 2018 Pew Research Center study, for example, finds that 72 percent of nones believe in God, and 17 percent of those describe that God as the God of the Bible ("When Americans Say They Believe in God"). Meanwhile, another 2018 Pew study found that only 21 percent of nones cite disbelief in God as a "very important" reason for religious disaffiliation. By contrast,

160 NOTES TO PAGES 7–13

51 percent cite their questioning of religious teachings as a very important reason, while 47 percent cite church leaders' political and social positions as very important reasons ("Why America's 'Nones' Don't Identify").

22. Burton, *Strange Rites*, 20–23.

23. Drescher, *Choosing Our Religion*, 28–29.

24. C. Taylor, *Secular Age*, 3.

25. Ibid., 299.

26. Ibid., 302.

27. Ibid., 595.

28. Altizer and Hamilton, *Radical Theology*, x.

29. Robbins, "Introduction," 2.

30. For Latour's early work in theology and its continuing influence on his work, see Lamy, "Sociology of a Disciplinary Bifurcation."

31. Latour, *Rejoicing*, 58.

32. Ibid., 60–61.

33. Ibid., 62.

34. Vahanian, *Death of God*, xxxi–xxxii.

35. Robbins, "Introduction," 13.

36. Poulakos, "Toward a Sophistic Definition," 36.

37. Boorstein, "Horn-Wearing 'Shaman.'" Some research suggests that the unchurched are more likely to succumb to Christian nationalism. When religious ideas or feelings become detached from institutional life, they are more prone to mutate into exclusionary identities: "As religious ideas and symbolism merge into secular life, they often lose much of their ethical and theological complexity but retain their power to draw group boundaries" (Stroope et al., "Unchurched Christian Nationalism," 406).

38. Wieseltier, "Christianism."

39. Elsewhere, Taylor writes of a "'neo-Durkheimian' effect, where the senses of belonging to a group and confession are fused, and the moral issues of the group's history tend to be coded in religious categories" (*Dilemmas and Connections*, 231). In the United States, Taylor notes, political identities can be easily woven into religious ones, with the result that powerful senses of in-groups and out-groups, along with senses of victimization, can metastasize. In addition, "the religious dimension also figures in what we might call the civilizational identity, the sense people have that the basic order by which they live, even imperfectly, is good and (usually) is superior to the ways of life of outsiders, be they 'barbarians,' 'savages,' or (in more polite contemporary language) 'less developed' peoples" (ibid., 151). This effect can lead to a "lashing out at such moments of threat in scapegoating violence against 'the enemy within'" (ibid.).

40. Dawson, *Flesh*, 134.

41. Ibid.

42. Flynn, "Emptying Town," 19.

43. Burke, *Rhetoric of Motives*, 23.

44. Ibid., 21.

45. Burke, "Rhetoric of Hitler's Battle," 219.

46. Haidt, *Righteous Mind*, 267–68.

47. Girard, *When These Things Begin*, 121.

48. Girard, *Violence and the Sacred*, 23. In this early work, Girard seemed to think religion was the source of violence, full stop. When he revealed the Christian turn in his thinking in his 1978 *Des choses cachées depuis la foundation du monde* (*Things Hidden Since the Foundation*

of the World), it came as something of a shock to his readers (Depoortere, *Christ in Postmodern Philosophy*, 34–35).

49. Latour, *Modern Cult*, 99.

50. Tracy, Westphal, and Zimmermann, "Theism, Atheism, Anatheism," 235.

51. E. Johnson, *Quest for the Living God*, 3.

52. Klemm, "Toward a Rhetoric," 444.

53. For the early decisive call, see Muilenburg, "Form Criticism and Beyond."

54. See Wuellner, "Where Is Rhetorical Criticism Taking Us?"

55. Ibid., 449.

56. Fiorenza, "Ethics of Biblical Interpretation," 15.

57. Milbank, *Theology and Social Theory*, 401.

58. Chase, "Christian Rhetorical Theory," 37.

59. Crosswhite, *Deep Rhetoric*, 28.

60. Ibid., 29.

61. Ibid., 79.

62. Ibid., 56.

63. White, *Kaironomia*, 14.

64. Ibid., 41.

65. Ibid. (emphasis added).

66. Muckelbauer, *Future of Invention*, 4.

67. Ibid., 12–13.

68. Lanham, *Style*, 152.

69. Muckelbauer, *Future of Invention*, 42, 43.

70. Booth, "Kenneth Burke's Religious Rhetoric," 32.

71. White, *Kaironomia*, 38–39.

72. Crosswhite, *Deep Rhetoric*, 17.

73. Medhurst, "Religious Belief and Scholarship," 43.

74. Fasching, *Ethical Challenge*, 5.

75. Bultmann, "What Does It Mean to Speak of God?," 53.

76. Grassi, *Rhetoric as Philosophy*, 113.

77. Wiman, *My Bright Abyss*, 75.

78. Norris, *Amazing Grace*, 2.

79. Muckelbauer, *Future of Invention*, 5.

80. The notable exception is C. Allen Carter's *Kenneth Burke and the Scapegoat Process*.

81. See Bernard-Donals and Jensen, "Introduction"; Bessette, "Rightness in Retrospect"; and Frank, "Engaging a Rhetorical God." See also Crowley, *Toward a Civil Discourse*; and Worsham, "Moving Beyond the Logic of Sacrifice."

82. Otto, *Idea of the Holy*, 6–7.

83. Ibid., 12.

Chapter 1

1. Kearney dubs his approach "onto-eschatology." If ontology risks permanently reifying God, eschatology risks permanently deferring God. By contrast, onto-eschatology places a wager on the God who is coming, the God who has made promises and asked for promises in return. By wedding ontology to eschatology, Kearney seeks "to respect the otherness of the Exodic God without succumbing to the extremes of mystical postmodernism" (*God Who May*

162   NOTES TO PAGES 24–28

Be, 34). In rejecting metaphysical certainty, Kearney does not mean to reject the idea that God might be known at all. Appropriate hesitation about assertion should not lead to a refusal to venture any claim whatsoever. Kearney writes, "it is wiser to interpret divinity as a possibility-to-be than as either pure being in the manner of ontotheology, or as pure non-being in the manner of negative theology" (ibid., 4).

2. Ibid., 7.

3. Kearney, *Strangers, Gods and Monsters*, 187.

4. Chase, "Christian Rhetorical Theory," 25.

5. Putt, "Imagination," 967.

6. Crosswhite, *Deep Rhetoric*, 17.

7. Keller, "Theopoetics," 29.

8. This will become especially important in chapter 3's examination of atonement theology, which has often been presented on the grounds of theory and argumentation rather than the poetic and narrative grounds from which the very idea initially emerges.

9. Caputo, *On Religion*, 9. The theologian Elizabeth Johnson, though not associated with theopoetics, concurs: "The God of these sacred writings cannot be neatly categorized. Not only are the books diverse in literary genre, historical context, and theological insight, but the subject referred to as G-o-d is incomparable, untamed, beyond imagination. This God cannot be captured in the net of our concepts; no single portrait will suffice" (*Creation and the Cross*, 60).

10. Kearney, *Poetics of Modernity*, 147.

11. Miller, "Theopoetry or Theopoetics?," 8. Like Miller, J. Denny Weaver resists the idea that theopoetics can be simply described as "a hybrid of poetry and theology." Rather, it is "an entire way of thinking," in which ideas are "more than abstractions. They have form—verbal, visual, sensual—and are thus experienced as least as much as they are thought" ("Series Editor's Foreword," 14).

12. Keller, "Kearney's Endless Morning," 355–56.

13. Kearney and Clemente, introduction to *The Art of Anatheism*, viii.

14. Quoted in Keller, "Theopoetics," 31.

15. Ibid.

16. A concrete idea of theopoetics began to coalesce at a series of meetings at Drew University in the 1960s, though some scholars date the formal beginning of theopoetics to an address delivered by Stanley Hopper at the 1971 annual meeting of the American Academy of Religion. Titled "Literary Imagination and the Doing of Theology," Hopper's address offers this justification for the theoretical project: "The traditional symbol systems have been sprung: the classical metaphysical model for talking about 'God' and the manifold of our experience is no longer our 'house of being.' We are shorn and bereft of these plain and comfortable prerequisites" ("Literary Imagination," 207). Founded on metaphysical sand, the theological house needed to be rebuilt. Theology could no longer rely on "the model of logic or mathematics, but the model of language—of Logos as primary utterance." In Hopper's understanding of Christian tradition, theology founded on "propositional logic is founded upon a profound metaphysical error," an error in which the Cross serves to fix the meaning of Christ rather than liberating it ("Literary Imagination," 224). Another early progenitor of theopoetic enterprise was Amos Wilder, whose *Theopoetic: Theology and the Religious Imagination* helped beat the path first indicated by Hopper's address. (Wilder's 1971 *Early Christian Rhetoric* was also a path-finding work in interdisciplinary study of theology and rhetoric.) "Religious communication," Wilder writes in an echo of Hopper, "generally must overcome a long addiction to the discursive, the rationalist, and the prosaic" (*Theopoetic*, 1). These modes of expression no longer seemed suitable to the era, including and especially the 1960s counterculture. In an echo of Tertullian,

NOTES TO PAGES 28–33   163

Wilder asks, "What has Zion to do with Bohemia?" (*Theopoetic*, 46). The "creative crisis" of that time demanded that "the Christian faith should be reshaped in the same crucible where our secular voices arise" (*Theopoetic*, 39).

17. Keller, "Theopoetics," 29. There is a danger here, as John Caputo notes. "My lingering worry," he writes, "is that the death of God theologies are themselves thinking disguised *grands récits*" ("Spectral Hermeneutics," 68). If the death of God becomes its own metanarrative, then metaphysics will have sneaked through the back door of the effort to dismantle metaphysics. Caputo also suggests that there is a danger of an inadvertent antisemitism in that particular expressions of such theologies may reinscribe the idea that Christianity has moved us all "beyond" Judaism ("Spectral Hermeneutics," 82–83). These are also questions that can be put to Girard, and we will revisit them in chapter 3. Yet, it seems impossible to deny that something has irrevocably shifted. "After the terrors of Verdun, after the traumas of the Holocaust, Hiroshima, and the gulags, to speak of God is an insult unless we speak in a new way" (Kearney, *Anatheism*, xvi).

18. Keller, *Intercarnations*, 105–6.

19. Keller, "Theopoetics," 30.

20. Caputo, "Theology, Poetry, and Theopoetics," 45.

21. Ibid., 46 (emphasis added).

22. Caputo, *On Religion*, 13.

23. Ibid., 37.

24. Kearney, "God After God," 10.

25. Wood and Kearney, "Theism, Atheism, and Anatheism," 15.

26. Miller, "Theopoetry or Theopoetics?," 8 (emphasis added).

27. Keller, "Theopoetics," 29 (emphasis added).

28. Caputo, *On Religion*, 69–70.

29. Crosswhite, *Deep Rhetoric*, 17.

30. Muckelbauer, "Returns of the Question."

31. Wess, *Kenneth Burke*, 27.

32. Girard, *Mimesis and Theory*, 287; Girard, *Theater of Envy*, 127, 349; Girard, *Violence and the Sacred*, 1.

33. Wess, *Kenneth Burke*, 38.

34. Latour, *Rejoicing*, 17.

35. Poulakos, "Toward a Sophistic Definition," 36.

36. White, *Kaironomia*, 17.

37. Ibid., 20.

38. Ibid., 39.

39. Ibid., 41 (emphasis added).

40. Ibid., 42–43.

41. Ibid., 38–39.

42. Medhurst, "Religious Belief and Scholarship," 43.

43. Wiman, *My Bright Abyss*, 16.

44. Ibid., 17.

45. Chase, "Christian Rhetorical Theory," 30. Theologically speaking, it is a mistake to construe the Incarnation as a kind of "persona" that God adopts, an idea that inserts a "hidden dualism" that separates actor and spectator. To construe God in this way is to subject God "to the structures of our own consciousness" (ibid., 32). It is also to deny the Trinity and the concomitant idea that Jesus is at once divine and human. To understand Jesus as a "persona" of God is to reassert the idea that "Truth" is "the transcendent content clothed in the immanent body and speech of Jesus. Rhetoric, accordingly, would be part of the immanence that must

164   NOTES TO PAGES 33–40

be discarded in the search for the truly transcendent" (ibid., 34). Chase continues, "From the perspective of the incarnation ... truth is not separable from the material world or from suasory appeal. In Christ, truth is embodied persuasion. That we ever came to believe anything other than this is, theologically speaking, heretical" (ibid., 35). Guided by Chase, we can read Medhurst's idea of "Truth/truths" not as a demarcation of transcendent and immanent but rather as the friendship with contingency offered by the Incarnation.

46. Ballif, "Divining Rhetoric's Future," 159.

47. D. Davis, *Inessential Solidarity*, 2.

48. Ibid., 3.

49. Crosswhite, *Deep Rhetoric*, 39.

50. Stormer and McGreavy, "Thinking Ecologically," 5.

51. Ibid., 3.

52. The *Westminster Theological Dictionary* defines "kenosis" as a "theological term for the 'self-emptying' of Jesus Christ in which he took the form of a slave or servant ... to accomplish the work of salvation through his death and resurrection" (Richardson and Boden, *Westminster Theological Dictionary*, 153). Theologically, that does not mean that Christ loses his divine nature but rather that he makes himself vulnerable in taking on a human nature. In classical Greek usage, *kenosis* has a negative connotation, referring to defect or lack. This is how Plato seems to use it (see *Republic* 585b and *Philebus* 35b). It can also refer to medical evacuation, such a purging or vomiting, or a deficient or restricted diet. Generally speaking, Paul tends to use the term in a similar way (Rom. 4:14; 1 Cor. 1:17, 9:15). The hymn of Philippians is unique in this regard.

53. E. Johnson, *Creation and the Cross*, 178.

54. Pender, *Techne*, 16.

55. Ibid., 32.

56. Quoted ibid., 137.

57. Gross, *Being-Moved*, 137.

58. Ratcliffe, *Rhetorical Listening*, 17.

59. Gross, *Being-Moved*, 132.

60. Muckelbauer, *Future of Invention*, 42.

61. Ibid., 43.

62. Lanham, "'Q' Question," 155.

63. Lanham is careful to point out that this runs counter to the spirit of Quintilian's work, which is a twelve-volume cradle-to-grave program for the education of the "good man speaking well." If Quintilian could reflexively insist that he was educating the good orator, it was because he was imagining a comprehensive liberal arts education in which an undergirding set of values would be consistently reinforced through years of study. Quintilian's curriculum "did not simply train, it created, the public person" (ibid., 189).

64. Ibid., 156.

65. Ibid.

66. Ernesto Grassi formulates the argument this way: "It is clear the first *archai* of any proof and hence of knowledge cannot be proved themselves because they cannot be the object of apodictic, demonstrative, logical speech; otherwise they would not be first assertions. Their nonderivable, primary character is evident from the fact that we neither can speak nor comport ourselves without them, for both speech and human activity simply presuppose them" (*Rhetoric as Philosophy*, 19). This is Grassi's version of the figure/ground shift of Lanham's strong defense.

67. Wess, *Kenneth Burke*, 37.

68. Lanham, "'Q' Question," 156.

NOTES TO PAGES 40–46   165

69. One finds an example of this virtuous virtuosity in St. Paul's First Letter to the Corinthians: "I have become all things to all, to save at least some" (1 Cor. 9:22). To be all things to all is perhaps the most ambitious wedding of *copia* and character and the surest means of rhetorical or religious salvation. In keeping with the meek defense, meanwhile, Corinthians is also where Paul makes a certain kind of weakness a virtue. "To the weak I became weak," he writes in the First Letter (1 Cor. 9:22). "If I must boast," he writes in the Second Letter, "I will boast of the things that show my weakness" (2 Cor. 11:30).

70. Crosswhite, *Deep Rhetoric*, 79.

71. Ibid., 79.

72. Grassi, *Rhetoric as Philosophy*, 113.

73. Lynch and Rivers, introduction to *Thinking with Bruno Latour*, 2.

74. Ibid., 4.

75. Ibid.

76. Mailloux, "Notes on Prayerful Rhetoric," 420.

77. Eagleton, "Lunging, Flailing, Mispunching."

78. Bultmann, "What Does It Mean to Speak of God?," 53.

79. Crosswhite, *Deep Rhetoric*, 188.

80. Mailloux, "Notes on Prayerful Rhetoric," 425.

81. Heidegger, *Being and Time*, 314.

82. Ibid., 320.

83. Ibid., 312.

84. Mailloux, "Notes on Prayerful Rhetoric," 428.

85. Marback, "Meditation," 3.

86. Ibid., 2.

87. Ibid., 4.

88. Ibid., 6.

89. Crosswhite, *Deep Rhetoric*, 188.

90. Marback, "Meditation," 10.

91. Butler, *Force of Nonviolence*, 71.

92. In the Christian scriptures, meekness (*praus, praeia, prau*) is distinguished from weakness (*astheneia*). "Meek," according to Danker and Krug's *Concise Greek-English Lexicon*, refers to having a temperate attitude, to being gentle or patient (296), as in "Take my yoke upon you and learn from me, for I am meek and humble of heart; and you will find rest for yourselves" (Matt. 11:29) or "Say to daughter Zion, / 'Behold, your king comes to you, / meek and riding on an ass, / and on a colt, the foal of a beast of burden'" (Matt. 21:5; cf. Isa. 62:11, Zech. 9:9) and, of course, "Blessed are the meek, for they will inherit the land" (Matt. 5:5). Danker and Krug explicitly contrast meekness to weakness (*astheneia*), which is a negation of the root *sthenos*, or strength (57–58). The antonym they offer is *dunamis*, the word Aristotle employs for "power" in the *Rhetoric*. There are understandable reasons to be wary of the idea of meekness, which in classical Greek was used to refer to the taming of animals, according to Liddell and Scott (*Greek-English Lexicon*). In *On the Art of Horsemanship*, Xenophon uses *praos* to describe the "gentle aids" that one should use when training a horse. The term *praos* was also used to describe people but often with context of unequal power relations. Plato uses the term in *Republic* to mean "gentle" (in opposition to *chalepous*, or "harsh") to refer to the guardians of the Republic, who must be both gentle and harsh (*Rep.* 375). Writing in late first-century CE Koine Greek, Flavius Josephus uses the term in *Jewish Antiquities* in reference to Herod giving a lighter punishment than expected to those who tried to overthrow him near the end of his life (*Antiquities* 17.6.4). In this light, the radicalness of Jesus's statement that the meek shall inherit the land becomes all the more clear.

166 NOTES TO PAGES 46–56

93. Elsewhere, invocations of meekness seem to recall the older sense of a social superior foregoing their status and power, as in Jesus's invocation of Sirach (51:23–26): "Take my yoke upon you and learn from me, for I am meek and humble of heart; and you will find rest for yourselves" (Matt. 11:29), and the evangelist's invocation of the prophet Zechariah: "Say to daughter Zion, / 'Behold, your king comes to you, / meek and riding on an ass, / and on a colt, the foal of a beast of burden'" (Matt. 21:5).

94. Wink, *Engaging the Powers*, 176.

95. Ibid., 176.

96. Butler, *Force of Nonviolence*, 195–96.

97. Ibid., 196.

98. Bobbio, "In Praise of Meekness," 29.

99. Wess, *Kenneth Burke*, 38.

100. Bobbio, "In Praise of Meekness," 24.

101. Ibid., 24.

102. Burke, *War of Words*, 46–47.

103. Ibid. (emphasis added).

104. Ibid., 140.

105. Ibid. (emphasis in original).

106. Ibid. (emphasis in original).

107. Ibid., 253.

108. Rivers, "Apathy," 141.

109. Ibid., 149.

110. Ibid., 147.

111. Wess, *Kenneth Burke*, 38.

112. Rivers, "Apathy," 147.

113. Brock and Parker, *Proverbs of Ashes*, 72–73.

114. See Haidt, *Righteous Mind*, 246–73.

115. Muckelbauer, *Future of Invention*, 4.

116. Ibid., 12.

117. Ibid., 13.

118. Ibid., 35.

119. Gross, *Being-Moved*, 135.

120. Girard, *Violence and the Sacred*, 23.

121. One of the challenges of working with Girard is whether and how to use the word "Bible," which means different things not only for Jews and Christians but also for Protestants, Catholics, and Orthodox Christians. Even the phrase "Christian Bible" seems to disregard disagreements about what is included. Wherever possible, I will specify the difference between the Hebrew Bible (i.e., the Tanakh) and the Christian scriptures (i.e., the "New Testament," as opposed to the "Old Testament"). I am wary of using these familiar terms, which can imply a supersessionist position: "new" as where we are headed, as opposed to "old" as what we have left behind. For a compelling argument against such relabeling, see Levine, *Misunderstood Jew*, 193–99.

Chapter 2

1. Dawson, *Flesh Becomes Word*, 134.

2. Girard, *When These Things Begin*, 121.

3. Burke, *Rhetoric of Religion*, 295.

NOTES TO PAGES 57–62   167

4. Knightley and Kennedy, *Affair of State*, 243.

5. Ward cannot be fully exonerated. Ward practiced a form of what we would now call grooming. It was he who often recruited young women to attend the parties with powerful associates such as Profumo (ibid., 173).

6. Davenport-Hines, "Ward, Stephen Thomas."

7. Knightley and Kennedy, *Affair of State*, 243.

8. Girard, *Violence and the Sacred*, 31.

9. Burke, *Rhetoric of Religion*, 5. Girard laments, "It is unpleasant to learn that the inner sanctum of human culture is really a putrefied core" (*Theatre of Envy*, 225).

10. Harrison, "Prophet of Envy."

11. Eagleton, *Radical Sacrifice*, 56.

12. Fleming, "Last of the Hedgehogs." See also Palaver, *Rene's Girard's Mimetic Theory*, vii.

13. Haven, *Evolution of Desire*, 113.

14. Latour, *We Have Never Been Modern*, 45.

15. Girard, *Resurrection from the Underground*, 88.

16. Girard, *When These Things Begin*, 121.

17. Wright, "Christian Challenge."

18. Kallscheuer, "Girard and Religion," 111. Regarding Girard's anthropology, Elizabeth Traube offers an important challenge. Like many critics of Girard, she describes Girard's work as having "the old-fashioned ring of a somewhat troubling voice from our own past" ("Incest and Mythology," 37). The past is one of confidence that human cultures could not only be explained but be explained by a single, overarching principle. Traube acknowledges that Girard's victimage principle can explain a wide variety of myths but also argues that he can accomplish this analysis only by removing those myths from their original context and meaning. "Anthropological analysis of myth is less a matter of performing a single type of operation on a text to elicit its meaning than of creating, through a multi-faceted investigation, the environment in which a text *has* meaning" ("Incest and Mythology," 44–45). The question Girard does not pursue is how the materials might be meaningful to the cultures from which they emerge. As a piece of anthropological critique, Traube's argument is quite persuasive, and it shows why some skepticism toward Girard's empirical claims is warranted. Yet, as a basis for religious critique, Girard's seemingly reductive hermeneutic—which Traube does admit has some explanatory power—indicates the lurking danger of violence in a great deal of religious expression.

19. Manning, "Emmanuel Levinas and René Girard," 23n1.

20. Girard, *When These Things Begin*, 120.

21. Alberg, "Return of Religion," 360.

22. Girard, *Things Hidden*, 249.

23. Latour, *Rejoicing*, 15 (emphasis added).

24. For excellent overviews of Girard, see both Kirwan, *Discovering Girard*, and Palaver, *René Girard's Mimetic Theory*.

25. Girard, *When These Things Begin*, 129.

26. Girard, *Deceit, Desire, and the Novel*, 2.

27. Ibid., 16.

28. Girard, *Things Hidden*, 8.

29. Ibid.

30. In this way, Girard's early work echoes Burke's even prior to their shared interest in scapegoating. William Rueckert has described Burke as "the only writer I know of who has ever developed an inclusive system out of a theory of literature" (*Kenneth Burke*, 5). Girard is another. He initially discovers his anthropological interest by reading European novelists,

168   NOTES TO PAGES 63–65

including Cervantes, Dostoyevsky, Flaubert, Proust, and Stendhal, before turning to the Bible, Athenian tragedy, and Shakespeare. Girard holds that "literature and religions reveal something *fundamental* about the real world—they are not simply imaginative exercises or unintelligible gibberish" (Darr, "Mimetic Desire," 358).

31. Adams and Girard, "Violence, Difference, Sacrifice," 23.

32. Ibid., 25.

33. To be sure, Girard had recognized this necessity of desire prior to his interview with Adams. In *Things Hidden*, Girard writes, "If human beings suddenly ceased imitating, all forms of culture would vanish" (7).

34. See Redekop, *From Violence to Blessing*, 260–69. To illustrate her point, Adams analyzes an episode of the television series *Star Trek: The Next Generation*. Captain Picard, commanding officer of the starship *Enterprise*, meets a "metamorph," a humanoid alien who has been engineered to mirror the desires of her companions to please them. In Girardian terms, her subjectivity has been deliberately distilled into pure and unadulterated mimesis. The *Enterprise* has been tasked with taking her to her final destination, where she will be offered as a peace gesture in some interplanetary conflict. When the metamorph meets Picard—who neither desires her nor approves of this mission—she begins inevitably to imitate his desire for her independence. She begins to achieve something that students of Paulo Freire might call "critical consciousness," though not with an entirely happy outcome. Because Picard feels bound by duty, the metamorph does, too. As a result, she concludes that it is her duty to go through with the arranged marriage. Though this conclusion is not entirely independent, it is closer to a free choice than was possible before. Picard has desired for her; she begins to desire for herself, even if the audience may lament rather than admire this outcome. As Adams notes, "fiction sometimes knows more than philosophy" (Redekop, *From Violence to Blessing*, 261).

35. Girard, *Violence and the Sacred*, 49.

36. Ibid., 241.

37. Bessette, "Rightness in Retrospect," 232.

38. Girard, *Violence and the Sacred*, 4.

39. Ibid.

40. Ibid., 8.

41. Worsham, "Moving Beyond the Logic of Sacrifice," 33.

42. Fiske and Rai, *Virtuous Violence*, 5.

43. Ibid. The relations Fiske and Rai describe tease out dynamics toward which Girard only gestures: *communal sharing, authority ranking, equality matching*, and *market pricing*. Communal sharing speaks to the need for unity and community identity; authority ranking, to the distinctions that maintain order; equality matching, to the management of reciprocity (e.g., the *lex talionis*); and market pricing, to ways communities calculate value among distinct goods (ibid., 18–21). Violence that maintains these relationships will be seen as moral precisely because it maintains these relationships.

44. Girard, *Theatre of Envy*, 204.

45. Burke, *Rhetoric of Religion*, 4–5.

46. Girard, *I See Satan Fall*, 70. Girard finds a thematization of this phenomenon in Shakespeare's *Julius Caesar*. When Decius tells Caesar, "from you great Rome shall suck / Reviving blood, and that great men shall press / For tinctures / stains, relics, and cognizance" (2.2.87–89), and when Brutus urges his fellow conspirators to "bathe [their] hands in Caesar's blood" (3.1.106), they both seem to agree that the victim is also a redeemer. For more, see Girard's *Theatre of Envy*, 185–226. In *Rhetoric of Motives*, Burke offers a more mundane example when he describes some boys who, playing in a vacant lot, stumble upon a rattlesnake and kill it. Afterward, the boys insist on having their pictures taken with the carcass and begin calling

NOTES TO PAGES 65–68   169

themselves the "Rattlesnake Club." "The snake was a sacred offering; by its death it provided the spirit for this magically united band" (*Rhetoric of Motives*, 266).

47. Girard, *Violence and the Sacred*, 19.

48. Ibid., 23.

49. Girard, *Things Hidden*, 34.

50. Caruana offers this phrase in an examination of a critique of the sacred offered by Emmanuel Levinas, who thematizes the issue in a much more sustained way (see "Not Ethics"). While these thinkers did not cross paths, their hesitations about the sacred resonate deeply with each other. Sandor Goodhart writes that Girard and Levinas "are both in the process of describing the passage from the sacred to the saintly or holy" (*Prophetic Law*, 204). Emmanuel Levinas describes himself as a thinker of the holy: "You know, one often speaks of ethics to describe what I do, but what really interests me in the end is not ethics, not ethics alone, but the holy, the holiness of the holy" (Derrida, *Adieu to Emmanuel Levinas*, 4).

51. Girard does make occasional references to the "holy" as an alternative (Hardin and Berry, *Reading the Bible*, loc. 105/181; Girard, Antonello, and Castro Rocha, *Evolution and Conversion*, 218). We will return to the topic in chapter 4.

52. For Freud, the motivating factor is sexual jealousy; for Girard, it is mimetic desire, which is the ultimate source of sexual jealousy. Girard reinterprets Freud in *Violence and the Sacred*, 193–222.

53. Girard, Antonello, and Castro Rocha, *Evolution and Conversion*, 138.

54. Girard, *Battling to the End*, ix.

55. Harrison, "Prophet of Envy." To Robertson-Smith and Frazer, Girard argues that the Jewish and Christian understandings of sacrifice represent an epochal religious innovation, which is to say—particularly contra Frazer—that those scriptures are not simply repetitions of archaic patterns of sacralized violence. Frazer, Girard argues, mistakenly takes scapegoating to be a metaphor rather than "a way of expressing a circumstance that has actually taken place at the threshold of human culture" (Girard, Antonello, and Castro Rocha, *Evolution and Conversion*, 138). To Freud, meanwhile, Girard argues that the "founding murder" described in *Totem and Taboo* is not the result of a primary sexual drive but rather is simply a subset of mimetic conflict (*Violence and the Sacred*, 193–222). The violence at the threshold of human culture is the product of mimesis. If Girard's argument to Frazer can be made with appeal to the Bible, Girard's argument with Freud depends entirely on speculative guesses about the evolution of *Homo sapiens*. For more on Girard's ideas of evolution, see Girard, Antonello, and Castro Rocha, *Evolution and Conversion*, especially chapters 3 and 4.

56. Gorringe, "Atonement," 369.

57. Leviticus 16 describes the annual rite of purification of the Tabernacle, elsewhere described (Lev. 23:27, 28, 25:9) as *yom hakippurim*, or "Day of Atonement." ("Atonement" is another Tyndale coinage.) The text reads, "the goat designated by lot for Azazel shall be left standing alive before the Lord, to make expiation with it and to send it off to the wilderness for Azazel" (Lev. 16:10). Azazel is understood to be a kind of demon. According to the *Jewish Study Bible*, the word "Azazel" can be divided into two words, *ez* and *azel*, which can be translated as "the goat that goes away," carrying the people's sins away as a kind of sacrifice to the wilderness demon (232n8). Tyndale's neologism "scapegoat" is meant to translate this word; only later does the word take on the modern meaning of someone who is unjustly blamed for community sins.

58. To take one example, in the story of Joseph in Genesis, we read of eleven brothers driven by envy who turn on their youngest brother, the twelfth and the favorite. They betray him and sell him into slavery in Egypt. Joseph is scapegoated for the unity of his brothers in a drama of mob violence, and he is again scapegoated in Egypt when he is falsely accused of seducing

170   NOTES TO PAGES 69–70

his master's wife. After languishing in prison, his ability to interpret dreams is made known to Pharaoh. When Joseph accurately predicts a famine, he is awarded the task of planning for it and thus becomes Pharaoh's right-hand man. Throughout his travails, the text makes clear that Joseph is innocent and that the stories his persecutors tell are lies. Moreover, he prospers despite the false accusations and suffering he endures. The text is telling the story of the victim, the story of the scapegoat. Later, when Joseph's brothers present themselves at Pharaoh's court in search of food during the famine, Joseph concocts a scheme in which he falsely accuses Benjamin, the youngest, of theft. He threatens to take him into slavery, a loss that will shatter their father, Jacob. In a sense, Joseph stages a scapegoating to see how his brothers will react. At this point, Judah, the oldest, steps forward and offers himself in place of Benjamin (Gen. 44:32–34). Judah offers to stand in the place of exclusion so that Benjamin will not have to, effectively reversing what happened to Joseph. This is a "sacrifice" in a positive sense: a self-forgetting for the sake of another.

59. Dawson, *Flesh Becomes Word*, 133. David Bentley Hart takes a somewhat similar view: "That Girard's arguments suffer from an occasional want of subtlety scarcely needs be said" (*Beauty of the Infinite*, 398).

60. Girard, *Things Hidden*, 131–32.

61. Ibid., 131.

62. Dawson, *Flesh Becomes Word*, 132.

63. Girard, *I See Satan Fall*, 116. That is not to deny that the Bible also features a fair bit of violence, some of it divinely endorsed. The Jesuit theologian Raymond Schwager counts more than six hundred passages of violence in the Tanakh and also notes that violent sacrifice remains an enduring theme of the Christian scriptures. But the question is not simply the presence of violence but rather what the violence means within the text. "The actual import of violence . . . becomes obvious only when one shifts from a quantitative to a qualitative consideration" (Schwager, *Must There Be Scapegoats?*, 47). Qualitative considerations transform the question from the sheer presence of violence in the text to its significance and import. "In the Hebrew Bible," says Girard, "there is clearly a dynamic that moves in the direction of the rehabilitation of the victims, but it is not a cut-and-dried thing. Rather, it is a process under way, a text in travail; it is not a chronologically progressive process, but a struggle that advances and retreats. I see the Gospels as the climactic achievement of that trend, and therefore as the essential text in the cultural upheaval of the modern world" (Burkert, Girard, and Smith, *Violent Origins*, 141).

64. Crowley, *Toward a Civil Discourse*, 98.

65. Girard's unusual notion of myth can lead to what may seem like ridiculous statements. As a colleague once put it to me, "I stopped reading Girard when he said that the evidence for his theory was that there was no evidence for his theory." The issue in question is Girard's notion of myth as stories whose primary purpose is to hide violence. So thoroughly do such stories work, Girard argues, that the stories sometimes lack violence altogether. If a myth includes such violence, Girard takes it as evidence of his hypothesis. But if a myth lacks violence, Girard also takes it as evidence for this theory by asserting that the myth is hiding the violence. At first hearing, this seems to create a "heads I win, tails you lose" argument. Yet the substance of Girard's argument is not so easily dismissed. Even in myths where violence seems absent, Girard notes the way in which a particular character disappears in some fashion. Perhaps a god leaps into heaven or becomes the earth or descends below the earth. It is this dynamic that Girard is referring to when he claims—with some measure of provocative mischief—that the evidence for violence is that there is no evidence.

66. Hardin and Berry, *Reading the Bible*, loc. 64/181.

67. Golsan, *René Girard and Myth*, 68.

NOTES TO PAGES 70–76   171

68. Girard, *Scapegoat*, 9.

69. Quoted ibid., 2.

70. Ibid., 6.

71. Crowley, *Toward a Civil Discourse*, 98.

72. Girard, *Things Hidden*, 126.

73. Girard, "Violence in Biblical Narrative," 392. See also Girard, *Job*.

74. Kearney, *Poetics of Modernity*, 143. See also Kearney, *Strangers, Gods and Monsters*, 26–46. Kearney also writes, "I have as much difficulty accepting that a single confessional theology has the remedy to the enigma of otherness as I would accepting similar claims for a positivist, Marxist, Freudian or any other interpretive model" (*Strangers, Gods and Monsters*, 41). That seems to be a reasonable conclusion. However, Kearney goes on to say, "Suffice it to say for now that what is needed, when confronted with extreme tendencies to demonize or deify monsters, is to look into our own psyche and examine our consciences in the mirror of our gods and monsters" (*Strangers, Gods and Monsters*, 42–43). This is precisely the conclusion that Girard draws from his reading of the Bible. That is not evidence that a *single* confessional theology *alone* has the remedy to the enigma of otherness, though it may be evidence that a particular theological tradition has gone a long way toward discerning the enigma of otherness. Kearney's laudable aversion to religious chauvinism does not undermine the possibility that the Hebrew and Christian scriptures have figured out an enduring, chronic problem of being human.

75. Kearney, *Poetics of Modernity*, 143.

76. Ibid., 145–46.

77. Ibid., 147.

78. Perelman and Olbrechts-Tyteca, *New Rhetoric*, 250.

79. Ibid.

80. Ibid., 251.

81. Eagleton, *Radical Sacrifice*, 4.

82. Houtman et al., introduction to *Actuality of Sacrifice*, 1.

83. Watts, "Rhetoric of Sacrifice," 4.

84. Detienne, "Culinary Practices," 20.

85. Detienne and Vernant, *Cuisine of Sacrifice*, 224n85.

86. Janzen, *Social Meanings of Sacrifice*, 3.

87. All Christian scriptural translations from the *New American Bible*.

88. Girard, *Things Hidden*, 200 (emphasis added).

89. Girard, *When These Things Begin*, 95.

90. Girard, *Battling to the End*, 49.

91. Goodhart, *Prophetic Law*, 68. Goodhart adds, "Girard never claims that Messianic status of Jesus, or his status as resurrected, has any methodological import. He argues theoretically only for the revelatory message of Jesus vis-à-vis sacrificial origins of culture" (ibid., 68). In a response to Goodhart, Girard nevertheless insists on the uniqueness of Jesus in that, through Jesus, God becomes the scapegoat. "What the Gospels and Christian theology really do is take this rapprochement . . . all the way to a complete identification" (ibid., 82). Goodhart replies, "The Christian Gospel . . . may be regarded as unique vis-à-vis Judaism. But its uniqueness does not necessarily reduce Judaism to its first step" (ibid., 90–91).

92. Ibid., 221.

93. Girard, *Battling to the End*, 113.

94. Burkert, Girard, and Smith, *Violent Origins*, 141.

95. In an essay on the presence of antisemitic attitudes in the Gospels, Girard writes, "Christianity, and prophetic Judaism, are the only examples of religions founded not on the

172 NOTES TO PAGES 76–78

blind acceptance of the founding murder but on a lucid rejection of it" ("Is There Antisemitism in the Gospels?," 346). In response to this essay, scholars cautioned Girard against dismissing the possibility of antisemitic or anti-Jewish readings of the Gospels. Joanna Dewey writes, "I find it crucial to distinguish between antisemitism encoded in the texts that would have been heard as such by their original audiences and the antisemitism that the texts in turn may generate when heard and used by later audiences" ("Response to René Girard," 355). Dewey argues that the latter problem troubles Girard's claim to the uniqueness of the Gospels. For more on this issue, see Darr, "Mimetic Desire."

96. Sacks, *Not in God's Name*, 76 (emphasis in original). For more, see ibid., chapters 4 and 5.

97. In 2021, for example, the Anti-Defamation League reported a massive spike in antisemitic violence, against both people and property (*Audit of Antisemitic Incidents*).

98. These include Girard, whose late work *Sacrifice* examines Vedic traditions from the perspective of mimetic theory. See also Palaver and Schenk, *Mimetic Theory and World Religions*, especially Collins, "Burning Desires, Burning Corpses"; Sheth, "Girard and Hindu Sacrifice"; Ericksen, "Tawhid"; and Lohlker, "Islam."

99. Girard, *Things Hidden*, 241–42.

100. This stance led Girard to reject the Epistle to the Hebrews because of its presentation of a theology of Jesus's death as a sacrifice. Girard was challenged on this point most intensely by Schwager, who began corresponding with Girard in the 1970s. In a letter to Girard dated April 22, 1978, Schwager writes, "Frankly, here I see a trace of sacrificial thinking. To *unify the NT, you throw out a text*" (Girard and Schwager, *Correspondence*, 59). The problem, they come to agree, is, as ever, one of vocabulary. "There is," Schwager wrote on March 29, 1978, "certainly a sacrificial *vocabulary* in this epistle [Hebrews]; but I think that we can demonstrate that it is only the *vocabulary* that remains sacrificial, and that the *content* is quite other than this" (*Correspondence*, 53). Girard eventually grants Schwager's point, conceding in an interview, "I give too much importance to that word [sacrifice]. That's one of the reasons of my misinterpreting Hebrews" (Adams and Girard, "Violence, Difference, Sacrifice," 28). For an "antisacrificial" (i.e., antiviolent sacred) reading of the Letter to Hebrews, see Poong-in Lee ("Is an Anti-sacrificial Reading of Hebrews Plausible?"), who defends the epistle against accusations of supersessionism by attending to its rhetorical function. Hebrews is a sermon exhorting its Jewish readers to persevere through a time of trial. Its appeal to the "new" example of the son as opposed to the "old" example of the prophets is therefore not intended as a supersessionist rejection of Judaism but rather as a motivating identification with Jesus. "Striking is the way the author's Christology develops out of a rhetorical engagement with his audience. Seeing them in their persecuted situation, the author sees Christ anew in them, even as he urges them to grow into a full conformity with Christ through mimesis" (Poong-in Lee, "Is an Anti-sacrificial Reading of Hebrews Plausible?," 432). But as Joanna Dewey would suggest ("Response to René Girard"), the meaning that contemporary readers might derive from that document makes it all the more imperative for ministers and theologians to challenge supersessionist assumptions that might lead to supersessionist readings.

101. Girard and Schwager, *Correspondence*, 99.

102. Girard, *One by Whom Scandal Comes*, 43.

103. Girard, "Literature and Christianity," 33.

104. Girard, *One by Whom Scandal Comes*, 44.

105. Girard, *I See Satan Fall*, 118.

106. I borrow the idea of a "rhetorical demand" from Ronald Arnett's *Levinas's Rhetorical Demand*, which similarly argues that Levinas, though uninterested and even hostile to rhetoric, produces insight that creates a need for rhetorical intervention (1–3, 7–13). See also David

Frank's "Origins of the Jewish Rhetorical Tradition," which extends Arnett's argument about Levinas to a larger Jewish rhetorical tradition.

107. Girard, *Things Hidden*, 233.

108. Girard, *One by Whom Scandal Comes*, 44.

109. Girard, *Things Hidden*, 241–42.

110. Vattimo and Girard, *Christianity, Truth, and Weakening Faith*, 37. This sense is confirmed, in the US context at least, by the ongoing reinvention of what constitutes "religion." See Burton, *Strange Rites*; Drescher, *Choosing Our Religion*; Pew Research Center, "When Americans Say They Believe in God"; and Pew Research Center, "Why America's 'Nones' Don't Identify."

111. Vattimo and Girard, *Christianity, Truth, and Weakening Faith*, 62.

112. Ibid., 63.

113. Girard, *Things Hidden*, 234.

114. Girard, *When These Things Begin*, 96.

115. Milbank, *Theology and Social Theory*, 399.

116. Ibid., 401.

117. Girard, *Battling to the End*, 50–51.

118. Milbank, *Theology and Social Theory*, 398.

119. Lucien Scubla also makes this point when he observes that Girard's interpretation of Christianity is "difficult to reconcile with the most solid parts of his fundamental anthropology. For . . . it is probably not knowledge which destroys the victimage mechanism" ("Christianity of René Girard," 178).

120. Hart, *Beauty of the Infinite*, 349.

121. Ibid.

122. Girard, *Things Hidden*, 399–400.

123. For some of those challenges, see Alison, *Joy of Being Wrong*; Kerr, "Rescuing Girard's Argument?"; and Kirwan, *Discovering Girard*. Grant Kaplan challenges Milbank on slightly different grounds, arguing that Milbank is ultimately mistaken to complain that Girard displaces theology in favor of anthropology (*René Girard*, 47–48). There is no doubt, Kaplan writes, that Girard is trying to present an anthropological theory that can stand on its own, apart from any faith claim. Yet at the same time, Girard's anthropological theory has clear implications for Christian apologetics. When Girard admits that he is searching "for the anthropology of the Cross, which turns out to rehabilitate orthodox theology" (*Girard Reader*, 288), he seems to give the game away as far as his claim to pursue a scientific hypothesis. Kaplan interprets this kind of position as a recognition of the limits of reason. Girard's pursuit of knowledge leads him toward the claims of faith; faith is necessary to turn the knowledge on one's own self and one's own culture. When Girard speaks of conversion, then, he is not speaking first and foremost of a religious conversion in a team-sport sense but rather a conversion to the realization that one cannot be saved by reason alone. Kaplan writes, "From Girard's admission of the limits of reason, however, there does not follow a plunge into irrationality. An admission of reason's limits, for Girard, is part and parcel with understanding reality under a graced horizon" (*René Girard*, 68).

124. Milbank, *Theology and Social Theory*, 401.

125. Scubla, "Christianity of René Girard," 160.

126. Alberg, "Return of Religion," 360.

127. Girard, *Things Hidden*, 249.

128. Girard, "Literature and Christianity," 32.

129. Kaplan, *René Girard*, 4. Kaplan frames his project as one of "fundamental theology," which seeks to "address the unbeliever and engage the reasons and the framework in which

174   NOTES TO PAGES 84–90

unbelief and even hostility toward the Christian message have become viable alternatives to believing" (ibid., 7). This is a project of apologetics, in which the purpose is not "*faith seeking understanding* but rather *unbelief* seeking *belief*" (ibid.). I understand the project of post-Christian theorhetoric in similar terms, though it does not seek belief but persuasion of probability. Put another way, a post-Christian theorhetoric seeks to be plausible and credible even in the absence of belief.

Chapter 3

1. Adams and Girard, "Violence, Difference, Sacrifice," 21.

2. For an examination of the rhetorical structure of Girard's arguments, see Bartlett, *Cross Purposes*, 160–66.

3. Girard, *Things Hidden*, 224.

4. Dawson, *Flesh Becomes Word*, 134 (emphasis added).

5. Girard, *Things Hidden*, 249.

6. Heidegger, "Overcoming Metaphysics," 85.

7. Ibid.

8. Vattimo, "Optimistic Nihilism," 38.

9. Vattimo, "Dialectics, Difference, and Weak Thought," 155.

10. Heidegger, "Overcoming Metaphysics," 85.

11. Ibid. Joan Stambaugh writes in a note to her translation, "Although Heidegger uses the familiar word *Überwindung* for 'overcoming,' he means it in the sense of the less familiar word *Verwindung*. When something is overcome in the sense of being *überwunden*, it is defeated and left behind. This is not the sense Heidegger intends here. When something is overcome in the sense of being *verwunden*, it is, so to speak, incorporated" (ibid., 84n1).

12. Heidegger, "Phenomenology and Theology," 51.

13. Ibid.

14. Vattimo, "Optimistic Nihilism," 37–38.

15. Ibid., 43.

16. Ibid., 38.

17. In a 1978 interview, Girard praises Burke for discerning the victimage principle, though he laments that it rates no higher than a "codicil" in Burke's "Definition of Man." But he also admires the way in which Burke's thought "points the way toward more rather than less 'danger,'" by which he means danger to entrenched critical habits. "That may be the reason he remains as marginal today as he was during the long reign of New Criticism. I am all for French influence, obviously, but I would like to see it sprout vigorous and truly independent offshoots on American soil. The day this happens, Kenneth Burke will be acknowledged as the great man he really is" (Girard, "Interview with René Girard," 220–21).

18. Burke, *Language as Symbolic Action*, 16.

19. Girard, "Interview with René Girard," 220.

20. Burke, *Rhetoric of Motives*, 31.

21. Mailloux, "Political Theologies of Sacred Rhetoric," 77.

22. Freccero, "Logology," 56.

23. Cavanaugh and Scott, introduction to *Blackwell Companion to Political Theology*, 2.

24. See Burke, *Rhetoric of Religion*, vi, 2, 4, 5. And yet, Burke also notes that there "is a sense in which language is *not* just 'natural,' but really *does* add a 'new dimension to the things of nature' (an observation that would be the logological equivalent of the theological statement that grace perfects nature)" (ibid., 8).

NOTES TO PAGES 90–96   175

25. Ibid., 268.

26. Rueckert, *Kenneth Burke*, 133–34.

27. Burke, *Permanence and Change*, 16.

28. Ibid.

29. Burke, "Rhetoric of Hitler's 'Battle,'" 218–19. Similarly, he adds, "People so dislike the idea of internal division that, where there is a real internal division, their dislike can easily be turned against the man or group who would so much as *name* it, let alone proposing to act upon it" (ibid., 206).

30. Burke, *Rhetoric of Religion*, 223.

31. Burke, "Philosophy of Literary Form," 26–27.

32. Biesecker, *Addressing Postmodernity*, 57.

33. Nelson, "Writing as the Accomplice of Language," 162.

34. Burke, "Rhetoric of Hitler's 'Battle,'" 208, 219.

35. See also Burke's late essay "Toward Hellhaven," where he imagines a dystopian future in which an elite has escaped the poisoned earth for a lunar "Culture-Bubble." These fortunates will spend their time in the "Super-Lookout, a kind of chapel, bare except for some small but powerful telescopes of a special competence. And on the wall, in ecclesiastical lettering, there will be these fundamental words from the *Summa Theologica*: 'And the blessed in Heaven shall look upon the sufferings of the damned, that they may love their blessedness the more'" (63).

36. Burke, *Rhetoric of Religion*, 217.

37. Ibid., 4–5. Part of the problem with critiquing religion may be the critical stance itself. As Carter notes, "Burke puts his faith in our ability to expose the darker side of myth to the light of critical analysis" (*Kenneth Burke*, 53). But as Worsham might observe, this stance describes "the dominant mode of cultural studies," which "reproduces a knowing subject that is deemed capable of critical consciousness through introspection and self-reflection" ("Moving Beyond the Logic of Sacrifice," 21). Given the psychology (Wess, *Kenneth Burke*, 221) underwritten by the iron law of history, Burke should have less faith in the critical stance.

38. Burke, *Rhetoric of Religion*, 295.

39. Ibid., 314.

40. Ibid., 181.

41. Wright, *Day the Revolution Began*, 76.

42. Ibid.

43. Maddux, "Finding Comedy in Theology," 222.

44. Crusius, "Case for Kenneth Burke's Rhetoric and Dialectic," 24.

45. Wess, *Kenneth Burke*, 221.

46. In his study of atonement theology, Stephen Finlan echoes Burke: "Underneath the shining sun of Christian triumphal faith, then, is the gloom of this ancient consciousness of *being stained*, which plays itself out in the extreme actions of ascetic saints and troubled believers throughout the centuries" (*Problems with Atonement*, 81). He continues, "Redemption-sacrificial doctrine perpetuates intense anxiety about a temperamental and judgmental God, firing a cycle of outbursts of rage or guilt, blame or self-blame. Superstition is a wolf that dons the sheep's clothing of 'selfless sacrifice' and 'innocent blood' and so enters into Christian theology and wreaks havoc in one generation after another" (ibid., 82).

47. Biesecker, *Addressing Postmodernity*, 67.

48. Burke, *Rhetoric of Religion*, 252.

49. Biesecker, *Addressing Postmodernity*, 71–72.

50. Ibid., 73.

51. Burke, *Rhetoric of Religion*, 314, 295.

176   NOTES TO PAGES 96–97

52. Cross and Livingstone, *Oxford Dictionary of the Christian Church*, s.v. "atonement," 124. As with "sacrifice," part of the problem with the word "atonement" is its provenance and translation history. Like "scapegoat," the word "atonement" (literally, to make "at one") is William Tyndale's coinage for the ritual described in Leviticus 16. The Hebrew word that it is meant to translate is *kaphar*, meaning "to wipe out or to cover, though it comes in time to stand for other things too—annulment, purging, and sometimes propitiation or appeasement" (Dawson, *Flesh Becomes Word*, 10). The Septuagint, however, translates the word as *exilaskomai*, "to propitiate" or "to appease," thus "adapting the expression considerably to specify the removal of guilt and defilement" (Dawson, *Flesh Becomes Word*, 10). As with the word "scapegoat," then, we can see how translation begins to distort the original sense of what is happening in the annual ritual known in English as the "Day of Atonement." As this Greek idea is grafted onto the original Hebrew meaning, the idea of propitiation, which was at best a minor motif in the original practice and meaning of Leviticus 16, starts to become a major one.

53. Heim, *Saved from Sacrifice*, 23.

54. Maddux, "Finding Comedy in Theology," 219.

55. Girard, *Things Hidden*, 182.

56. John Stoner, quoted in Hardin, "Practical Reflections," 251.

57. Cahill, "Atonement Paradigm," 418. This lack of clarity is echoed throughout the literature. One theologian describes the atonement as "the central doctrine of Christianity" (Eleonore Stump, quoted in Dawson, *Flesh Becomes Word*, 9). But another counters, "The first point to be made and always kept in mind, is that 'the atonement'—especially when one means by that any particular theory of atonement—is not a central Christian doctrine" (Daly, *Sacrifice Unveiled*, 100). A third theologian writes, "it is a remarkable fact about Christian theology that there is no such thing as an official or even generally accepted doctrine of the atonement" (Jenson, *Theology in Outline*, 78). A fourth adds, "No council of the church ever laid down what had to be believed about what we call, in English, the atonement" (Gorringe, "Atonement," 364). A fifth concurs, "Atonement is not an essential doctrine of Christianity but is in fact derivative. The more central doctrine is the Incarnation" (Finlan, *Problems with Atonement*, 104).

58. Cahill, "Atonement Paradigm," 419.

59. Aulén, *Christus Victor*, 78. While some scholars count seven distinct theories, the usual modern typology set by Aulén counts three major strands of thought. These emerge chronologically, with the first round of ideas being articulated by the church fathers, the second major round in the Middle Ages, a third major round in the reformation, and the fourth round in the contemporary period. Aulén's system includes (1) the "dramatic" view, which Aulén calls "Christus Victor," (2) the "Latin" view articulated most enduringly by Anselm (1033–1109), and (3) "subjective" theories that include the "moral exemplar" idea articulated by Peter Abelard (1079–1142). In Christus Victor, Jesus wins a victory over the devil or the powers, or rather, the devil's seeming victory over Jesus is recognized as pyrrhic. The "Latin" or Anselmian view will be discussed in a moment. Finally, the "moral exemplar" view rejects Anselm on the grounds that the issue is not a matter of changing God's attitude toward human beings but rather changing human beings' attitude toward God. The idea in moral exemplar theory is that "Jesus died as the demonstration of God's love. And the change that results from that loving death is not in God but in the subjective consciousness of the sinners, who repent" (Weaver, *Nonviolent Atonement*, 18). For more on the basic typologies, see McCormack, "Atonement"; Cross and Livingstone, *Oxford Dictionary of the Christian Church*, s.v. "atonement"; Richardson and Boden, *Westminster Dictionary of Christian Theology*, s.v. "atonement."

60. E. Johnson, *Creation and the Cross*, 118.

61. Finlan, *Problems with Atonement*, 62.

NOTES TO PAGES 97–100   177

62. Ibid.

63. Alison, "Some Thoughts on the Atonement."

64. Richardson and Boden, *Westminster Dictionary of Christian Theology*, s.v. "atonement," 52.

65. E. Johnson, *Creation and the Cross*, 7.

66. Ibid., xiii. Anselm's explanation would eventually evolve, through the writings of Luther and Calvin, into what becomes the "penal substitution" theory, which alters satisfaction slightly but significantly to say that "Christ's death satisfied . . . the divine law" (Weaver, *Nonviolent Atonement*, 17). In other words, it is the law, rather than God's honor, that needs to be answered so that one upholds the idea that God is righteous and just.

67. E. Johnson, *Creation and the Cross*, 15. Even closer to its own time, theologians objected to the image of God suggested by Anselm's thought. Within a generation, Peter Abelard objected; within a few centuries, both Thomas Aquinas and Duns Scotus objected.

68. Ibid., 21.

69. Brown and Parker, "For God So Loved the World?," 2. For challenges to this damning impression of Anselm, see Hart, "Gift Exceeding Every Debt"; and Schwager, *Jesus in the Drama of Salvation*, 13–16. Both authors suggest that Anselm himself has often been confused with a popular caricature and distortion of his meaning.

70. Cone, *God of the Oppressed*, 212.

71. Ibid., 213.

72. Ibid. John Caputo puts it in a different context: "no debt is lifted from us in this scene but a responsibility imposed upon us" ("Spectral Hermeneutics," 66). This notion echoes the Levinasian ideas that Diane Davis draws on to detect a "prior rhetoricity" that calls us to responsibility as the enabling condition of our very subjectivity. Davis's notion rejects any idea of *rhetorical heroism*; our obligations choose us. Agency, Davis writes, "is always already for-the-other: it is not spontaneous or self-determined or heroic but thoroughly rhetorical, responsive, assigned" (*Inessential Solidarity*, 113). This rhetorical structure enables us to understand this persuasion of God as something decisive and even objective in the obligation it places on its witnesses.

73. Brown and Parker, "For God So Loved the World?," 2. Brown and Parker systematically reject the three major forms of atonement theology. Christus Victor suggests that suffering may eventually have good outcomes, even if those outcomes cannot yet be seen; satisfaction suggests that suffering is necessary to appease an insulted God; the moral influence tradition imagines that the victim is obliged to suffer so that the other might be persuaded (ibid., 4–13). In all of these theories, they argue, suffering is a necessity for some good to emerge.

74. Brock and Parker, *Proverbs of Ashes*, 148.

75. Quoted in Brown and Parker, "For God So Loved the World?," 2–3.

76. Williams, *Sisters in the Wilderness*, xiv.

77. Ibid., 162.

78. Ibid., 164.

79. For her, the paradigmatic example is Hagar, the Egyptian slave to Abram's wife Sarah, whose suffering includes not only slavery, homelessness, and poverty but also surrogacy and rape when she is forced to bear Abram a child (Gen. 16:3–4). Later, Paul uses Hagar as an image of the earthly city, born into slavery like Hagar's child, as opposed to Sarah and her children, born into freedom (Gal. 4:22–27). Yet Hagar also has "radical encounters with God," though in those encounters, God does not liberate Hagar so much as help her survive (Williams, *Sisters in the Wilderness*, 4–6). For Williams, then, Hagar is paradigmatic for the experience of African American women, whose liberation struggle begins with simple survival in the wilderness, which becomes a key image for Williams.

80. Brown and Parker, "For God So Loved the World?," 27.

178   NOTES TO PAGES 101–105

81. Megill-Cobbler, "Feminist Rethinking," 14. Finlan makes a related point, complaining that many critiques of atonement simply ignore scripture. These critics, he writes, "do not fill this [their criticism] out with any biblical scholarship, any background in cultic theology or the metaphorical appropriation of cultic images, or any history of the phases of doctrinal development" (*Problems with Atonement*, 104). In other words, they do not operate from the inside out. Girard concurs: "the Cross is the source of all knowledge of God" (Girard, Antonello, and Castro Rocha, *Evolution and Conversion*, 262).

82. Vattimo and Girard, *Christianity, Truth, and Weakening Faith*, 26.

83. Watts, "Rhetoric of Sacrifice," 12n33.

84. Girard, "Conversion in Literature and Christianity," 272. The complex relation to precedent creates fundamental rhetorical challenges for the *kerygma*, or "announcement" of the good news. "In order to secure the attention of his listeners," therefore, "Jesus is obliged to speak their language up to a certain point and take into account illusions that cannot yet be eradicated. If his audience conceives of the deity as vengeful, then the audience can only approach the truth if it is still partly clothed in myth" (Girard, *Things Hidden*, 189). The myth of the violent sacred becomes the available means by which Jesus attempts to warn his listeners that God's favor can be lost. Girard relates these passages to the parable of the sower (Matt. 13:1–23; Mark 4:1–20; Luke 8:4–10), whose presence in the Gospel texts encourages a hermeneutic humility in the readers. In this parable, Jesus raises the possibility—a possibility frequently confirmed by his own disciples—that his message will be misunderstood. In Matthew, Jesus quotes Isaiah. "You shall indeed hear but not understand, you shall indeed look but never see" (Matt. 13:14; Isa. 6:9–10). What is interesting about Girard's argument here is not simply that it characterizes Jesus as a very able rhetorician but also that the text appeals to the sacred topoi that Girard insists the Gospel is trying to dislodge. This is the essence of complicit invention.

85. Girard, Antonello, and Castro Rocha, *Evolution and Conversion*, 262. J. Denny Weaver offers some confirmation of Girard's take, acknowledging that part of the reason that Christus Victor fell out of favor is that the battle metaphors on which it relies seem incompatible with both a loving God and a suffering messiah (Weaver, *Nonviolent Atonement*, 15). Christus Victor theories can also oppose Satan to God in ways that reduce God to Satan's equal.

86. Galvin, "Marvelous Exchange," 677–78.

87. Girard, *I See Satan Fall*, 139–40.

88. Girard, *Girard Reader*, 287.

89. Ibid., 286.

90. Gorringe, "Atonement," 373. The only exception he notes, echoing Cone, are the spirituals of African American religious tradition.

91. Williams, *Sisters in the Wilderness*, 166.

92. Moltmann, *Crucified God*, 68.

93. Ibid.

94. Gorringe, "Atonement," 373–74.

95. As Raymund Schwager puts it to Girard in a letter dated September 3, 1980, "If we abandon the word sacrifice, the danger would be to not sufficiently underline the *solidarity* of Christ with *us*, who are still terribly embedded in a sacrificial world" (Girard and Schwager, *Correspondence*, 99).

96. Eagleton, *Radical Sacrifice*, 22.

97. Brown and Parker, "For God So Loved the World?," 27.

98. Moltmann, *Crucified God*, 51.

99. Ibid., 45–46.

100. Wright, *Day the Revolution Began*, 20.

NOTES TO PAGES 105–109   179

101. Ibid., 57.

102. Quoted in Kaufman, *Jewhooing the Sixties*, 127. In *Jewhooing the Sixties*, David Kaufman writes, "Only Lenny Bruce could find the humor in this ugly but persistent belief, the basis of much of historical antisemitism. And what chutzpah (effrontery) on his part, because raising this aspect of antisemitism is necessarily an affront to Catholicism. How could devout Christians have believed such nonsense, he seemed to imply, and how could their leaders have allowed it to persist? When Bruce first performed this routine, the Catholic Church had yet to repudiate the deicide charge—as it did in the Second Vatican Council of 1965" (128).

103. Quoted ibid., 128. The scene fictionalizes actual Bruce routines in which he condemns Catholic hypocrisy for focusing on sins of sexuality far more than sins of violence. See Bruce, *How to Talk Dirty*, 70–72; and Bruce, *Essential Lenny Bruce*, 40–41. Lest anyone accuse Bruce of mere mockery, one might also cite Jorge Mario Bergoglio, the future Pope Francis. According to a former student, at the College of the Immaculate Conception in Argentina, Bergoglio was giving a lesson on the true meaning of the cross: "Over time, art has stereotyped this instrument of torture, turned it into an object of costume jewelry. Would you hang the image of a hanged man around your neck? . . . Think about it: it would not have been very different to hang a cross around your neck in the first century. Don't look at it with eyes of today, but with those of that time. Try to think. Reason. Would you hang a guillotine or an electric chair around your neck? Difficult to imagine, isn't it?" (quoted in Borghese, *Mind of Pope Francis*, 233).

104. Girard, *One by Whom Scandal Comes*, 43.

105. Heim, *Saved from Sacrifice*, 116.

106. Vattimo, *Belief*, 75.

107. Ibid.

108. Carravetta, "What Is 'Weak Thought?,'" 1.

109. Vattimo, "Dialectics, Difference, and Weak Thought," 155.

110. Ibid., 156.

111. Ibid.

112. Vattimo, *Belief*, 35.

113. Vattimo, "Optimistic Nihilism," 43.

114. Vattimo with Paterlini, *Not Being God*, 150.

115. Vattimo is careful to say that he is not suggesting "that postmodern nihilism opens the way to an authentic religiosity, finally uncovered in its true essence." Such an argument would violate the terms of his project. "Rather, my thesis is that nihilism is the (most likely probable) form of religiosity of our epoch, to the extent that it can be called a postmodern one" ("Nihilism as Postmodern Christianity," 48).

116. Vattimo, *Belief*, 36.

117. Vattimo, "Dialectics, Difference, and Weak Thought," 162. In *The End of Modernity*, drawing on Gadamer, Vattimo insists that rhetoric and hermeneutics are necessary to give truth some purchase on our common social life (135). Without persuasion, truth remains inert and ineffective.

118. Vattimo, "Dialectics, Difference, and Weak Thought," 161.

119. Carravetta, "What Is 'Weak Thought?,'" 4.

120. Vattimo, "Dialectics, Difference, and Weak Thought," 159.

121. Ibid.; Vattimo, "*Verwindung*," 14.

122. Vattimo, "Toward a Nonreligious Christianity," 42.

123. This connection to tradition characterizes Vattimo's own religious and philosophical development. Though on the one hand he frames his reconversion as an outgrowth of his philosophy, he also acknowledges, "in all probability I constructed my philosophy with a

preference for these authors precisely because I started with the Christian inheritance, which I have now found again, though, in reality, I had never abandoned it" (*Belief*, 33). As he recounts in his short autobiography *Not Being God*, he never fully shed the early formative influence of religion (Vattimo with Paterlini, *Not Being God*, 40–43). No one ever starts from scratch. Cynthia Haven's biography of Girard, *Evolution of Desire*, raises similar questions. Haven suggests that Girard arrived at his religious conclusions through his scholarly project. However, Haven suggests that Girard arrived at a religious conclusion that he was intellectually inclined against. She depicts his friends as being "incredulous" at his conversion (Haven, *Evolution of Desire*, 111). But not all were entirely surprised. John Freccero insisted that he could observe in Girard the lingering religious influence of his Catholic youth (Haven, *Evolution of Desire*, 112).

124. Vattimo, "Dialectics, Difference, and Weak Thought," 162.

125. Vattimo, "Myth and the Fate of Secularization," 34.

126. Vattimo, *After Christianity*, 24.

127. Vattimo and Girard, *Christianity, Truth, and Weakening Faith*, 28.

128. Vattimo, *Belief*, 21–22.

129. Some have critiqued Vattimo for remaining "stuck in an oppositional way of thinking" that is entirely "typical of the metaphysical tradition" (Jonkers, "In the World," 382). See also Antonello, "Sacred and the Secular"; and Depoortere, *Christ in Postmodern Philosophy*, on this point. In addition, Vattimo's endorsement of *caritas* seems to constitute the very sort of "strong" gesture that his project would eschew. As Jonkers writes, "once secularised reason begins to demythologise morality and dogma as historical constructions etc., then it cannot stop short at the commandment of love as something sacrosanct anymore" ("In the World," 386). In a similar vein, Depoortere notes that Vattimo's repeated appeal to the kenosis passage in Philippians skips the second half of the hymn, which reads, "Because of this [kenosis], God greatly exalted him [Jesus] and bestowed on him the name that is above every other name, that at the name of Jesus every knee should bend" (2:9–10). As Depoortere explains, this exaltation hardly seems consistent with ideas of weakening and secularization (*Christ in Postmodern Philosophy*, 21). But perhaps the most important challenge is put by Thomas Guarino, who asks, "Does *caritas* have any purchase if Christianity and its central truths have themselves no metaphysical force? How long can society live off expended Christian capital?" (*Vattimo and Theology*, 100).

130. Vattimo and Girard, *Christianity, Truth, and Weakening Faith*, 36.

131. Vattimo, "Toward a Nonreligious Christianity," 42.

132. Vattimo and Girard, *Christianity, Truth, and Weakening Faith*, 39.

133. Ibid., 28.

134. Ibid., 35.

135. "When the pope meets the Dalai Lama," Vattimo asks, "is he worried that the poor fellow will go to hell because he is not Catholic?" (ibid., 40). If the pope is not concerned, it is ultimately because of what Vattimo identifies as a "self-consuming dynamic within Christianity" (ibid., 35). That is to say, Christianity becomes most itself when it sheds an overt, team-sport sort of expression.

136. Vattimo, *Belief*, 21–22.

137. Vattimo and Girard, *Christianity, Truth, and Weakening Faith*, 90.

138. Ibid., 88–89.

139. Ibid., 57. Pierpaolo Antonello also senses the danger. In his introduction to *Christianity, Truth, and Weakening Faith*, Antonello observes that Vattimo's idea of "weak faith" seems shaped by an individualism that undermines bonds and belonging-to, the elements not only of Christian faith but also of Vattimo's own idea of truth. Though weak faith responds "to a legitimate demand for emancipation," Antonello writes, it also risks devolving into a form of "'de-christianized' Christianity, . . . an increasingly individual and unstructured faith, 'made to

measure' to suit the needs and expectations of the individual." How, Antonello wonders, does a notion of weak faith account for "truth as the truth of the victim, the truth of Christian revelation" (introduction to *Christianity, Truth, and Weakening Faith*, 16)? Vattimo responds by saying, "In debates I always tend to exaggerate. . . . Naturally I have the greatest respect for the Ten Commandments" (Vattimo and Girard, *Christianity, Truth, and Weakening Faith*, 57).

140. Vattimo and Girard, *Christianity, Truth, and Weakening Faith*, 43.

141. Ibid., 46–47.

142. Moltmann, *Crucified God*, 51.

143. A. Davis, "Bavaria Orders All Government Buildings." See also Benhold, "Crosses Go Up in Public Offices."

144. Heneghan, "Fending Off the Rising Right."

145. Ibid.

146. Pongratz-Lippitt, "Nuncio Berates Cardinal Marx."

147. Ibid.

Chapter 4

1. French distinguishes between *christianisme* and *chrétienté*. The former refers to the faith itself, the latter to civilizations based on the faith in a sense closer to the English world "Christendom." Ellul uses the word *christianisme* purposefully: "The real essence of the subversion is indicated by the very term 'Christianity,' which gives to the matter the force of an 'ism.' A word ending in 'ism' denotes an ideological or doctrinal trend deriving from a philosophy. Thus we have positivism, socialism, republicanism, spiritualism, idealism, materialism, etc. None of these words, however, denotes the philosophy itself." He continues, "The moment the mutation takes place from existential thinking to existentialism, a living stream is transformed into a more or less regulated stagnant irrigation channel" (*Subversion of Christianity*, 10).

2. Ibid., 36.

3. Government of Canada, *Residential School System*.

4. Ibid.

5. In *Postsecular Catholicism*, Michele Dillon argues for what she calls a "contrite Catholicism," which has included papal acknowledgment of the Catholic Church's complicity in egregious crimes, including not only the Canadian residential boarding school system but also the worldwide child sex abuse scandal (10–11). Contrite Catholicism refers to the ways in which the Church finds itself in a posture of public contrition. This posture means that the Church can no longer rely on older forms of appeal. Dillon borrows the phrase "contrite Catholicism" from Jürgen Habermas. In dialogues with Joseph Ratzinger (Benedict XVI), Habermas refers to a "contrite modernity," the idea that modernity has failed to deliver on its promises (quoted ibid., 2–3). For Dillon, postsecularity refers to the ways in which contrite modernity and contrite Christianity will dialogue and interact with each other.

6. As I was completing the revisions on this manuscript, the Vatican finally announced that it was repudiating the Doctrine of Discovery (Povoledo, "Vatican Repudiates 'Doctrine of Discovery'"). Some Indigenous leaders welcomed the announcement, while others insisted that it was only a first and long-overdue step toward a full accounting of the church's role in colonization (Hertzler-McCain, "Indigenous Call Vatican's Repudiation").

7. Ellul, *Subversion of Christianity*, 11.

8. Ibid., 35. Ellul is careful not to fall into the all-too-familiar commonplaces by which this argument has been made, according to a (quite literally) killer dichotomy "between the pure message of Jesus and either the terrible God of the Jews or the detestable Paul, a false

NOTES TO PAGES 116–121

interpreter. There is complete coherence between what we know of Jesus the Christ and the God of Abraham, Isaac, and Jacob" (ibid., 6).

9. Girard, *When These Things Begin*, 121.

10. Hardin and Berry, *Reading the Bible*, loc. 105/181.

11. Girard, Antonello, and Castro Rocha, *Evolution and Conversion*, 218. There is a supersessionist tone in this statement.

12. I borrow the idea of disarticulation from Sharon Crowley, who borrows it from Stuart Hall. Within ideologies, writes Crowley, "beliefs, symbols, and images are articulated in such a way that they assemble a more or less coherent depiction of reality and/or establish a hierarchy of values" (*Toward a Civil Discourse*, 65). Rhetorical criticism aspires "to invent means of disarticulating beliefs that circulate within a given ideology, and the exposure of untenable connections might assist with the project of disarticulating systems of belief" (ibid., 77).

13. Bernard-Donals and Jensen, "Introduction," 1.

14. Lundberg, "Rhetoric's Affective Reckoning," 269–70.

15. Derrida, *Adieu to Emmanuel Levinas*, 4.

16. Bernard-Donals, "Divine Cruelty," 402–3.

17. Bernard-Donals and Jensen, "Introduction," 1.

18. Mailloux, "Notes on Prayerful Rhetoric," 420.

19. Dupuy, "Neither Dawkins nor Durkheim," 3.

20. Tarot, "Émile Durkheim and After," 12.

21. Girard, *Violence and the Sacred*, 23.

22. Bernard-Donals and Jensen, "Introduction," 5.

23. Friedrich Feigel, quoted in Alles, introduction to *Rudolf Otto*, 30.

24. Kearney, *God Who May Be*, 7.

25. See Evans-Pritchard, *Theories of Primitive Religion*, 9.

26. Agamben, *Homo Sacer*, 78. Agamben thinks there is no mystery to what makes the sacred frightening (ibid., 71–74). Agamben's idea of the *homo sacer* has nothing to do with "the sacred" as an independent force or entity. The *homo sacer*, argues Agamben, is neither sacrificeable to the gods nor punishable by law and therefore may be killed by anyone. That double exclusion constitutes political sovereignty; it is "an originary *political* structure that is located in a zone prior to the distinction between sacred and profane, religious and juridical" (ibid., 74). Through expulsion from the community, *homo sacer* simultaneously constitutes sovereign power, for it is only sovereign power that can declare someone sacred. Such distinctions—along with the century-long conversation that produced them—are no longer necessary. There may be something frightening and fascinating here, but it requires no reference to any supposed "ambivalence" to explain—hence his dismissal of the "science" of "shivers and goosebumps." For a critical examination of Agamben's interpretation of the Roman sources he uses to produce the idea of *homo sacer*, see Depoortere, "Reading Giorgio Agamben's *Homo Sacer*," 154–57.

27. Poland, "Idea of the Holy," 187–88.

28. Colpe, "Sacred and the Profane," 511.

29. Booth, "Kenneth Burke's Religious Rhetoric," 32.

30. Oxtoby, "Holy (the Sacred)," 514.

31. Palaver, *Transforming the Sacred*, 23.

32. In addition, Palaver notes that Girard's *La violence et le sacré* was initially rendered in German as *Das Heilige und die Gewalt*, thus substituting German's word for "holy" in place of French's word for "sacred" (Palaver, *Transforming the Sacred*, 23). One sees a similar challenge in English translations of Levinas. Those translations, notes John Caruana, sometimes render both *le saint* and *le sainteté*—along with *le sacré*—as "the sacred," thus risking the obscuring of Levinas's meaning (Caruana, "'Not Ethics,'" 562n2).

NOTES TO PAGES 121–124   183

33. Schwager, *Must There Be Scapegoats?*, 19.

34. Colpe, "Sacred and the Profane," 513.

35. Tarot, "Émile Durkheim," 12–13.

36. Durkheim, *Elementary Forms of Religious Life*, 38.

37. Ibid., 36.

38. Ibid., 413.

39. Ibid., 41.

40. Ibid., 44 (emphasis in original).

41. Tarot, "Émile Durkheim," 13.

42. Ibid., 18.

43. "For nearly eighty years this text has been used as a yardstick against which subsequent studies of holiness have declared and defined their own position" (Raphael, *Rudolf Otto*, 1). Yet Colin Crowder suggests that *The Idea of the Holy* has become a "classic" in Mark Twain's sense of the word: a book that everyone wants to have read but no one wants to read ("Rudolf Otto's *The Idea of the Holy* Revisited," 22).

44. Otto, *Idea of the Holy*, 5. Notice again the shift between "sacred" and "holy."

45. Ibid., 59 (emphasis added).

46. Raphael, *Rudolf Otto*, 25.

47. In addition, Otto quite explicitly invokes his ideal audience: "whoever knows no such moments [of the numinous] in his experience, is requested to read no farther; for it is not easy to discuss questions of religious psychology with one who . . . cannot recall any intrinsically religious feelings" (*Idea of the Holy*, 8). Wayne Proudfoot complains that "the rules [of Otto's book] have been drawn up so as to preclude any naturalistic explanation of whatever feeling the reader may have attended to in his or her own experience" (*Religious Experience*, 118). One might ask why a "naturalistic explanation" should be more secure.

48. Otto, *Idea of the Holy*, 31.

49. Ibid.

50. Ibid., 109.

51. Ibid., 75. Unlike Girard, however, Otto has no compunction about speaking in supersessionist terms. Otto writes, "The culmination of the process [of the development of the holy] is found in the Prophets and the Gospels" (ibid.). Though this pairing may initially suggest otherwise, there is no doubt that Otto sees Christianity as the ultimate fulfillment of this progress.

52. The scripture scholar Walter Brueggemann confirms Otto's understanding. The focus on purity prevents holiness from being reduced to a mere moral requirement; the demand for justice prevents holiness from being reduced to ceremonial function. "This unresolvable tension in the very life of God shapes Israel's faith and evokes Israel as a community of both doxology and commandment, amazement and obedience" ("Editor's Foreword," xi).

53. Like Girard, Otto finds the fullest expression of holiness within the Jewish and Christian scriptures, though unlike Girard, Otto has unabashed supersessionist attitudes (Crowder, "Rudolf Otto's *The Idea of the Holy* Revisited," 45–47).

54. Eliade, *Sacred and the Profane*, 10. The original French uses "le sacré" at this point: "Ce n'est pas la rapport entre les éléments non-rationnel et rationnel de la religion qui nous intéresse, mais le sacré dans sa totalité" (*Le sacré et le profane*, 16). The book was originally published as part of Rowohlt's *German Encyclopedia* under the title *Das Heilige und Das Profane* and the editorship of Ernesto Grassi.

55. Eliade, *Sacred and the Profane*, 21.

56. Ibid., 12.

57. Ibid., 11.

184   NOTES TO PAGES 124–131

58. Eliade echoes Durkheim in defining the sacred against the profane: "The first possible definition of the *sacred* is that it is *the opposite of the profane*" (ibid., 10). The sacred and profane "are two modes of being in the world, two existential situations assumed by man in the course of his history" (ibid., 14). A profane thing may be made sacred, but the relation remains binary.

59. Ibid., 27.

60. Ibid., 13.

61. Bernard-Donals and Jensen, "Introduction," 6 (emphasis added).

62. Depoortere, "Reading Giorgio Agamben's *Homo Sacer*," 161.

63. Girard, Antonello, and Castro Rocha, *Evolution and Conversion*, 218.

64. In addition to health and well-being, *halio-* also suggests "good omen, auspice, augury." It is thus related to the long-obsolete English verb *halse*, meaning to "augur, divine, or exorcise." In Latin, meanwhile, there is a recognizable distinction between *sanctus* and *sacer*, one that would seem to be a precursor of Romance-language usages like the French *le sainteté* and *le sacré*. For more on the languages issue, see Colpe, "Sacred and the Profane," 511–16.

65. Miles, *God*, 221.

66. Minear, "Holy and the Sacred," 5.

67. Oxtoby, "Holy (the Sacred)," 511–12.

68. Ibid.

69. Rogerson, "What Is Holiness?," 3.

70. Blumenthal, *Facing the Abusing God*, 24–25 (emphasis added).

71. Rogerson, "What Is Holiness?," 21.

72. Brueggemann, "Editor's Foreword," xi.

73. Daniel Gross argues that most writing and speaking classrooms construe rhetoric as "a type of know-how designed to enhance a student's capacity for communicating in a variety of secular circumstances" ("Historiography," 236).

74. Lundberg and Gunn, "Ouija Board," 88.

75. Ibid., 97.

76. Nicotra, "Hacking the Sacred," 142.

77. Eliade, *Sacred and the Profane*, 29.

78. D. Davis, *Inessential Solidarity*, 3.

79. Scult, *Being Jewish*, 46.

80. D. Davis, *Inessential Solidarity*, 11.

81. Caputo, "Theology, Poetry, and Theopoetics," 46.

82. Bernard-Donals and Jensen, "Introduction," 1.

83. Girard, *I See Satan Fall*, 70.

84. Scult, *Being Jewish*, 51.

85. Bernard-Donals, "Divine Cruelty," 400–401.

86. Bernard-Donals and Jensen, "Introduction," 5.

87. Bernard-Donals, "Call of the Sacred," 404.

88. Bernard-Donals, "Divine Cruelty," 408.

89. Ibid., 408–9.

90. Frank, "Engaging a Rhetorical God," 57.

91. Frank's evidence for the rhetorical God is also drawn from the *Aggadah*, "or the body of work designed to translate sacred texts into practice" (ibid., 56). These include "interpretations offered by Rashi, the Talmud, the Zohar (the teachings of the Kabbalah), the Targum (Aramaic translations and interpretations of the Hebrew Bible), and Jewish folklore," the last of which is contained in a wide variety of sources (ibid., 55). This background is crucial for understanding the depth of God's rhetoricity.

92. Ibid., 58–59.

NOTES TO PAGES 132–137   185

93. Ibid., 73–74.

94. Ibid., 52.

95. Bernard-Donals, "Call of the Sacred," 404.

96. Lundberg, "Rhetoric's Affective Reckoning," 271.

97. Ibid., 271.

98. Ibid., 269–70.

99. Crosswhite, *Deep Rhetoric*, 17.

100. Lundberg, "Rhetoric's Affective Reckoning," 261.

101. Ibid., 262.

102. The title, "Rejoice and Be Glad," comes from the final verse of the Beatitudes: "Rejoice and be glad, for your reward is great in heaven, for so men persecuted the prophets who were before you" (5:12).

103. For a more likely example, we might be tempted to turn to Francis's much-better-known environmental encyclical *Laudato Si'*, addressed not only to Christians but to "every person living on this planet" (3). Unlike most papal documents, *Laudato Si'* resonated far beyond the confines of the Catholic Church, receiving favorable treatment from a wide variety of public intellectuals, including Bruno Latour (*Facing Gaia*, 287–88) and Amitav Ghosh (*Great Derangement*, 150–59). It has also received a great deal of attention from rhetoricians (see P. Lynch, "On Care for Our Common Discourse"; C. Lynch, "Religion and the Environment"; and a special issue of the *Journal of Communication and Religion* 44, no. 2 [2022]). GE, by contrast, has not received nearly as much attention, either outside or inside the Roman Catholic Church.

104. The Vatican journalist Alessandro Gisotti describes Francis's language as "Ignatian in rhythm, Franciscan in style" ("El perfil humano," 28). In his daily sermons, Francis tends to focus on three central points, in keeping with the structure of the *Spiritual Exercises*. His phrasing, meanwhile, is brief, "with few subordinate clauses and a vocabulary drawn from everyday usage" (ibid., 28). Antonio Sporado adds, "Francis's language is not speculative, but missionary, attentive to the interlocutor as much as to the message, which is uttered not to be 'studied' but to be 'heard,' immediately compelling one who hears it to react. In reality, more than 'communicating,' he creates 'communicative events,' in which the recipient of the message actively participates" (quoted in Borghesi, *Mind of Pope Francis*, 224).

105. Borghesi, *Mind of Pope Francis*, 131.

106. Jiménez Rodríguez, "Concepto teológico," 25.

107. Ibid., 3. Jiménez Rodríguez also notes that "style" plays a central role in *Laudato Si'*.

108. Faggioli, "Pope Francis's *Gaudete et Exsultate*." Likewise, Jiménez Rodríguez writes that Francis "accepts that the Church has been mistaken in failing at times to live according to the style proposed by Jesus" ("Concepto teológico," 13). Francis writes, "In the Church we have often erred by not embracing this demand of God's word" (*GE*, 73). In this particular section, Francis reminds the reader of Paul's injunction to approach the mistakes of others "'with a spirit of meekness,' since 'you too could be tempted' (Gal 6:1). Even when we defend our faith and convictions, we are to do so 'with meekness' (cf. 1 Pet 3:16). Our enemies too are to be treated 'with meekness' (2 Tim 2:25)" (*GE*, 73).

109. Sparado, "Big Heart Open to God."

110. Pope Francis, GE, 134. Hereafter cited parenthetically in the text. The numbers refer to sections rather than pages.

111. Jiménez Rodríguez, "Concepto teológico," 5.

112. Orsuto, *Holiness*, 1.

113. Ekpo, "Gaudete et Exsultate," 442.

114. Latour, *Rejoicing*, 18.

115. Girard, "Literature and Christianity," 33.

186   NOTES TO PAGES 137–147

116. Lamb, "Pope Francis."

117. Bustos, "Pope Addresses Genocide."

118. Girard, *Battling to the End*, 82.

119. The Second Vatican Council was a series of meetings that took place from 1962 to 1965. The purpose of the council was to radically rethink the church's relationship to modernity.

120. *Lumen Gentium*, 42.

121. Though Francis never speaks of atonement theology, it is hard not to sense a gnostic tendency in the urge to articulate a "theory," which becomes not so much a theory but an answer. "When someone has an answer for every question, it is a sign that they are not on the right road" (*GE*, 41).

122. Manson, "Should Women Rejoice over *Gaudete et Exsultate*?" Massimo Faggioli agrees, writing, "The short paragraph on holiness and the 'feminine genius' shows Francis's weakness on the issue of women in the church" ("Pope Francis's *Gaudete et Exsultate*").

123. In addition, Francis makes clear—despite the impression one might gather from certain American church leaders—that abortion cannot be the only issue on which Christians speak. "Equally sacred . . . are the lives of the poor, those already born, the destitute, the abandoned and the underprivileged, the vulnerable infirm and elderly exposed to covert euthanasia, the victims of human trafficking, new forms of slavery, and every form of rejection" (*GE*, 101).

124. Quoted in Borghesi, *Mind of Pope Francis*, 61.

125. Borghesi writes, "Unlike Hegel and his ascending dialectic, *which never returns*, Bergoglio's [Francis's] dialectic lives by antimonies. This means that it is 'circular,' that its third moment—a deepening social awareness and the reform of structures—implies a turn to the first stage: direct contact, *really and not merely theoretical*, with people and in particular the poor" (ibid., 67). He adds that in Hegel's thought, "the particular is only apparently 'conserved' in the universal. In Catholicism the concrete universal calls for *the care of the particular*, the awareness that that the smallest is, in the kingdom of God, the greatest" (ibid., 65). This is why the unity Francis pursues is one that still attends to the care of the particular, without it being resolved into some universal transcendent idea.

126. Ibid., 83.

127. Quoted ibid., 89. "You have to run the same risk every time and it will be different every time" (Latour, *Rejoicing*, 17).

128. Quoted in Borghesi, *Mind of Pope Francis*, 105.

129. Ibid., 64.

130. "How often we are tempted to keep close to the shore! Yet the Lord calls us to put out into the deep and let down our nets (cf. Luke 5:4)" (*GE*, 130). In Luke 5:4, Jesus instructs Simon to go out into the deeper water. Despite the fact that he has fished all night and caught nothing, Simon does it and hauls in a catch so large that he needs help bringing it in.

131. Pope Paul VI, *Evangelii Nuntiandi*, 41. The line comes from an earlier *Address to the Members of the Consilium de Laicis* (October 2, 1974): AAS 66 (1974).

132. Pope Paul VI, *Evangelii Nuntiandi*, 22.

133. Ibid., 21.

134. Girard, *When These Things Begin*, 121.

135. Girard, *Girard Reader*, 287.

Postscript

1. See Palaver and Schenk, *Mimetic Theory and World Religions*, especially Collins, "Burning Desires, Burning Corpses"; Sheth, "Girard and Hindu Sacrifice"; Ericksen, "Tawhid"; and Lohlker, "Islam."

NOTES TO PAGES 147–155   187

2. Girard, *Battling to the End*, xi.

3. My thanks to David Frank for recommending this book.

4. Sacks, *Not in God's Name*, 98.

5. Ibid., 76.

6. Anti-Defamation League, *Audit of Antisemitic Incidents 2022*.

7. Girard, *I See Satan Fall*, 157.

8. Girard, *Battling to the End*, 21.

9. Ibid., xiii.

10. Ibid., 35.

11. Ibid., xvii.

12. Stendahl articulated this idea during a 1985 press conference in Stockholm, Sweden, defending the opening of a Mormon temple in Stockholm. Stendhal articulated three basic principles: "1. When trying to understand another religion, you should ask the adherents of that religion and not its enemies. 2. Don't compare your best to their worst. 3. Leave room for holy envy" (B. Taylor, *Holy Envy*, 65). For more, see chapter 4 of Barbara Brown Taylor's *Holy Envy*. In a recent study of holy envy in Jewish-Christian relations (one that challenges Taylor's take), Maeera Y. Shreiber defines holy envy this way: "Calling for a more active, demanding, and affective condition than the dispassionate tolerance that typically presides over such meetings, Stendahl challenges us to be genuinely vulnerable and to recognize that there may be something about another faith that is genuinely lacking in one's own. He challenges us thus to risk experiencing, in all its pain and discomfort, the shameful condition we call *envy*" (*Holy Envy*, 2).

13. Harrison, "Prophet of Envy."

14. Sacks, *Not in God's Name*, 99.

15. Ibid., 53.

16. Ibid., 184.

17. Ibid., 51.

18. Ibid. (emphasis in original).

19. Johnstone, "Some Reflections on Argumentation," 1.

20. Frank, "Arguing with God," 75.

21. Ibid., 72.

22. Ibid., 79.

23. Miles, *God*, 325.

24. Frank, "Arguing with God," 80.

25. See Greenbaum and Holdstein, *Judaic Perspectives*; and Bernard-Donals and Fernheimer, *Jewish Rhetorics*.

26. Chase, "Christian Rhetorical Theory," 35.

27. Foucault, "About the Beginning"; Foucault, *Hermeneutics of the Subject*; Foucault, "Self-Writing"; Foucault, "Technologies of the Self"; Hadot, *Philosophy as a Way of Life*.

28. Gross, *Being-Moved*, 14.

29. See Gandhi, *Non-Violent Resistance*, 37–47, 87–88.

30. Hadot, *Philosophy as a Way of Life*, 107.

31. Ibid. Hadot does draw the conventional and somewhat invidious distinction between rhetoric and dialectic: "What is needed is *persuasion*, and for that one must use psychology, the art of seducing souls. Even at that, it is not enough to use only rhetoric, which, as it were, tries to persuade from a distance, by means of continuous discourse. What is needed above all is *dialectic*, which demands the explicit consent of the interlocutor at every moment" (ibid., 92).

32. Foucault, *Hermeneutics of the Subject*, 15.

33. Hadot, *Philosophy as a Way of Life*, 83.

34. Sheldrake, *Befriending Our Desires*, 11.
35. Burke, *War of Words*, 159.
36. Ibid.
37. Siegel, *Why Argument Matters*, 74.
38. Burke, *War of Words*, 160 (emphasis added).
39. Ibid.

Bibliography

Adams, Rebecca, and René Girard. "Violence, Difference, Sacrifice: A Conversation with René Girard." *Religion and Literature* 25, no. 2 (1993): 9–33.

Agamben, Giorgio. *Homo Sacer: Sovereign Power and Bare Life*. Translated by David-Heller Roazen. Stanford: Stanford University Press, 1998.

Alberg, Jeremiah. "The Return of Religion." In *The Palgrave Handbook of Mimetic Theory and Religion*, edited by James Alison and Wolfgang Palaver, 357–61. New York: Palgrave, 2017.

Alison, James. *The Joy of Being Wrong: Original Sin Through Easter Eyes*. New York: Crossroad, 1998.

———. "Some Thoughts on the Atonement." James Alison [website], 2004. https://james alison.com/some-thoughts-on-the-atonement/.

Alles, Gregory D. Introduction to *Rudolf Otto: Autobiographical and Social Essays*, by Rudolf Otto, edited and translated by Gregory D. Alles, 1–49. Berlin: Mouton de Gruyter, 1996.

Altizer, Thomas, and William Hamilton. *Radical Theology and the Death of God*. Indianapolis: Bobbs-Merrill, 1966.

Anti-Defamation League. *Audit of Antisemitic Incidents 2021*. April 21, 2022. https://www .adl.org/resources/report/audit-antisemitic-incidents-2021.

———. *Audit of Antisemitic Incidents 2022*. March 23, 2023. https://www.adl.org/resources /report/audit-antisemitic-incidents-2022.

Antonello, Pierpaolo. Introduction to *Christianity, Truth, and Weakening Faith*, by Gianni Vattimo and René Girard, 1–22. Translated by William McCuaig. New York: Columbia University Press, 2010.

———. "The Sacred and the Secular: René Girard and Gianni Vattimo on Modernity and Violence." In *The Sacred and the Political: Explorations on Mimesis, Violence and Religion*, edited by Elisabetta Brighi and Antonio Cerella, 189–211. New York: Bloomsbury Academic, 2016.

Arnett, Ronald C. *Levinas's Rhetorical Demand: The Unending Obligation of Communication Ethics*. Carbondale: Southern Illinois University Press, 2017.

Augustine. *On Christian Teaching*. Translated by R. P. H. Green. Oxford: Oxford University Press, 1997.

Aulén, Gustav. *Christus Victor: An Historical Study of the Three Main Types of the Idea of Atonement*. Translated by A. G. Herbert. New York: Macmillan, 1956.

Ballif, Michelle. "Divining Rhetoric's Future." In Bernard-Donals and Jensen, *Responding to the Sacred*, 157–71.

Bartlett, Anthony W. *Cross Purposes: The Violent Grammar of Christian Atonement*. Harrisburg, PA: Trinity, 2001.

Bendavid, Naftali. "Europe's Empty Churches Go on Sale." *Wall Street Journal*, January 2, 2015. https://www.wsj.com/articles/europes-empty-churches-go-on-sale-1420245359.

BIBLIOGRAPHY

Benhold, Katrin. "Crosses Go Up in Public Offices. It's Culture, Bavaria Says, Not Religion." *New York Times*, May 30, 2018. https://www.nytimes.com/2018/05/30/world/europe/bavaria-germany-crucifix-migrants.html.

Berger, Peter L. "The Desecularization of the World: A Global Overview." In *The Desecularization of the World: Resurgent Religion and World Politics*, edited by Peter Berger, 1–18. Grand Rapids, MI: Eerdmans, 1999.

Bernard-Donals, Michael. "The Call of the Sacred and the Language of Deterritorialization." *Rhetoric Society Quarterly* 41, no. 5 (2011): 397–415.

———. "Divine Cruelty and Rhetorical Violence." *Philosophy and Rhetoric* 47, no. 4 (2014): 400–418.

Bernard-Donals, Michael, and Janice W. Fernheimer, eds. *Jewish Rhetorics: History, Theory, and Practice*. Waltham, MA: Brandeis University Press, 2014.

Bernard-Donals, Michael, and Kyle Jensen. "Introduction: Taking Rhetoric to Its Limits; or, How to Respond to a Sacred Call." In Bernard-Donals and Jensen, *Responding to the Sacred*, 1–23.

———, eds. *Responding to the Sacred: An Inquiry into the Limits of Rhetoric*. University Park: Penn State University Press, 2021.

Bessette, Jean. "Rightness in Retrospect: Stonewall and the Sacred Call of Kairos." In Bernard-Donals and Jensen, *Responding to the Sacred*, 214–35.

Biesecker, Barbara A. *Addressing Postmodernity: Kenneth Burke, Rhetoric, and a Theory of Social Change*. Tuscaloosa: University of Alabama Press, 1997.

Blumenthal, David R. *Facing the Abusing God: A Theology of Protest*. Louisville, KY: Westminster / John Knox, 1993.

Bobbio, Norberto. "In Praise of Meekness." In *In Praise of Meekness: Essays on Ethics and Politics*, translated by Teresa Chataway, 19–36. Cambridge, UK: Polity, 2000.

Boorstein, Michelle. "A Horn-Wearing 'Shaman.' A Cowboy Evangelist. For Some, the Capitol Attack Was a Kind of Christian Revolt." *Washington Post*, July 6, 2021. https://www.washingtonpost.com/religion/2021/07/06/capitol-insurrection-trump-christian-nationalism-shaman/.

Booth, Wayne C. "Kenneth Burke's Religious Rhetoric: 'God-Terms' and the Ontological Proof." In *Rhetorical Invention and Religious Inquiry*, edited by Walter Jost and Wendy Olmstead, 25–39. New Haven: Yale University Press, 2000.

Borghesi, Massimo. *The Mind of Pope Francis: Jorge Mario Bergoglio's Intellectual Journey*. Translated by Barry Haddock. Collegeville, MN: Liturgical Press, 2018.

Brock, Rita Nakashima, and Rebecca Ann Parker. *Proverbs of Ashes: Violence, Redemptive Suffering, and the Search for What Saves Us*. Boston: Beacon Press, 2001.

Brown, Joanne Carlson, and Rebecca Parker. "For God So Loved the World?" In *Christianity, Patriarchy, and Abuse: A Feminist Critique*, 1–30. New York: Pilgrim Press, 1989.

Bruce, Lenny. *The Essential Lenny Bruce*. Edited by John Cohen. New York: Ballantine Books, 1967.

———. *How to Talk Dirty and Influence People: An Autobiography*. New York: Fireside, 1963.

Brueggemann, Walter. "Editor's Foreword." In *Holiness in Israel*, by John G. Gammie, ix–xii. Minneapolis: Fortress Press, 1989.

Bultmann, Rudolf. "What Does It Mean to Speak of God?" 1925. In *Faith and Understanding*, edited by Robert W. Funk, translated by Louise Pettibone Smith, 53–65. New York: Harper and Row, 1969.

Burke, Kenneth. *Language as Symbolic Action: Essays on Life, Literature, and Method*. Berkeley: University of California Press, 1966.

————. *Permanence and Change: An Anatomy of Purpose*. 3rd ed. Berkeley: University of California Press, 1984.

————. "The Philosophy of Literary Form." In *The Philosophy of Literary Form: Studies in Symbolic Action*, 3rd ed., 1–137. Berkeley: University of California Press, 1973.

————. "The Rhetoric of Hitler's 'Battle.'" In *The Philosophy of Literary Form: Studies in Symbolic Action*, 3rd ed., 191–220. Berkeley: University of California Press, 1973.

————. *A Rhetoric of Motives*. Berkeley: University of California Press, 1969.

————. *The Rhetoric of Religion*. Boston: Beacon Press, 1961.

————. "Toward Hellhaven." In *On Human Nature: A Gathering While Everything Flows, 1967–1984*, edited by William H. Rueckert and Angelo Bonadonna, 54–65. Berkeley: University of California Press, 2003.

————. *The War of Words*. Edited by Anthony Burke, Kyle Jensen, and Jack Selzer. Berkeley: University of California Press, 2018.

Burkert, Walter, René Girard, and Jonathan Smith. *Violent Origins: Walter Burkert, René Girard, and Jonathan Smith on Ritual Killing and Cultural Formation*. Edited by Robert G. Hamerton-Kelly. Stanford: Stanford University Press, 1987.

Burton, Tara Isabella. *Strange Rites: New Religions for a Godless World*. New York: Public Affairs, 2020.

Bustos, Aida. "Pope Addresses Genocide, 'Backwardists' and His Health." *Southern Cross: The Official Newspaper of the Diocese of San Diego*, July 31, 2022. https://www.thesouthern cross.org/news/pope-addresses-genocide-backwardists-and-his-health/.

Butler, Judith. *The Force of Nonviolence: An Ethico-Political Bind*. London: Verso, 2020.

Cahill, Lisa Sowle. "The Atonement Paradigm: Does It Still Have Explanatory Value?" *Theological Studies* 68, no. 2 (2007): 418–32.

Caputo, John. *On Religion*. 2nd ed. New York: Routledge, 2019.

————. "Spectral Hermeneutics: On the Weakness of God and the Theology of the Event." In *After the Death of God*, by John Caputo and Gianni Vattimo, 47–88. New York: Columbia University Press, 2007.

————. "Theology, Poetry, and Theopoetics." In Kearney and Clemente, *Reimagining the Sacred*, 43–48.

Carravetta, Peter. "What Is 'Weak Thought'? The Original Theses and Context of *il pensiero debole*." In *Weak Thought*, edited by Gianni Vattimo and Pier Aldo Rovatti, translated by Peter Carravetta, 1–38. Albany: State University of New York Press, 2012.

Carter, C. Allen. *Kenneth Burke and the Scapegoat Process*. Norman: University of Oklahoma Press, 1996.

Caruana, John. "'Not Ethics, Not Ethics Alone, but the Holy': Levinas on Ethics and Holiness." *Journal of Religious Ethics* 34, no. 4 (2006): 561–83.

Cavanaugh, William T., and Peter Scott. Introduction to *The Blackwell Companion to Political Theology*, edited by Peter Scott and William T. Cavanaugh, 1–3. Oxford: Blackwell, 2004.

Chase, Kenneth R. "Christian Rhetorical Theory: A New (Re)Turn." *Journal of Communication and Religion* 36, no. 1 (2013): 25–49.

Collins, Brian. "Burning Desires, Burning Corpses: Girardian Reflections on Fire in Hinduism and Buddhism." In Palaver and Schenk, *Mimetic Theory and World Religions*, 303–22.

Colpe, Carsten. "The Sacred and the Profane." In *Encyclopedia of Religion*, edited by Mircea Eliade, vol. 12, 511–26. Detroit: Macmillan Reference USA, 2005.

Cone, James H. *Black Theology and Black Power*. New York: Seabury, 1969.

————. *God of the Oppressed*. New rev. ed. Maryknoll, NY: Orbis, 1997.

192   BIBLIOGRAPHY

Cross, Frank L., and Elizabeth A. Livingstone, eds. *The Oxford Dictionary of the Christian Church*. 3rd ed. Oxford: Oxford University Press, 2005.

Crosswhite, James. *Deep Rhetoric: Philosophy, Reason, Violence, Justice, Wisdom*. Chicago: University of Chicago Press, 2013.

Crowder, Colin. "Rudolf Otto's *The Idea of the Holy* Revisited." In Barton, *Holiness*, 22–47.

Crowley, Sharon. *Toward a Civil Discourse: Rhetoric and Fundamentalism*. Pittsburgh: University of Pittsburgh Press, 2006.

Crusius, Timothy W. "A Case for Kenneth Burke's Rhetoric and Dialectic." *Philosophy and Rhetoric* 19, no. 1 (1986): 23–37.

Daly, Robert J. *Sacrifice Unveiled: The True Meaning of Christian Sacrifice*. London: T&T Clark, 2009.

Danker, Frederick William, and Kathryn Krug. *The Concise Greek-English Lexicon of the New Testament*. Chicago: University of Chicago Press, 2009.

Darr, John A. "Mimetic Desire, the Gospels, and Early Christianity: A Response to René Girard." *Biblical Interpretation* 1, no. 3 (1993): 357–67.

Davenport-Hines, Richard. "Ward, Stephen Thomas (1912–1963), Osteopath and Scapegoat." In *Oxford Dictionary of National Biography*. Oxford: Oxford University Press, 2013. https://www.oxforddnb.com/view/10.1093/ref:odnb/9780198614128.001.0001/odnb-9780198614128-e-40839.

Davis, Austin. "Bavaria Orders All Government Buildings to Display Crosses." *USA Today*, April 25, 2018. https://www.usatoday.com/story/news/world/2018/04/25/bavaria-crosses-government-buildings/550653002/.

Davis, Diane. *Inessential Solidarity: Rhetoric and Foreigner Relations*. Pittsburgh: University of Pittsburgh Press, 2010.

Dawson, David. *Flesh Becomes Word: A Lexicography of the Scapegoat or, the History of an Idea*. East Lansing: Michigan State University Press, 2013.

Depoortere, Frederiek. *Christ in Postmodern Philosophy*. London: T&T Clark, 2008.

———. "Reading Giorgio Agamben's *Homo Sacer* with René Girard." *Philosophy Today* 56, no. 2 (2012): 154–63.

Derrida, Jacques. *Adieu to Emmanuel Levinas*. Translated by Pascale-Ann Brault and Michael Naas. Stanford: Stanford University Press, 1999.

Detienne, Marcel. "Culinary Practices and the Spirit of Sacrifice." In Detienne and Vernant, *Cuisine of Sacrifice Among the Greeks*, 1–20.

Detienne, Marcel, and Jean-Pierre Vernant. *The Cuisine of Sacrifice Among the Greeks*. Translated by Paula Wissing. Chicago: University of Chicago Press, 1989.

Dewey, Joanna. "A Response to René Girard: 'Is There Anti-Semitism in the Gospels?'" *Biblical Interpretation* 1, no. 3 (1993): 353–56.

Dillon, Michele. *Postsecular Catholicism: Relevance and Renewal*. New York: Oxford University Press, 2018.

Drescher, Elizabeth. *Choosing Our Religion: The Spiritual Lives of America's Nones*. New York: Oxford University Press, 2016.

Dupuy, Jean-Pierre. "Neither Dawkins nor Durkheim: On René Girard's Theory of Religion." In Palaver and Schenk, *Mimetic Theory and World Religions*, 3–11.

Durkheim, Émile. *The Elementary Forms of Religious Life*. 1912. Translated by Karen E. Fields. New York: Free Press, 1995.

Duve, Thierry de. "Come On, Humans, One More Effort If You Want to Be Post-Christians!" In *Political Theologies: Public Religions in a Post-Secular World*, edited by Hent de Vries and Lawrence E. Sullivan, 652–70. New York: Fordham University Press, 2006.

Eagleton, Terry. "Lunging, Flailing, Mispunching." *London Review of Books* 28, no. 19 (2006): 406. https://www.lrb.co.uk/the-paper/v28/n20/terry-eagleton/lunging-flailing-mispunching.

———. *Radical Sacrifice.* New Haven: Yale University Press, 2018.

Ekpo, Anthony. "*Gaudete et Exsultate*: Pope Francis and the Call to Holiness." *Australasian Catholic Record* 95, no. 4 (2018): 441–54.

Eliade, Mircea. *The Sacred and the Profane: The Nature of Religion.* 1957. Translated by Willard R. Trask. Orlando, FL: Harvest, 1959.

———. *Le sacré et le profane.* Paris: Gallimard, 1965.

Ellul, Jacques. *The Subversion of Christianity.* Grand Rapids, MI: Eerdmans, 1986.

Ericksen, Adam. "Tawhid: The Oneness of God and the Desire for the Good." In Palaver and Schenk, *Mimetic Theory and World Religions*, 401–12.

Evans-Pritchard, E. E. *Theories of Primitive Religion.* Oxford: Clarendon Press, 1965.

Faggioli, Massimo. "Pope Francis's *Gaudete et Exsultate.*" *Commonweal*, April 9, 2018. https://www.commonwealmagazine.org/pope-franciss-gaudete-et-exsultate-0.

Fasching, Darrell. *The Ethical Challenge of Auschwitz and Hiroshima: Apocalypse or Utopia?* Albany: State University of New York Press, 1993.

Finlan, Stephen. *Problems with Atonement.* Collegeville, MN: Liturgical Press, 2005.

Fiorenza, Elisabeth Schüssler. "The Ethics of Biblical Interpretation: Decentering Biblical Scholarship." *Journal of Biblical Literature* 107, no. 1 (1988): 3–17.

Fiske, Alan Page, and Tage Shakti Rai. *Virtuous Violence: Hurting and Killing to Create Sustain, End, and Honor Social Relationships.* Cambridge: Cambridge University Press, 2015.

Flavius Josephus. *Antiquities of the Jews.* In *The Complete Works of Flavius Josephus, the Celebrated Jewish Historian*, translated by William Whiston, 29–498. Philadelphia: Potter, 1895.

Fleming, Chris. "The Last of the Hedgehogs." *Los Angeles Review of Books*, August 16, 2020. https://lareviewofbooks.org/article/the-last-of-the-hedgehogs/.

Flynn, Nick. "Emptying Town." In *Some Ether*, 19. Minneapolis: Graywolf Press, 2000.

Foucault, Michel. "About the Beginning of the Hermeneutics of the Self." In *Religion and Culture*, edited by Jeremy R. Carrette, 158–81. New York: Routledge, 1999.

———. *The Hermeneutics of the Subject: Lectures at the Collège de France, 1981–82.* New York: Picador, 2001.

———. "Self Writing." In *Ethics: Subjectivity and Truth*, edited by Paul Rabinow, 207–22. New York: New Press, 1994.

———. "Technologies of the Self." In *Technologies of the Self: A Seminar with Michel Foucault*, edited by Luther H. Martin, Huck Gutman, and Patrick H. Hutton, 16–49. Amherst: University of Massachusetts Press, 1988.

Frank, David. "Arguing with God, Talmudic Discourse, and the Jewish Countermodel: Implications for the Study of Argumentation." *Argumentation and Advocacy* 41 (2004): 71–86.

———. "Engaging a Rhetorical God: Developing the Capacities of Mercy and Justice" In Bernard-Donals and Jensen, *Responding to the Sacred*, 51–76.

———. "The Origins of the Jewish Rhetorical Tradition: Levinas's Rhetorical Demand and Rhetoric's Demand on Levinas." *Journal of Communication and Religion* 44, no. 1 (2021): 5–29.

Freccero, John. "Logology: Burke on St. Augustine." In *Representing Kenneth Burke*, edited by Hayden White and Margaret Brose, 52–67. Baltimore: Johns Hopkins University Press, 1982.

Galvin, John. "The Marvelous Exchange: Raymund Schwager's Interpretation of the History of Soteriology." *Thomist* 53, no. 4 (1989): 675–91.

194 BIBLIOGRAPHY

Gandhi, M. K. *Non-Violent Resistance (Satyagraha)*. New York: Schocken Books, 1951.

Gauchet, Marcel. *The Disenchantment of the World: A Political History of Religion*. Translated by Oscar Burge. Princeton: Princeton University Press, 1997.

Ghosh, Amitav. *The Great Derangement: Climate Change and the Unthinkable*. Chicago: University of Chicago Press, 2016.

Girard, René. *Battling to the End: Conversations with Benoît Chantre*. Translated by Mary Baker. East Lansing: Michigan State University, 2010.

———. "Conversion in Literature and Christianity." In *Mimesis and Theory: Essays on Literature and Criticism, 1953–2005*, 263–73. Stanford: Stanford University Press, 2011.

———. *Deceit, Desire, and the Novel: Self and Other in Literary Structure*. Translated by Yvonne Freccero. Baltimore: Johns Hopkins University Press, 1965.

———. *The Girard Reader*. Edited by James G. Williams. New York: Crossroad, 2002.

———. "An Interview with René Girard." In *To Double Business Bound: Essays on Literature, Mimesis, and Anthropology*, 199–229. Baltimore: Johns Hopkins University Press, 1978.

———. *I See Satan Fall like Lightning*. Translated by James G. Williams. Maryknoll, NY: Orbis, 2001.

———. "Is There Antisemitism in the Gospels?" *Biblical Interpretation* 1, no. 3 (1993): 339–52.

———. *Job: The Victim of His People*. Translated by Yvonne Freccero. Stanford: Stanford University Press, 1987.

———. "Literature and Christianity: A Personal View." *Philosophy and Literature* 23, no. 1 (1999): 32–43.

———. *Mimesis and Theory: Essays on Literature and Criticism, 1953–2005*. Edited by Robert Doran. Stanford: Stanford University Press, 2008.

———. *The One by Whom Scandal Comes*. Translated by M. B. DeBevoise. East Lansing: Michigan State University Press, 2014.

———. "The Passionate Oxymoron in Shakespeare's *Romeo and Juliet*." 2005. In *Mimesis and Theory: Essays on Literature and Criticism, 1953–2005*, edited by Robert Doran, 274–89. Stanford: Stanford University Press, 2008.

———. *Resurrection from the Underground: Feodor Dostoyevsky*. Edited and translated by James G. Williams. East Lansing: Michigan State University Press, 2012.

———. *Sacrifice*. Translated by Matthew Pattillo and David Dawson. East Lansing: Michigan State the University Press, 2011.

———. *The Scapegoat*. Translated by Yvonne Freccero. Baltimore: Johns Hopkins University Press, 1989.

———. *A Theater of Envy: William Shakespeare*. New York: Oxford University Press, 1991.

———. *Things Hidden Since the Foundation of the World*. Translated by Stephen Bann and Michael Metteer. Stanford: Stanford University Press, 1987.

———. *Violence and the Sacred*. Translated by Patrick Gregory. Baltimore: Johns Hopkins University Press, 1977.

———. "Violence in Biblical Narrative." *Philosophy and Literature* 23, no. 2 (1999): 387–92.

———. *When These Things Begin: Conversations with Michel Treguer*. Translated by Trevor Cribben Merrill. East Lansing: Michigan State University Press, 2014.

Girard, René, Pierpaolo Antonello, and João Cezar de Castro Rocha. *Evolution and Conversion: Dialogues on the Origin of Culture*. London: Continuum, 2008.

Girard, René, and Raymund Schwager. *Correspondence, 1974–1991*. Edited by Scott Cowdell, Chris Fleming, Joel Hodge, and Mathias Moosbrugger. Translated by Chris Fleming and Sheelah Treflé Hidden. New York: Bloomsbury Academic, 2016.

Gisotti, Alessandro. "El perfil humano y pastoral del Papa Bergoglio." In *Los lenguages del Papa Francisco*, edited by Jacinto Núñez Regodón, 15–32. Salamanca: Universidad Pontifica de Salamanca, 2015.

Golsan, Richard J. *René Girard and Myth: An Introduction*. New York: Routledge, 2002.

Goodhart, Sandor. *The Prophetic Law: Essays in Judaism, Girardianism, Literary Studies, and the Ethical*. East Lansing: Michigan State University Press, 2014.

Gorringe, Timothy J. "Atonement." In Scott and Cavanaugh, *Blackwell Companion to Political Theology*, 363–76.

Government of Canada. *The Residential School System*. September 1, 2020. https://www .canada.ca/en/parks-canada/news/2020/09/the-residential-school-system.html.

Grassi, Ernesto. *Rhetoric as Philosophy: The Humanist Tradition*. 1980. Translated by John Michael Krois and Azizeh Azodi. Carbondale: Southern Illinois University Press, 2001.

Greenbaum, Andrea, and Deborah Holdstein, eds. *Judaic Perspectives in Rhetoric and Composition*. New York: Hampton Press, 2008.

Gross, Daniel. *Being-Moved: Rhetoric as the Art of Listening*. Berkeley: University of California Press, 2020.

———. "Historiography and the Limits of (Sacred) Rhetoric." In Bernard-Donals and Jensen, *Responding to the Sacred*, 236–56.

Guarino, Thomas G. *Vattimo and Theology*. London: T&T Clark, 2009.

Hadot, Pierre. *Philosophy as a Way of Life*. Edited by Arnold I. Davidson. Translated by Michael Chase. Malden, MA: Blackwell, 2005.

Haidt, Jonathan. *The Righteous Mind: Why Good People Are Divided by Politics and Religion*. New York: Pantheon, 2012.

Hardin, Michael. "Practical Reflections on Nonviolent Atonement." In *Violence, Desire, and the Sacred*, vol. 2, *René Girard and Sacrifice in Life, Love, and Literature*, edited by Scott Cowdell, Chris Fleming, and Joel Hodge, 247–58. New York: Bloomsbury Academic, 2014.

Hardin, Michael, and Steven E. Berry. *Reading the Bible with René Girard: Conversations with Steven E. Berry*. Edited by Michael Hardin. Lancaster, PA: JDL Press, 2015. ebook.

Harrison, Robert Pogue. "The Prophet of Envy." *New York Review of Books*, December 20, 2018. https://www.nybooks.com/articles/2018/12/20/rene-girard-prophet-envy/.

Hart, David Bentley. *The Beauty of the Infinite: The Aesthetics of Christian Truth*. Grand Rapids, MI: Eerdmans, 2003.

———. "A Gift Exceeding Every Debt: An Eastern Orthodox Appreciation of Anselm's *Cur Deus Homo*." *Doctores Ecclesiae* 7, no. 3 (1998): 333–49.

Haven, Cynthia L. *Evolution of Desire: A Life of René Girard*. East Lansing: Michigan State University Press, 2018.

Heidegger, Martin. *Being and Time*. 1962. Translated by John Macquarrie and Edward Robinson. New York: Harper Perennial, 2008.

———. "Overcoming Metaphysics." In *The End of Philosophy*, translated by Joan Stambaugh, 84–110. Chicago: University of Chicago Press, 2003.

———. "Phenomenology and Theology." Translated by James G. Hart and John C. Maraldo. In *Pathmarks*, edited by William McNeill, 38–62. New York: Cambridge University Press, 1998.

Heim, S. Mark. *Saved from Sacrifice: A Theology of the Cross*. Grand Rapids, MI: Eerdmans, 2006.

Heneghan, Tom. "Fending Off the Rising Right, Bavarian Leader Puts Crosses in State Offices." *National Catholic Reporter*, June 7, 2018. https://www.ncronline.org/news /world/fending-rising-right-bavarian-leader-puts-crosses-state-offices.

Hertzler-McCain, Aleja. "Indigenous Call Vatican's Repudiation of Doctrine of Discovery 'Only a Step.'" *National Catholic Reporter*, April 6, 2023. https://www.ncronline.org /news/indigenous-call-vaticans-repudiation-doctrine-discovery-only-step.

Hopkins, Julie M. *Toward a Feminist Christology: Jesus of Nazareth, European Women, and the Christological Crisis*. Grand Rapids, MI: Eerdmans, 1995.

Hopper, Stanley Romaine. "The Literary Imagination and the Doing of Theology." In *The Way of Transfiguration: Religious Imagination as Theopoiesis*, edited by R. Melvin Keiser and Tony Stoneburner, 207–29. Louisville, KY: Westminster / John Knox Press, 1992.

Houtman, Alberdina, Marcel Poorthuis, Joshua Schwartz, and Yossi Turner. Introduction to *The Actuality of Sacrifice: Past and Present*, edited by Alberdina Houtman, Marcel Poorthuis, Joshua Schwartz, and Yossi Turner, 1–5. Leiden: Brill, 2014.

Hyde, Michael J. "Introduction: Rhetorically, We Dwell." In *The Ethos of Rhetoric*, edited by Michael J. Hyde, xiii–xxviii. Columbia: University of South Carolina Press, 2004.

Janzen, David. *The Social Meanings of Sacrifice in the Hebrew Bible: A Study of Four Writings*. Berlin: Walter de Gruyter, 2004.

Jenson, Robert W. *A Theology in Outline: Can These Bones Live?* Edited by Adam Eitel. New York: Oxford University Press, 2016.

The Jewish Study Bible. 2nd ed. Edited by Adele Berlin and Marc Zvi Brettler. New York: Oxford University Press, 2014.

Jiménez Rodríguez, Luis Orlando. "El concepto teológico de 'estilo' como clave de lectura de *Laudato si'* y *Gaudete et exsultate*: Una manera de encontrar a Dios en la acción transformadora del mundo." *Theologica Xaveriana* 70 (2020): 1–28.

Johnson, Elizabeth A. *Creation and the Cross: The Mercy of God for a Planet in Peril*. Maryknoll, NY: Orbis, 2018.

———. *Quest for the Living God: Mapping Frontiers in the Theology of God*. New York: Continuum, 2007.

Johnstone, Henry W. "Some Reflections on Argumentation." In *Philosophy, Rhetoric, and Argumentation*, edited by Maurice Natanson and Henry W. Johnstone, 1–9. University Park: Penn State University Press, 1965.

Jonkers, Peter. "In the World, but Not of the World: The Prospects of Christianity in the Modern World." *Bijdragen: International Journal for Philosophy and Theology* 61, no. 4 (2000): 370–89.

Kallscheuer, Otto. "Girard and Religion in the Age of Secularism." In Palaver and Schenk, *Mimetic Theory and World Religions*, 111–37.

Kaplan, Grant. *René Girard, Unlikely Apologist: Mimetic Theory and Fundamental Theology*, Notre Dame: University of Notre Dame Press, 2016.

Kaufman, David. *Jewhooing the Sixties: American Celebrity and Jewish Identity*. Waltham, MA: Brandeis University Press, 2012.

Kearney, Richard. *Anatheism: Returning to God After God*. New York: Columbia University Press, 2010.

———. "God After God: An Anatheist Attempt to Reimagine God." In Kearney and Zimmermann, *Reimagining the Sacred*, 6–18.

———. *The God Who May Be: A Hermeneutics of Religion*. Bloomington: Indiana University Press, 2001.

———. *Poetics of Modernity: Toward a Hermeneutic Imagination*. Amherst, NY: Humanity Books, 1999.

———. *Strangers, Gods and Monsters: Interpreting Otherness*. London: Routledge, 2003.

Kearney, Richard, and Matthew Clemente. Introduction to *The Art of Anatheism*, edited by Richard Kearney and Matthew Clemente, vii–ix. Lanham, MD: Rowman and Littlefield, 2018.

Kearney, Richard, and Jens Zimmermann, eds. *Reimagining the Sacred: Richard Kearney Debates God*. New York: Columbia University Press, 2016.

Keller, Catherine. *Intercarnations: Exercises in Theological Possibility*. New York: Fordham University Press, 2017.

———. "Kearney's Endless Morning." In *After God: Richard Kearney and the Religious Turn in Continental Philosophy*, edited by John Panteleimon Manoussakis, 355–61. New York: Fordham University Press, 2006.

———. "Theopoetics: A Becoming History." In Kearney and Clemente, *Art of Anatheism*, 29–41.

Kennedy, George A. "A Hoot in the Dark: The Evolution of a General Rhetoric." *Philosophy and Rhetoric* 25, no. 1 (1992): 1–21.

Kerr, Fergus. "Rescuing Girard's Argument?" *Modern Theology* 8, no. 4 (1992), 385–99.

Kirwan, Michael. *Discovering Girard*. Lanham, MD: Cowley, 2005.

Klemm, David E. "Toward a Rhetoric of Postmodern Theology: Through Barth and Heidegger." *Journal of the American Academy of Religion* 55, no. 3 (1987): 443–69.

Knightley, Phillip, and Caroline Kennedy. *An Affair of State: The Profumo Case and the Framing of Stephen Ward*. New York: Atheneum, 1987.

Lamb, Christopher. "Pope Francis on Tradition and the Development of Doctrine." *Chicago Catholic*, August 3, 2022. https://www.chicagocatholic.com/vatican/-/article/2022 /08/03/pope-francis-on-tradition-and-the-development-of-doctrine.

Lamy, Jérôme. "Sociology of a Disciplinary Bifurcation: Bruno Latour and His Move from Philosophy/Theology to Sociology." *Social Science Information* 60, no. 1 (2021): 107–30.

Lanham, Richard A. "The 'Q' Question." In *The Electronic Word: Democracy, Technology, and the Arts*, 155–94. Chicago: University of Chicago Press, 1994.

———. *Style: An Anti-Textbook*. 2nd rev. ed. Philadelphia: Paul Dry Books, 2007.

Latour, Bruno. *Facing Gaia: Eight Lectures on the New Climatic Regime*. Translated by Catherine Porter. London: Polity, 2017.

———. *An Inquiry into Modes of Existence: An Anthropology of the Moderns*. Translated by Catherine Porter. Cambridge: Harvard University Press, 2013.

———. *On the Modern Cult of the Factish Gods*. Durham, NC: Duke University Press, 2010.

———. *Rejoicing: Or the Torments of Religious Speech*. Translated by Julie Rose. Cambridge, UK: Polity, 2013.

———. *We Have Never Been Modern*. Translated by Catherine Porter. Cambridge: Harvard University Press, 1993.

Lee, Poong-in. "Is an Anti-sacrificial Reading of Hebrews Plausible?" In *Sacrifice, Scripture, and Substitution: Readings in Ancient Judaism and Christianity*, edited by Ann W. Astell and Sandor Goodhart, 424–44. Notre Dame, IN: University of Notre Dame Press, 2011.

Levertov, Denise. *A Door in the Hive*. New York: New Directions, 1989.

Levine, Amy-Jill. *The Misunderstood Jew: The Church and the Scandal of the Jewish Jesus*. San Francisco: Harper San Francisco, 2006.

Liddell, Henry George, and Robert Scott. *A Greek-English Lexicon*. Edited by Henry Stuart Jones and Roderick McKenzie. Oxford: Clarendon Press, 1940.

Lohlker, Rüdiger. "Islam: Law and Violence (and Nonviolence)." In Palaver and Schenk, *Mimetic Theory and World Religions*, 413–26.

Lumen Gentium. November 21, 1964. https://www.vatican.va/archive/hist_councils/ii_vati
can_council/documents/vat-ii_const_19641121_lumen-gentium_en.html.

Lundberg, Christian. "Rhetoric's Affective Reckoning: Holy Icons and Sacred Commitments."
In *New Directions in Rhetoric and Religion: Exploring Emerging Intersections of Religion, Public Discourse, and Rhetorical Scholarship,* edited by James W. Vining, 259–84. Lanham, MD: Lexington Books, 2021.

Lundberg, Christian, and Joshua Gunn. "'Ouija Board, Are There Any Communications?': Agency, Ontotheology, and the Death of the Humanist Subject, or, Continuing the ARS Conversation." *Rhetoric Society Quarterly* 35, no. 4 (2005): 83–105.

Lynch, Christopher. "Religion and the Environment in the Rhetoric of Thomas Berry and Pope Francis." *Journal of Communication and Religion* 45, no. 1. (2022): 111–29.

Lynch, Paul. "On Care for Our Common Discourse: Pope Francis's Nonmodern Epideictic." *Rhetoric Society Quarterly* 47, no. 5 (2017): 463–82.

Lynch, Paul, and Nathaniel Rivers. Introduction to *Thinking with Bruno Latour in Rhetoric and Composition,* edited by Paul Lynch and Nathaniel Rivers, 1–22. Carbondale: Southern Illinois University Press, 2015.

Maddux, Kristy. "Finding Comedy in Theology: A Hopeful Supplement to Kenneth Burke's Logology." *Philosophy and Rhetoric* 39, no. 3 (2006): 208–32.

Mailloux, Steven. "Notes on Prayerful Rhetoric with Divinities." *Philosophy and Rhetoric* 47, no. 4 (2014): 419–33.

———. "Political Theologies of Sacred Rhetoric." In Bernard-Donals and Jensen, *Responding to the Sacred,* 77–98.

———. *Rhetoric's Pragmatism: Essays in Rhetorical Hermeneutics.* University Park: Penn University Press, 2017.

Manning, Robert J. S. "Emmanuel Levinas and René Girard: Religious Prophets of Nonviolence." *Philosophical Journal of Conflict and Violence* 1, no. 1 (2017): 22–38.

Manson, Jamie. "Should Women Rejoice over *Gaudete et Exsultate*?" *National Catholic Reporter,* April 13, 2018. https://www.ncronline.org/news/opinion/grace-margins/should-women-rejoice-over-gaudete-et-exsultate.

Marback, Richard. "A Meditation on Vulnerability in Rhetoric." *Rhetoric Review* 29, no. 1 (2010): 1–13.

McCormack, Bruce Lindley. "Atonement." In *The Cambridge Dictionary of Christian Theology,* edited by Ian A. MacFarland et al., 43–45. Cambridge: Cambridge University Press, 2011.

Medhurst, Martin J. "Religious Belief and Scholarship: A Complex Relationship." *JCR* 27 (2004): 40–47.

Megill-Cobbler, Thelma. "A Feminist Rethinking of Punishment Imagery in Atonement." *Dialog* 35, no. 1 (1996): 14–20.

Meister Eckhart. *The Complete Mystical Works of Meister Eckhart.* Edited by Bernard McGinn. Translated by Maurice O'C. Walshe. New York: Herder and Herder, 2009.

Milbank, John. *Theology and Social Theory.* 2nd ed. Malden, MA: Blackwell, 2006.

Miles, Jack. *God: A Biography.* New York: Vintage, 1996.

Miller, David L. "Theopoetry or Theopoetics?" *CrossCurrents* 60, no. 1 (2010): 6–23.

Minear, Paul S. "The Holy and the Sacred." *Theology Today* 47, no. 1 (1990): 5–12.

Moltmann, Jürgen. *The Crucified God.* Minneapolis: Fortress Press, 2015.

Muckelbauer, John. *The Future of Invention: Rhetoric, Postmodernism, and the Problem of Change.* Albany: State University of New York Press, 2008.

———. "Returns of the Question." *Enculturation* 5, no. 2 (2004). https://www.enculturation.net/5_2/muckelbauer.html.

Muilenburg, James. "Form Criticism and Beyond." *Journal of Biblical Literature* 88, no. 1 (1969): 1–18.

Nelson, Cary. "Writing as the Accomplice of Language: Kenneth Burke and Poststructuralism." In *The Legacy of Kenneth Burke*, edited by Herbert W. Simons and Trevor Metia, 156–73. Madison: University of Wisconsin Press, 1989.

The New American Bible. Washington, DC: Confraternity of Christian Doctrine, 1991.

Nicotra, Jodie. "Hacking the Sacred (or Not): Rhetorical Attunements for Ecodelic Imbrication." In Bernard-Donals and Jensen, *Responding to the Sacred*, 141–56.

Norris, Kathleen. *Amazing Grace: A Vocabulary of Faith*. New York: Riverhead, 1998.

OED Online. Oxford University Press, December 2021. http://www.oed.com.

Orsuto, Donna. *Holiness*. London: Bloomsbury, 2006.

Otto, Rudolf. *The Idea of the Holy*. 1917. Translated by John W. Harvey. New York: Oxford University Press, 1967.

Oxtoby, Willard G. "The Idea of the Holy." In *The Encyclopedia of Religion*, edited by Mircea Eliade, vol. 6, 431–38. New York: Macmillan, 1987.

Palaver, Wolfgang. *René Girard's Mimetic Theory*. Translated by Gabriel Borrud. East Lansing: Michigan State University Press, 2013.

———. *Transforming the Sacred into Saintliness: Reflecting on Violence and Religion with René Girard*. Cambridge: Cambridge University Press, 2020.

Palaver, Wolfgang, and Richard Schenk, eds. *Mimetic Theory and World Religions*. East Lansing: Michigan State University Press, 2018.

Pender, Kelly. *Techne, from Neoclassicism to Postmodernism*. Anderson, SC: Parlor Press, 2011.

Perelman, Chaim, and Lucie Olbrechts-Tyteca. *The New Rhetoric: A Treatise on Argumentation*. Translated by John Wilkinson and Purcell Weaver. Notre Dame, IN: University of Notre Dame Press, 1971.

Pew Research Center. "When Americans Say They Believe in God, What Do They Mean?" April 25, 2018. https://www.pewforum.org/2018/04/25/when-americans-say-they-believe-in-god-what-do-they-mean/.

———. "Why America's 'Nones' Don't Identify with a Religion." August 8, 2018. https://www.pewresearch.org/fact-tank/2018/08/08/why-americas-nones-dont-identify-with-a-religion/.

Plato. *Republic, Books 1–5*. Ca. 375 BC. Edited and translated by Chris Emlyn-Jones and William Preddy. Cambridge: Harvard University Press, 2013.

Poland, Lynn. "The Idea of the Holy and the History of the Sublime." *Journal of Religion* 72, no. 2 (1992): 175–97.

Pongratz-Lippitt, Christa. "Nuncio Berates Cardinal Marx over Bavarian Crosses." *The Tablet*, May 2, 2018. https://www.thetablet.co.uk/news/9004/nuncio-berates-cardinal-marx-over-bavarian-crosses.

Pope Francis. *Gaudete et Exsultate*. Huntington, IN: Our Sunday Visitor, 2018.

———. *Laudato Si': On Care for Our Common Home*. Huntington, IN: Our Sunday Visitor, 2015.

Pope Paul VI. *Evangelii Nuntiandi: On Evangelization in the Modern World*. Boston: Pauline Books and Media, 1975.

Poulakos, John. "Toward a Sophistic Definition of Rhetoric." *Philosophy and Rhetoric* 16, no. 1 (1983): 35–48.

Povoledo, Elisabetta. "Vatican Repudiates 'Doctrine of Discovery,' Used as Justification for Colonization." *New York Times*, March 30, 2023. https://www.nytimes.com/2023/03/30/world/europe/vatican-repudiates-doctrine-of-discovery-colonization.html.

Proudfoot, Wayne. *Religious Experience*. Berkeley: University of California Press, 1985.

Putt, B. Keith. "Imagination, Kenosis, and Repetition: Richard Kearney's Theopoetics of the Possible God." *Revista Portuguesa de Filosofia* 60, no. 4 (2004): 953–83.

Raphael, Melissa. *Rudolf Otto and the Concept of Holiness*. New York: Oxford University Press, 1997.

Ratcliffe, Krista. *Rhetorical Listening: Identification, Gender, Whiteness*. Carbondale: Southern Illinois University Press, 2005.

Redekop, Vern Neufeld. *From Violence to Blessing: How and Understanding of Deep-Rooted Conflict Can Open Paths to Reconciliation*. Ottawa: Novalis, 2002.

Richardson, Alan, and John Boden, eds. *The Westminster Dictionary of Christian Theology*. Philadelphia: Westminster Press, 1983.

Rickert, Thomas. *Ambient Rhetoric: The Attunements of Rhetorical Being*. Pittsburgh: University of Pittsburgh Press, 2013.

Rivers, Nathaniel. "Apathy." In *A New Handbook of Rhetoric: Inverting the Classical Vocabulary*, edited by Michele Kennerly, 139–54. University Park: Penn State University Press, 2021.

Robbins, Jeffrey W. "Introduction: After the Death of God." In Caputo and Vattimo, *After the Death of God*, 1–24.

Rogerson, John. W. "What Is Holiness?" In Barton, *Holiness*, 3–21.

Rueckert, William. *Kenneth Burke and the Drama of Human Relations*. 2nd ed. Berkeley: University of California Press, 1983.

Sacks, Jonathan. *Not in God's Name: Confronting Religious Violence*. New York: Schocken, 2015.

Schwager, Raymund. *Jesus in the Drama of Salvation: Toward a Biblical Doctrine of Redemption*. New York: Crossroad, 1999.

———. *Must There Be Scapegoats? Violence and Redemption in the Bible*. Translated by Maria L. Assad. San Francisco: Harper and Row, 1987.

Scubla, Lucien. "The Christianity of René Girard and the Nature of Religion." Translated by Mark R. Anspach. In *Violence and Truth: On the Work of René Girard*, edited by Paul Dumouchel, 160–78. Stanford: Stanford University Press, 1988.

Scult, Allen. *Being Jewish/Reading Heidegger*. New York: Fordham University Press, 2004.

Sheldrake, Philip. *Befriending Our Desires*. 3rd ed. Collegeville, MN: Liturgical Press, 2016.

Sheth, Noel. "Girard and Hindu Sacrifice." In Palaver and Schenk, *Mimetic Theory and World Religions*, 323–38.

Shreiber, Maeera Y. *Holy Envy: Writing in the Jewish Christian Borderzone*. New York: Fordham University Press, 2022.

Siegel, Lee. *Why Argument Matters*. New Haven: Yale University Press, 2022.

Sparado, Antonio. "A Big Heart Open to God: An Interview with Pope Francis." *America*, September 30, 2013. https://www.americamagazine.org/faith/2013/09/30/big-heart-open-god-interview-pope-francis.

Stormer, Nathan, and Bridie McGreavy. "Thinking Ecologically About Rhetoric's Ontology: Capacity, Vulnerability, and Resilience." *Philosophy and Rhetoric* 50, no. 1 (2017): 1–25.

Stroope, Samuel, Paul Froese, Heather M. Rackin, and Jack Delehanty. "Unchurched Christian Nationalism and the 2016 Presidential Election." *Sociological Forum* 36, no. 2 (2021): 405–25.

Tarot, Camille. "Émile Durkheim and After: The War over the Sacred in French Sociology in the 20th Century." *Distinktion: Scandinavian Journal of Social Theory* 10, no. 2 (2009): 11–30.

Taylor, Barbara Brown. *Holy Envy*. New York: Harper One, 2019.

Taylor, Charles. *Dilemmas and Connections: Selected Essays*. Cambridge: Harvard University Press, 2011.

———. *A Secular Age*. Cambridge: Harvard University Press, 2007.

Tracy, David, Merold Westphal, and Jens Zimmermann. "Theism, Atheism, Anatheism." In Kearney and Zimmermann, *Reimagining the Sacred*, 219–39.

Traube, Elizabeth. "Incest and Mythology: Anthropological and Girardian Perspectives." *Berkshire Review* 14 (1979): 37–53.

Vahanian, Gabriel. *The Death of God: The Culture of Our Post-Christian Era*. New York: George Braziller, 1961.

Vattimo, Gianni. *After Christianity*. Translated by Luca D'Isanto. New York: Columbia University Press, 2002.

———. *Belief*. Translated by Luca D'Isanto and David Webb. Stanford: Stanford University Press, 1999.

———. "Dialectics, Difference, and Weak Thought." Translated by Thomas Harrison. *Graduate Faculty Philosophy Journal* 10, no. 1 (1984): 151–64.

———. *The End of Modernity: Nihilism and Hermeneutics in Postmodern Culture*. Baltimore: Johns Hopkins University Press, 1988.

———. "Myth and the Fate of Secularization." *RES: Anthropology and Aesthetics* 9 (1985): 29–35.

———. "Nihilism as Postmodern Christianity." In *Transcendence and Beyond: A Postmodern Inquiry*, edited by John D. Caputo and Michael J. Scanlon, 44–48. Bloomington: Indiana University Press, 2007.

———. "Optimistic Nihilism." *Common Knowledge* 1, no. 3 (1992): 37–44.

———. "Toward a Nonreligious Christianity." In *After the Death of God*, by John Caputo and Gianni Vattimo, 27–46. New York: Columbia University Press, 2007.

———. "'Verwindung': Nihilism and the Postmodern in Philosophy." *SubStance* 16, no. 2, iss. 53 (1987): 7–17.

Vattimo, Gianni, and René Girard. *Christianity, Truth, and Weakening Faith*. Edited by Pierpaolo Antonello. Translated by William McCuaig. New York: Columbia University Press, 2010.

Vattimo, Gianni, with Piergiorgio Paterlini. *Not Being God: A Collaborative Autobiography*. Translated by William McCuaig. New York: Columbia University Press, 2009.

Watts, James W. "The Rhetoric of Sacrifice." In *Ritual and Metaphor: Sacrifice in the Bible*, edited by Christian A. Eberhart, 3–16. Atlanta: Society of Biblical Literature, 2011.

Weaver, J. Denny. *The Nonviolent Atonement*. Grand Rapids, MI: Eerdmans, 2001.

———. "Series Editor's Foreword." In *Songs from an Empty Cage: Poetry, Mystery, Anabaptism and Peace*, by Jeff Gundy, 13–14. Telford, PA: Cascadis, 2013.

Wess, Robert. *Kenneth Burke: Rhetoric, Subjectivity, Postmodernism*. Cambridge: Cambridge University Press, 1996.

White, Eric Charles. *Kaironomia: On the Will-to-Invent*. Ithaca: Cornell University Press, 1987.

Wieseltier, Leon. "Christianism." *Liberties* 2, no. 3 (2022). https://libertiesjournal.com/articles/issue/volume-02-number-03/.

Wilder, Amos. *Theopoetic: Theology and the Religious Imagination*. Philadelphia: Fortress Press, 1976.

Williams, Delores. *Sisters in the Wilderness: The Challenge of Womanist God-Talk*. Maryknoll, NY: Orbis, 1993.

Wiman, Christian. *My Bright Abyss: Meditation of a Modern Believer*. New York: Farrar, Straus and Giroux, 2014.

BIBLIOGRAPHY

Wink, Walter. *Engaging the Powers: Discernment and Resistance in a World of Domination.* Minneapolis: Fortress Press, 1992.

Wood, James, and Richard Kearney. "Theism, Atheism, and Anatheism." In *Richard Kearney's Anatheistic Wager: Philosophy, Theology, Poetics*, edited by Chris Doude van Troostwijk and Matthew Clemente, 7–39. Bloomington: Indiana University Press, 2018.

Worsham, Lynn. "Moving Beyond the Logic of Sacrifice: Animal Studies, Trauma Studies, and the Path to Posthumanism." In *Writing Posthumanism: Posthuman Writing*, edited by Sidney I. Dobrin, 19–55. Anderson, SC: Parlor Press, 2015.

Wright, N. T. "The Christian Challenge in the Postmodern World." *Response* 28, no. 2 (2005). https://spu.edu/depts/uc/response/summer2k5/features/postmodern.asp.

———. *The Day the Revolution Began: Reconsidering the Meaning of Jesus's Crucifixion.* San Francisco: HarperOne, 2016.

Wuellner, Wilhelm. "Where Is Rhetorical Criticism Taking Us?" *Catholic Biblical Quarterly* 49, no. 3 (1987): 448–63.

Xenophon. *On the Art of Horsemanship.* In *Xenophon in Seven Volumes*, translated by E. C. Marchant and G. W. Bowersock, vol. 7. Cambridge: Harvard University Press, 1925.

Index

Abel, 69
Abelard, Peter, 177n67
abortion, 186n123
Abraham, 46, 132–33
Adam, 94–95
Adams, Rebecca, 62–63, 71, 80, 82, 168nn33–34
Agamben, Giorgio, 23, 120, 131, 182n26
agency, 33–35, 44, 93–94, 153, 177n72
Alberg, Jeremiah, 60
Alison, James, 98
Ambient Rhetoric (Pickert), 3
ambiguous rhetoric, 118–21
ambivalent rheotric, 127–35
Anselm of Canterbury, 98–99, 176n59, 177n66
antimyth, 70–72
antisemitism, 25, 179n102
    "death of God" and, 163n17
    in Gospels, 171n95
    mimetic theory and, 148
    original sin and, 105
    persistence of, 76
    resurgence of, 148–49, 172n97
Antonello, Pierpaolo, 180n139
apathy, 49–51
Aquinas, Thomas, 175n35, 177n67
Arnett, Ronald, 172n106
atonement, 10–11, 86–89, 93–104, 113–14, 178n81
    in Brown and Parker, 177n73
    in Francis, 186n121
    as persuasion, 22
    scapegoating and, 68
    in Stump, 176n57
    as term, 176n52
Augustine of Hippo, 2, 92, 110
Aulén, Gustav, 97, 176n59

Ballif, Michelle, 25, 33–34, 36
Balthasar, Hans Urs von, 138
Battling to the End (Girard), 75, 80, 146–47
Beatitudes, 141, 185n102
Being-Moved (Gross), 38, 154
Bergoglio, Jorge Mario, 143, 179n103
    See also Francis (pope)

Bernard-Donals, Michael, 117, 119, 129–30, 132–34, 152
Berrigan, Daniel, 147
Bessette, Jean, 64
Bible
    in Girard, 55, 59
    as term, 166n121
    victimhood and, 71–72
    See also specific books
Biesecker, Barbara, 93–95
Bizzell, Patricia, 152
Black liberation theology, 99, 159n14
Black Power, 159n14
blandness, 48
Bloy, León, 138
Blumenthal, David, 126–27
boarding schools, Canadian, 115–16
Bobbio, Norberto, 47–48
Booth, Wayne, 17–18, 120–21
Borghesi, Massimo, 135, 143, 186n125
bringing forth, 37
Brock, Rita Nakashima, 50–51
Brown, Joanne Carlson, 99–100, 104, 177n73
Bruce, Lenny, 105, 179nn102–3
Brueggermann, Walter, 183n52
Buddhism, 35
Bultmann, Rudolf, 41
Burke, Kenneth, 2, 11–12, 22, 88, 94–95, 99, 175n29, 175n35
    agency in, 93–94
    atonement in, 95–96, 175n46
    Carter on, 175n37
    complicity in, 86
    Girard on, 89
    language in, 174n24
    meekness in, 48–49
    redemption in, 168n46
    rhetoric as way of life in, 155–56
    scapegoating in, 59, 65, 67, 167n30
    violence in, 55–56, 90–92
    vulnerability in, 156–57
burning bush, 24
Butler, Judith, 45, 47
Butmann, Rudolph, 19

204   INDEX

Cahill, Lisa Sowle, 97
Cain, 69, 131–32
Canadian boarding schools, 115–16
capacity, 35, 37
Caputo, John, 27–28, 30, 53, 129, 163n17, 177n72
Carter, C. Allen, 175n37
Caruana, John, 66, 169n50, 182n32
Cassirer, Ernst, 42
Catholic Social Teaching, 10
Cavanaugh, William, 90
Charney, Davida, 152
Chase, Kenneth, 15, 24–25, 33, 153, 163n45
"Christianists," 9–10
Christian nationalism, 9–10, 160n37
Christis Victor (Aulén), 97
Clemente, Matthew, 27
colonialism, 25, 116, 181n6
colonization, 48–49
Colossians, Epistle to, 101
Colpe, Carsten, 120
complicity, 16–17, 30–34, 47, 53, 86, 106
Cone, James, 99, 159n14
Confessions (Augustine), 92
confrontation, 26, 38–39, 45, 47–48, 80
conscientious objection, 38–39
consecration, 121–22
contingency, 33, 36
control, 30, 35
conversion, 102–3
Corinthians, First, 96, 164n52, 165n69
Corinthians, Second, 52, 165n69
Council of Nicaea, 28
cross, the, 10–11, 96, 104–5, 111–13
      See also Crucifixion
"cross pressure," 7–8
Crosswhite, James, 15–16, 25, 28, 36–37, 41–42, 44
Crowder, Colin, 183n43
Crowley, Sharon, 70, 182n12
Crucified God (Moltmann), 103
Crucifixion, 11, 78, 101
      See also cross, the
Crusius, Timothy, 94–95
Cur Deus Homo (Why the God-Man?) (Anselm of Canterbury), 98

Dasein, 42, 87
Davis, Diane, 3, 25, 33, 36–37, 63, 128, 177n72
Dawson, David, 10–11, 85
Death of God, The (Vahanian), 5, 8–9, 11
"death of God" theology, 5, 8–9, 159n14–159n15, 163n17

de Duve, Thierry, 6
Deep Rhetoric (Crosswhite), 15
deification, 27–28, 36
Depoortere, Frederiek, 125, 180n129
desire, 57–58, 61–63, 81, 157, 169n52
Detienne, Marcel, 74
Deuteronomy, Book of, 93
Dewey, Joanna, 172n95, 172n100
dialectic, negative, 17, 39
Dillon, Michele, 181n5
discipleship, 2
Doctrine of Discovery, 116, 181n6
Duns Scotus, 177n67
Durkheim, Émile, 23, 66, 118, 121–23, 184n58

Eagleton, Terry, 41, 104
Eckhart, Meister, 2
Elements of Eloquence, The (Forsyth), 1
Eliade, Mircea, 23, 118, 121, 124–25, 130, 134, 184n58
Elizabeth (cousin of Mary), 39
Ellul, Jacques, 19, 115–16, 143, 181n1, 181n8
"Emptying Town" (Flynn), 11
empty rhetoric, 35–38
End of Modernity, The (Vattimo), 179n117
eschatology, 24, 143, 161n1
ethics, 43, 71, 124, 169n50
ethos, 4, 18–20
Evangelii Gaudium (Francis), 140
Evangelii Nuntiandi (Paul VI), 144
Evans-Pritchard, E. E., 119–20
evocation, 123
Exodus, Book of, 24, 130–31, 150
Ezekiel, Book of, 1

Faggioli, Massimo, 136, 186n122
faith, 15
      Berrigan on, 147
      knowledge and, 173n123
      returning and renewal of, 29
      in Vattimo, 180n139
      weak, 108–9
Fasching, Darrell, 19
feminist theology, 99–100
Fernheimer, Janice, 152
Finlan, Stephen, 97, 175n46, 178n81
Fiske, Alan Page, 65, 168n43
Fitzgerald, Lauren, 152
Flavius Josephus, 165n92
Flynn, Nick, 11, 19
Forsyth, Mark, 1

INDEX

Foucault, Michel, 153, 155
Francis (pope), 23, 186n121
  on abortion, 186n123
  on the cross, as symbol, 179n103
  holiness in, 115–16, 118, 135–45
  Laudato Si', 185n103
Frank, David, 131–32, 151, 184n91
Frazer, James, 118, 160n55
Freccero, John, 89, 180n123
Freire, Paulo, 168n34
Freud, Sigmund, 67, 118, 169n52, 169n55
Future of Invention, The (Muckelbauer), 17

Gabriel (angel), 38, 45
Galatians, Epistle to, 185n108
Gandhi, Mahatma, 38, 154
Gauchet, Marcel, 6
Gaudete et Exsultate (Francis), 23, 115, 118, 135–43, 186n121
generosity, sacrifice and, 73
Genesis, Book of, 92, 95, 131–32, 151, 170n58, 177n79
Girard, René, 10–11
  Bible in, 55, 59
  conversion in, 102–3
  desire in, 57–58, 61–63, 169n52
  as distrustful of rhetoric, 31
  Gospels in, 66, 80, 171n95, 178n84
  humanism in, 59–60
  Jesus in, 80, 171n91
  meekness and, 54
  myth in, 70–72, 170n65
  persuasion in, 60–61
  post-Christian and, 56, 78–79, 83, 85
  religion defined in, 13
  rivalry in, 12, 21
  sacred in, 64–67
  sacrifice in, 73–78, 172n100
  scapegoating in, 67–70, 105
  subjectivity in, 59, 62
  supersessionism and, 74–76
  theorhetoric in, 78–82
  Vattimo and, 107–11
  violence in, 55, 57–58, 64
Gisotti, Alessandro, 185n104
Gnosticism, 140
God
  in Burke, 92, 96
  "death of," 5, 8–9, 159n5, 159n14, 163n17
  in definition of theorhetoric, 1–2
  love and, 19–20

  naming, 24
  onto-eschatology and, 161n1
  persuasion and, 3, 152
  solidarity of, with suffering, 103
  theorhetoric and, 133
  theorhetoric and question of, 15–16
  vulnerability and, 25
  who-is-probably, 25
God of the Oppressed (Cone), 99
God Who May Be, The (Kearney), 24
Gomorrah, 132, 151
Goodhart, Sandor, 75, 169n50, 171n91
Gorgias (Plato), 16, 18
Gorringe, Timothy, 103–4
Gospels, 11, 13, 66, 80, 171n95, 178n84
  See also specific Gospels
Grassi, Ernesto, 20, 164n66
Gross, Daniel, 38, 46, 104, 154, 184n73
Guarino, Thomas, 180n129
Gündüz, Erdem, 47
Gunn, Joshua, 128

Habermas, Jürgen, 181n5
Hadot, Pierre, 153–55, 187n31
Hagar, 177n79
Haidt, Jonathan, 12, 52
Hall, Stuart, 182n12
Handelman, Susan, 152
Harrison, Robert Pogue, 67
Hart, David Bentley, 81–82, 170n59
Haven, Cynthia, 180n123
Hebrews, Letter to, 74, 172n100
Hegel, Georg Wilhelm Friedrich, 186n125
Heidegger, Martin, 37, 41, 85–88, 106–7
Heim, S. Mark, 106
hierophany, 124–25, 130
Hölderlin, Friedrich, 149
Holdstein, Deborah, 152
holiness, 117–19, 126–27, 133–34, 137–40
holy, 22–23, 125–27
homophobia, 25
"Hoot in the Dark, A" (Kennedy), 24
hope, 149
Hopper, Stanley, 29, 162n16
humanism, 59–60, 128
Hyde, Michael, 4
hypocrisy, sacrifice and, 73

Idea of the Holy, The (Otto), 121, 123, 183n43
Ignatius of Loyola, 155, 185n104
imitation, 47, 51, 53, 62

206   INDEX

inaction, directed, 46
  See also *satyagraha*
Incarnation, 27–28, 42, 81, 176n57
Indigenous boarding schools, in Canada, 115–16
integralists, 9–10
interdividuals, 62
Isaiah, Book of, 75

James, William, 118, 159n5
January 6 Capitol attack, 9
Janzen, David, 74
Jensen, Kyle, 117, 119, 129
Jesus Christ
  audience of, 46, 178n84
  comprehensibility of, 80
  as contingency, 33, 36
  in Girard, 80, 171n91
  kenosis and, 36
  on meekness, 46
  mustard seed analogy of, 1
  salvation and, 97
  solidarity of, 77, 178n95
  vulnerability of, 36, 164n52
  as withdrawing, 80–81
Jewhooing the Sixties (Kaufman), 179n102
Jewish Antiquities (Flavius Josephus), 165n92
Jiménez Rodríguez, Luis Orlando, 135–36, 185n108
Job, Book of, 71, 131, 152
John, Gospel of, 76–77, 80
Johnson, Elizabeth, 14, 97, 99, 162n9
Jonkers, Peter, 180n129
Joseph, 169n58
Joseph (Genesis), 69
Judaism
  in supersessionism, 74–76
  See also antisemitism
Julius Caesar (Shakespeare), 168n46

kaironomia, 16, 31, 33
Kaironomia (White), 16
kairos, 3–13, 31–32
Kaplan, Grant, 173n123, 173n129
Kaufman, David, 179n102
Kearney, Richard, 19, 24, 27, 29, 71–72, 161n1, 171n74
Keeler, Christine, 56–58
Keller, Catherine, 19, 26–27, 159n5
Kennedy, George, 14–15, 24
kenosis, 36, 103, 164n52
Kinneavy, James, 15

Klemm, David, 14
Kripal, Jeffrey, 119

Language as Symbolic Action (Burke), 91
Lanham, Richard, 17, 25, 39–44, 164n63
Latour, Bruno, 8, 13, 19, 61, 137, 159n5, 185n103
Laudato Si' (Francis), 185n103
Levertov, Denise, 1
Levinas, Emmanuel, 77, 130, 169n50, 172n106, 182n32
Levinas's Rhetorical Demand (Arnett), 172n106
Leviticus, Book of, 68–69, 160n57, 176n52
listening, rhetorical, 38–39, 104, 154
logology, 22, 86, 90–92, 94–95, 97, 174n24
Logos, 27, 162n16
love, 19–20, 110
loving mimesis, 63
Luke, Gospel of, 178n84
  in Francis, 141, 186n130
  Mary in, 38–39, 45
  mustard seed parable in, 1
  Prodigal Son in, 99
  sacred in, 66
Lumen Gentium (Second Vatican Council), 139
Lundberg, Christian, 117, 128, 133–35

Maddux, Kristy, 93–94
"Magnificat, The" (prayer), 39
Mailloux, Steven, 1–2, 41–42, 89, 118
Manning, Robert, 60
Marback, Richard, 25, 43–44, 52
Mark, Gospel of, 178n84
Mary, 38–39, 45
materialism, 28, 35
Matthew, Gospel of, 87, 178n84
  conflict in, 47
  in Francis, 141
  meekness in, 20, 46, 165n92, 166n93
  misunderstanding of apostles in, 101
  sacrifice in, 74
  theopoeisis and, 36
McGreavy, Bridie, 25, 35–36
Medhurst, Martin, 18–19, 33
"Medication on Vulnerability in Rhetoric, A" (Marback), 43
meekness, 20–21, 85
  apathy and, 49–51
  colonization and, 48–49
  complicit rhetoric and, 30–34
  confrontation and, 26, 38–39, 45, 47–48
  defining, 26, 45–46

empty rhetoric and, 35–38
in Francis, 141–42
holiness and, 133
Jesus on, 46
post-Christian and, 25–26, 28, 33, 39, 50–53, 55
rhetoric of, 25, 38–52, 55
suffering and, 50, 103–4
weakness *vs.*, 28, 44–45, 52, 165n92
Megill-Cobbler, Thelma, 101
Milbank, John, 15, 80–82, 173n123
mildness, 26, 45, 47–48
Miles, Jack, 126, 152
Miller, David, 27, 29, 162n11
mimesis, 11, 62–63
mimetic desire, 21–22, 26, 47, 61–65, 80–81, 157, 169n52
mimetic rivalry, 26, 63
mimetic theory, 61–62, 75–76, 146, 148, 153
Minear, Paul S, 126
Moltmann, Jürgen, 103–4, 111
Moses, 130–31, 152
Muckelbauer, John, 16–17, 34, 39, 52–53
mustard seed analogy, 1
myth, 70–72, 167n18, 170n65

name, of God, 24
nationalism, Christian, 9–10, 160n37
negative dialectic, 17, 39, 52
Nelson, Cary, 91
New Rhetoric, The (Perelman and Olbrechts-Tyteca), 73
New Testament, 133, 166n121
Nicotra, Jody, 128
Nietzsche, Friedrich, 5, 106, 118
nihilism, 88, 106–13, 179n115
nomos, 16, 31
"nones" (demographic category), 6–7, 159n21
Norris, Kathleen, 20
Not Being God (Vattimo), 180n123
Not in God's Name (Sacks), 76, 147–48
"nova effect," 7–8

Olbrechts-Tyteca, Lucy, 73
Old Testament, 75, 133, 166n121
One by Whom Scandal Comes, The (Girard), 84
On the Art of Horsemanship (Xenophon), 165n92
On the Modern Cult of the Factish Gods (Latour), 13
"On the Parables of the Mustard Seed" (Levertov), 1
onto-eschatology, 161n1

ontology, 11, 25, 41–42, 161n1
Otto, Rudolf, 22–23, 66, 118–19, 121, 123, 183nn51–53
Oujia board, 128
overcoming, 85–88, 95, 102–3
"Overcoming Metaphysics" (Heidegger), 87
Oxtoby, Willard G., 126

Palaver, Wolfgang, 121, 182n32
Parker, Rebecca Ann, 50–51, 99–100, 104, 177n73
passivity, 38–39, 47
paternalism, 45
patriarchy, 25
Paul, 36, 96–97, 164n52, 165n69, 185n108
Paul VI, 144
Pelagianism, 140
Pelikan, Jaroslav, 137
Pender, Kelly, 25, 37
Perelman, Chaim, 73
"Perfect Mate, The" (*Star Trek: The Next Generation* episode), 168n34
permutation, 3–4, 16
persuasion, 2–3, 22
complicity and, 34
evocation and, 123
in Girard, 60–61
in Hadot, 187n31
post-Christian and, 25
in strong defense of rhetoric, 25
vulnerability and, 18
in weak defense of rhetoric, 39
Peter, 101
Peter, First, 185n108
Philebus (Plato), 164n52
Philippians, Epistle to, 36, 103
Philosophy as a Way of Life (Hadot), 154
phronesis, 29
pilgrimage, 2
Plato, 16, 18, 39, 164n52, 165n92
poesis, 27–28
poetics. *See* theopoetics
post-Christian, 3–4, 15, 17–18, 22, 25–26
complicity and, 33
Girard and, 56, 78–79, 83, 85
holiness and, 127
meekness and, 25–26, 28, 33, 39, 50–53, 55
overcoming and, 102
Vattimo and, 106–7
poststructuralism, 118
Poulakos, John, 31
prayer, in theorhetoric-to, 2

208 INDEX

prior rhetoricity, 3, 36, 53, 55, 63, 177n72
Prodigal Son, 99
Profumo Affair, 56–57, 167n5
Psalms, Book of, 46

"'Q' Question, The" (Lanham), 39
Quintilian, 39, 164n63

Rai, Tage Shakti, 65, 168n43
Ratcliffe, Krista, 38
Ratzinger, Joseph, 181n5
realism, rhetorical, 40, 48
reconciliation, 95–106
redemption, 50, 65, 92–96, 99–100, 105–6, 168n46
reflection, theological, 14–15
Rejoicing (Latour), 61
relationality, 30, 34, 41–42, 44
replacement theology, 74–75
Republic (Plato), 164n52, 165n92
Responding to the Sacred (Bernard-Donals and Kensen, eds.), 117
Resurrection, 78–79, 93, 99, 164n52
rhetoric
  ambiguous, 118–21
  ambivalent, 127–35
  as-ontology, 25
  in Burke, 11–12
  complicit, 30–34
  in Crosswhite, 15
  empty, 35–38
  of holiness, 133–34
  of meekness, 25, 38–52, 55, 85
  in Rickert, 3
  strong defense of, 25, 40–44
  struggle and, 35
  weak defense of, 25, 39–40, 43
rhetorical listening, 38–39, 104, 154
rhetorical realism, 40, 48
Rhetoric of Motives (Burke), 168n46
Rhetoric of Religion, The (Burke), 11, 22, 67, 86, 88–96
  See also Burke, Kenneth
"Rhetoric of Sacrifice, The" (Watts), 74
Rickert, Thomas, 3
Righteous Mind, The (Haidt), 12, 52
rivalry, 11–12, 21
  desire and, 58, 81
  meekness and, 26, 47
  mimetic, 26
Rivers, Nathaniel, 25, 43, 49–50
Robertson-Smith, William, 118, 160n55

Rogerson, John, 126–27
Romans, Epistle to, 164n52
Rueckert, William, 90, 167n30

Sacks, Jonathan, 76, 147–48, 150–51
sacred, 22–23, 121–25
  amenability of, to rhetoric, 129–30
  in Girard, 64–67
  holiness and, 116–19
Sacred and the Profane, The (Eliade), 121, 124
sacrifice, 10–11, 50, 172n100
  reconciliation and, 96
  sacred and, 64–68, 73–78
  violence and, 89–92
saints, 138–39
salvation, 81, 97, 139, 149, 164n52, 165n69
satyagraha, 38, 46, 51, 154
Scandal (film), 56–58
scapegoating, 12, 58–59, 65–66, 71–72, 77, 167n30, 169n57
  antisemitism and, 149
  complicity and, 106
  in Girard, 67–70, 105
  Joseph and, 169n58
  as metaphor, 169n55
  rivalry and, 101
  violence and, 160n39
Schüssler Fiorenza, Elisabeth, 14
Schwager, Raymund, 77, 121, 170n63, 172n100, 178n95
Scott, Peter, 90
Scubla, Lucien, 82, 173n119
Scult, Allen, 128–30
Second Vatican Council, 139, 186n119
Secular Age, A (Taylor), 7
secularization, 5–9, 109, 113, 127
segregation, 25
Shakespeare, William, 168n46
Siegel, Lee, 156
slavery, 25
Söder, Markus, 112–13
Sodom, 132–33, 151
solidarity, 45, 77, 103, 113, 178n95
Song of the Suffering Servant, 75
Spiritual Exercises (Ignatius of Loyola), 155, 185n104
Sporado, Antonio, 185n104
Star Trek: The Next Generation (television show), 168n34
Stendahl, Krister, 150, 187n12
Stoicism, 38, 154–55
Stoner, John, 96

Stormer, Nathan, 25, 35–36
Strangers, Gods and Monsters (Kearney), 171n74
structuralism, 118
struggle, 35
Stump, Eleonore, 176n57
subjectivity, 44, 59, 62, 153, 155, 168n34
Subversion of Christianity, The (Ellul), 115
suffering, 5, 71, 75, 96, 103
    abuse and, 142
    atonement and, 93
    God's solidarity with, 103
    meekness and, 50, 103–4
    redemptive, 99–100, 105–6
Summa Theologica (Aquinas), 175n35
supersessionism, 74–76

Taksim Square protests 2013, 47
Tarot, Camille, 119, 122
Taylor, Charles, 7, 10
Tertullian, 162n16
Theatre of Envy (Girard), 168n46
theological reflection, 14–15
theology
    Black liberation, 99, 159n14
    "death of God," 5, 8–9
    feminist, 99–100
    logology and, 90
    politics and, 90, 93
    replacement, 74–75
    theopoetics and, 27
    womanist, 100
theopoeisis, 36
theopoetics, 26–31, 162n11, 162n16
Theopoetic: Theology and the Religious Imagination (Wilder), 162n16
theorhetoric
    defined, 1–2
    empty rhetoric and, 35–36
    in Girard, 78–82
    God and, 133
    post-Christian, 25
    question of God and, 15–16
theorhetoric-about, 2–3
theorhetoric-for, 2
theorhetorics-beyond, 2
theorhetorics-from, 2
theorhetorics-in, 2
theorhetorics-through, 2
theorhetoric-to, 2
Theories of Primitive Religion (Evans-Pritchard), 119–20

theosis, 27–28
Things Hidden Since the Foundation of the World (Girard), 74, 82, 168n33
Timothy, Second, 185n108
topoi, 17–18
Totem and Taboo (Freud), 67, 160n55
Traube, Elizabeth, 167n18
Treguer, Michel, 55
Trinity, 163n45
Turkey, 47
Tyndale, William, 68, 160n57, 176n52

Überwindung, 85–86

Vahanian, Gabriel, 5, 7–9, 11
Vattimo, Gianni, 6, 22, 85–87, 103–13, 116, 179n115, 179n117, 179n123, 180n129, 180n135, 180n139
Verwindung, 85–88, 95, 108–10
victimhood, 65, 69, 71–72, 149
violence, 55–58, 64–65, 89–90, 167n18
    in Burke, 91–93
    redemptive, 92–93, 105–6
    sacred and, 119
Violence and the Sacred (Girard), 10, 13, 59, 65, 160n48, 169n52
virtue, 40–41, 45, 48, 139–40, 153, 165n69
Virtuous Violence (Fiske and Rai), 65
vulnerability, 21, 37
    in Burke, 156–57
    control and, 30, 35
    fear of, 44
    God and, 25
    in Gospels, 11
    Incarnation and, 36
    of Jesus, 36, 164n52
    in Marback, 43–44
    of Mary, 39
    paternalism and, 45
    persuasion and, 18
    virtue and, 44–45

Ward, Stephen, 56–57, 68, 167n5
War Games (film), 49–50
Watts, James, 74
weakness, 28, 44–45, 52, 165n92
Weaver, J. Denny, 162n11, 178n85
Wess, Robert, 31, 40, 94
When These Things Begin (Treguer), 55
White, Eric Charles, 16, 18, 31–32
white supremacy, 25

INDEX

Wholly Other, 2, 53
 mediation and, 132
 meekness and, 45
 Otto and, 22–23, 119, 123
 persuasion and, 18
 vulnerability and, 30, 36
Wieseltier, Leon, 9
Wilder, Amos, 162n16
Williams, Delores, 100, 103, 177n79
Wiman, Christian, 20

Wink, Walter, 46–47
womanism, 100
women, 50–51, 99–100, 142
Worsham, Lynn, 65–66, 175n37
Wright, N.T., 60, 93
Wuellner, Wilhelm, 14

Xenophon, 165n92

Zimmerman, Jens, 14

Milton Keynes UK
Ingram Content Group UK Ltd.
UKHW012255060324
438913UK00003B/77